THE ATLAS OF
MYSTERIOUS
PLACES

THE ATLAS OF MYSTERIOUS PLACES

THE WORLD'S UNEXPLAINED SACRED SITES,
SYMBOLIC LANDSCAPES, ANCIENT CITIES
AND LOST LANDS

EDITED BY JENNIFER WESTWOOD

TORSTAR BOOKS

NEW YORK · TORONTO

CONTENTS

A Marshall Edition
The Atlas of Mysterious Places
was conceived, edited and designed by
Marshall Editions Limited
170 Piccadilly
London W1V 9DD

This edition published 1987 by
Torstar Books Inc.
300 East 42nd Street
New York, NY 10017
by arrangement with
Marshall Editions Limited, London.
Published in the USA by
Weidenfeld & Nicolson, New York.

EDITOR	Pip Morgan
EDITORIAL COORDINATOR	Carole Devaney
MANAGING EDITOR	Ruth Binney
ART DIRECTOR	John Bigg
DESIGN ASSISTANT	Jonathan Bigg
PICTURE EDITOR	Zilda Tandy
PRODUCTION	Barry Baker
	Janice Storr
	Rosanna Scott

Originated by Imago Publishing Ltd, Thame, UK
Typeset by Hourds Typographica, Stafford, UK
Printed and bound in West Germany by
Mohndruck Graphische Betriebe GMBH

ISBN 1-55001-090-5

10 9 8 7 6 5 4 3 2 1

In conjunction with *The Atlas of
Mysterious Places*
Torstar Books offers a 12-inch raised
relief world globe.
     For more information write to:
     Torstar Books Inc.
     300 East 42nd Street
     New York, NY10017

CONTRIBUTORS

Jennifer Westwood
Cumae; Malta; Jerusalem; Takht-i Sulaiman;
Tower of Babel; Earth Mounds of North
America; Susa; Mohenjo-Daro; Atlantis;
Lyonesse; Lemuria; Shangri-La; Eldorado

Janet and Colin Bord
Glastonbury; Stonehenge; Avebury;
Newgrange; Mazes and Labyrinths;
Cerne Abbas

Nigel Pennick
Carnac; The Externsteine; Geomancy;
Great Zimbabwe

Richard Bluer
Machu Picchu; Chaco Canyon; Teotihuacan

Patricia Stoat
T'ai Shan; Easter Island

Garry Kilworth
Mecca; Ayers Rock

Patricia Quaife
Santiago de Compostela; Petra

John Griffiths
Knossos

Humphrey Evans
Giza

Polly Dyne Steel
Troy

INTRODUCTION

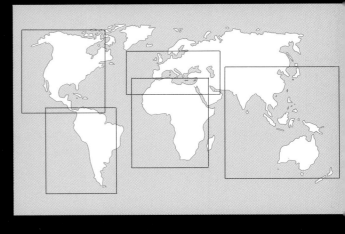

*'. . . and in these ancient lands
Enchased and lettered as a tomb
And scored with prints of perished hands,
And chronicled with dates of doom . . .
I trace the lives such scenes enshrine
And their experience count as mine.'*

Thomas Hardy

The past has left a legacy of enigmas. All about us are sacred sites, symbolic landscapes, ancient cities and lost lands, fascinating alike to scholars and adventurers, curiosity-seekers and tourists. Yet still they keep their secrets.

Such mysterious places fire the imagination and generate awe. They raise questions about the religion, astronomy, engineering, history and intentions of ancient peoples throughout the world. They challenge modern thinking and its ideas about the supremacy of 20th-century technology and the 'foolproof' dogma of the scientific method. The riddles enshrined in the world's mysterious places undermine, time and again, any condescending assumptions about the so-called 'primitive' cultures of our ancestors.

This atlas courts no fixed persuasion and champions no point of view. The authors have applied the research expertise of their separate and various scholarly disciplines to explore each mysterious place and reveal its secrets. As myth and legend intermingle with current archaeological and historical findings, so rich tales have taken form. But it is clear that many of these mysteries will never be resolved, essentially for lack of conclusive evidence. . . Perhaps it is better that way.

These maps show the locations of the mysterious places featured in this atlas. Places in bold type are the subject of major essays; the remainder are described in the Gazetteer (pp. 226–231) or referred to in the text.

SACRED SITES

'To you, to me,
Stonehenge and Chartres Cathedral . . .
are works by the same Old Man
under different names: we know what He did,
what, even, He thought He thought,
but we don't see why.'

W. H. Auden

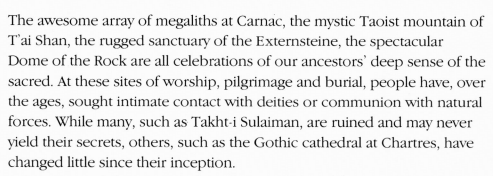

The awesome array of megaliths at Carnac, the mystic Taoist mountain of T'ai Shan, the rugged sanctuary of the Externsteine, the spectacular Dome of the Rock are all celebrations of our ancestors' deep sense of the sacred. At these sites of worship, pilgrimage and burial, people have, over the ages, sought intimate contact with deities or communion with natural forces. While many, such as Takht-i Sulaiman, are ruined and may never yield their secrets, others, such as the Gothic cathedral at Chartres, have changed little since their inception.

Many sacred sites seem to have an astronomical function, certain features of their construction being aligned to planetary events in the heavens. The orientation of Stonehenge to the midsummer sunrise and the alignment of the passage-grave at Newgrange to the midwinter sunrise are two of the most famous examples. The ancient and widespread incorporation of celestial events into the fabric of holy places demonstrates the yearning of our ancestors to unite their spirits with the forces of heaven and earth.

GLASTONBURY: THE LEGENDARY AVALON

EUROPE: ENGLAND

The legends surrounding one of England's most sacred sites attract a multitude of visitors and pilgrims. Was King Arthur really buried in the abbey grounds? Is the Holy Grail hidden in Chalice Well? Does a maze spiral its way to the summit of Glastonbury Tor?

Rising above the flat plains of the Somerset Levels, Glastonbury Tor, with a ruined church tower at its peak, provides an unmistakable landmark for one of England's most mysterious places. For Glastonbury, the site of one of the country's earliest Christian buildings, is steeped in a wealth of tradition and legend, myth and romance. This small bustling country town attracts visitors of all kinds. Romantics are drawn by the legends of King Arthur, pilgrims by its ancient Christian heritage, mystics look to find the Holy Grail, while astrologers are lured by the rumour of a zodiac said to be laid out upon the landscape.

Glastonbury was almost an island surrounded by marshland or floodwater where early Christians settled, though quite when is uncertain. The earliest reliable date is about AD 705 when King Ine founded a monastery here, which became a Benedictine house in the 10th century. Archaeological excavations have uncovered traces of earlier buildings made of wattle and daub, while over the centuries many fine stone edifices were constructed, most now traceable in outline only. Substantial remains exist of the main abbey church built in the 13th and 14th centuries, with a mystique all of its own.

The abbey's 12th-century Lady Chapel stands on the site of an earlier church destroyed by fire in AD 1184. This was the 'Old Church', built, according to tradition, by Joseph of Arimathea, the rich man who wrapped up the body of Jesus and carried it to his tomb. Legend tells how Joseph later emigrated to Glastonbury and established a church there. Another legend relates how Joseph landed by boat on Wearyall Hill and leaned on his staff in prayer. The staff took root and became the Glastonbury Thorn, which still flowers at Easter and Christmas time in the abbey grounds and in front of St John's Church.

Was King Arthur buried here?

Glastonbury's greatest mystery is arguably whether the body of King Arthur lies buried in the abbey grounds. Despite the monks' claim to have discovered his remains, and those of his wife Guinevere, in AD 1190, there is still considerable uncertainty as to the truth of the story – recent evidence suggests he may have been buried near Bridgend in south Wales. After Arthur's last battle at Camlann, whose location is unknown, the dying king was taken to the mystical Isle of Avalon. He commanded Sir Bedivere to throw away his mighty sword Excalibur and when the knight tossed it into a lake, a hand reached out of the water and grasped it. Where did this strange event take place? The most popular answer is at the mere, since drained, at Pomparles Bridge near Glastonbury.

The grave in the abbey grounds was discovered after the secret of the burial was revealed by a Welsh bard to King Henry II. The

The terraces encircling the Tor may mark a winding pilgrim's path, a kind of spiral maze leading to the summit and dating from the time when the first Christians settled in Glastonbury. The Tor also forms part of the Aquarius figure in the Glastonbury Zodiac said to be laid out in a 16km (10mi) diameter circle in the Somerset countryside. There is also an old straight track or ley passing through the hill and linking it with other sacred sites in the area. The town of Glastonbury, the abbey and St John's Church lie beyond the bottom of the photograph.

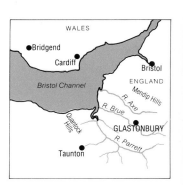

In early times, Glastonbury was almost an island for the sea covered the low lands of the Somerset Levels between the Mendips and the Quantock Hills. The remains of Iron Age lake villages found nearby confirm this and indicate that boats could have sailed to Glastonbury.

king then informed the Abbot of Glastonbury and, eventually, when rebuilding the abbey after the fire of AD 1184, the monks searched for the grave. About 2m (7ft) down they found a stone slab and lead cross inscribed *hic iacet sepultus inclitus rex arturius in insula avalonia*, 'Here lies buried the renowned King Arthur in the Isle of Avalon'. About 2.7m (9ft) below the slab was a coffin cut from a hollow log containing the bones of a 2.4m (8ft) man with a damaged skull, as well as smaller bones identified as Guinevere's by the scrap of yellow hair lying with them.

British archaeologist Dr Ralegh Radford confirmed, in 1962, that a burial really had been discovered, but he had no way of showing to whom the grave belonged. The site in the abbey grounds marked today as Arthur's Grave is in fact the place where the bones were reinterred in 1278 in a black marble tomb before the high altar. The original grave is unmarked, but lies 15m (50ft) from the south door of the Lady Chapel.

The legends of the Tor

King Arthur has an older connection with Glastonbury in a tale told long before the claimed discovery of his tomb. Melwas, a king of Somerset, kidnapped Guinevere and kept her prisoner at Glastonbury. Arthur came with a band of men to rescue his wife from the king's stronghold believed to have been on the Tor, but a settlement was arranged by the Abbot before fighting began.

During excavations in the 1960s, traces of early timber buildings were found on top of the 150m (500ft) Tor, but whether this was really the king's dwelling place or a monastic settlement could not be established. Whoever lived there had lived comfortably: among the finds were metal-working hearths, animal bones representing many joints of beef, mutton and pork, and pieces of pottery suggesting Mediterranean wine had been drunk.

During medieval times Glastonbury's monks built a church on top of the Tor and dedicated it to St Michael the Archangel, but it fell during an earthquake. The tower that stands there today is all that remains of a subsequent church built to replace the earlier one. The monks' intention was probably to christianize the pagan Tor. In legend it was the entrance to Annwn, a hidden realm of the Underworld whose lord was Gwyn ap Nudd, king of the Fairies. When the 6th-century St Collen visited Gwyn on the Tor he went through a secret entrance and found himself inside a palace. Subjected to temptations, he sprinkled holy water all around, only to find the palace had disappeared and he was all alone on the Tor.

The Chalice Well

At the foot of the Tor is an old well whose spring waters sound like the beating of a heart. Because the waters are tinted red with iron oxide, the well is also called Blood Spring. But its most famous name is Chalice Well, for a tradition has arisen that the priceless Holy Grail was hidden there. This legendary vessel was the chalice used by Jesus at the Last Supper and was brought by Joseph of Arimathea to England. The Grail was said to have miraculous powers and after its disappearance was sought in vain by several of King Arthur's Knights of the Round Table.

The Glastonbury legends may have a tenuous basis in fact but they have imbued the area with an aura of mystery that few other places generate. The 12th-century chronicler William of Malmesbury wrote of Glastonbury Abbey that 'It savoured somewhat of heavenly sanctity even from its very foundation, and exhaled it over the whole country . . .' Despite subsequent changes and modern development, Glastonbury remains still, in William's words, 'a heavenly sanctuary on earth'.

A medieval fair was held at the foot of Glastonbury Tor every year from 1127 until 1825. In honour of St Michael, the fair lasted for six days – five before the feast day, and on the saint's day itself. All that remains of St Michael's church on the Tor is the tower – its frontage bears some curious carvings. One shows the devil weighing a human soul against the world; another shows a woman milking a cow; yet another shows a pelican plucking its breast.

The ruins of Glastonbury Abbey stand on hallowed ground. From the wattle-and-daub 'Old Church' traditionally built by Joseph of Arimathea to the large and wealthy abbey destroyed in the 16th century, this site was one of the most sacred in England. Tradition points to this place as Avalon, an island of the dead where King Arthur and St Patrick are said to be buried.

On Chalice Hill, between the Tor and the Abbey, lies the magical Chalice Well. Legend tells how the shaft of the well was built of huge stones by the Druids and that later the Chalice used at the Last Supper was thrown into its rust-coloured waters.

GLASTONBURY'S TEMPLE OF THE STARS

THE LADY OF THE ZODIAC

English sculptor Katharine Maltwood created a wave of controversy in 1929 with the publication of her book *The Glastonbury Temple of the Stars.* While illustrating the *High History of the Holy Grail* (written *c.*1200 in Glastonbury), she claimed to have discovered a group of enormous figures laid out in the Somerset countryside south of Glastonbury. Outlined by the natural contours of rivers, paths, roads, hills, ditches and earthworks, these figures represented the 12 signs of the zodiac. Moreover, Katharine Maltwood was able to link the symbolism of these giants with the history of the Holy Grail and the legends of King Arthur.

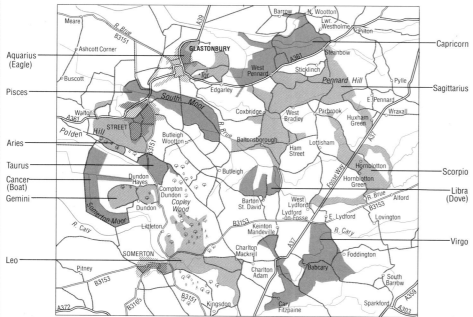

THE GLASTONBURY ZODIAC

Old as the hills that constitute its effigies and the rivers that partly outline them, the Glastonbury Zodiac is spread over the natural landscape in a great circle 16km (10mi) across. Early man completed the astrological pattern with roads, canals and earthworks. This Temple of the Stars is a synthesis of astrology, Arthurian legend and New Age philosophy. Grasping its significance requires considerable patience and imagination, for it is based largely on the associations of place-names and legends rather than on historical fact.

Arthur is Sagittarius, Guinevere his wife is Virgo, Merlin the magician is Capricorn, and Sir Lancelot is Leo. Glastonbury is located in Aquarius which is represented by a phoenix – the New Age rising from the ashes of the old. Chalice Well is in the bird's beak, the Tor is its head and the abbey, Grail Castle.

THE ZODIAC'S LEADING LIGHT
English art teacher Mary Caine is the
leading light in the study of the
Glastonbury Zodiac. A member of the
London Order of Druids, she has added
a wealth of additional detail to the
Zodiac's rich symbolism and has filmed
the Zodiac, some of it from the air. Her
main contribution to knowledge of the
Zodiac was the discovery of a Messianic
face in the Gemini figure at Dundon Hill
Camp, halfway between the towns of
Glastonbury and Somerton. Mary Caine
further contributed to the study of such
earth patterns with her discovery of a
similar Zodiac around Kingston-on-
Thames in Surrey, England.

T'AI SHAN: A SACRED CHINESE MOUNTAIN

The temples and shrines built on a mountain in eastern China have long been places of pilgrimage. Why do the Chinese venerate this mountain? What gods have their sanctuaries there? Why is T'ai Shan important to the Taoist faith?

The revered mountain of T'ai Shan watches over the wide flood plain of the Yellow River, the birthplace of Chinese civilization. At the dawn of the Chinese Empire, the mountain stood at the boundary between the known and the unknown, between the world of taxes, flood control works, labour and death, and the wild world of Shantung to the east. In Shantung lived magicians who studied the secrets of eternal life and who visited the immortals dwelling on the islands of the eastern sea.

The early Han peoples worshipped nature, honouring rivers and mountains among their many gods. T'ai Shan has been venerated since those times. The legendary Emperor Shun is traditionally believed to have made the great sacrifices to Heaven and Earth at T'ai Shan 2,000 years before the birth of Christ. The first Ch'in Emperor, who conquered and then united the Warring States, came to worship at T'ai Shan in 219 BC. Emperor Wu Ti made the pilgrimage to the mountain for the great sacrifices in 110 BC. And through the centuries, imperial patronage continued: T'ai Shan was honoured as Equal of Heaven by an 11th-century Sung Emperor and presented with a magnificent and magical slab of jade by the Emperor Chien Lung in 1736.

But T'ai Shan has never been linked with the faith of official China, the teachings of Confucius. It is, in fact, the most sacred of the five mountains of Taoism, faith of the magician and the alchemist, the outsider and the rebel.

Rudiments of the Taoist faith

Taoism is at once the most austere and the most earthy of religions. In the 4th century BC, the lands of the Han peoples were torn by bitter warfare. Peace, thought the first Taoists, could be found only by abandoning material ambitions and seeking instead to observe and understand the inner and outer worlds. Of the Way taught by Lao Tzu, the father of Taoism, it is said: 'Those who know do not speak, those who speak do not know.'

The Taoist ethic was individualist and democratic, based on the return to the small, self-governing communities of free individuals which Taoists believed existed in former times. They regarded strife as the result of failing to act in accordance with the true nature of reality, the Tao.

Taoism stresses the receptive, passive and observing aspect of human nature. In Chinese philosophy, this is the *yin* or feminine force. The early Taoists refused to distinguish between 'higher' and 'lower' in the human and animal worlds, but chose instead to observe and seek the essential unity and harmony in all things. As a result they became skilled in alchemy and divination. As time passed, Taoism became increasingly identified with magical and mysterious popular cults. Indeed, in the minds of most people, the Taoist pantheon was confused with the gods and demons associated with the new Buddhist faith.

Since ancient times, pilgrims have made their way up the thousands of steps leading to the temple of the Jade Emperor at the summit of T'ai Shan, China's most sacred mountain. It has been revered for centuries by followers of both the Buddhist and the Taoist faiths, and the many deities that inhabit its stony slopes have been credited with controlling man's fate on earth. Pilgrims start the 6- or 7-hour ascent in the evening and, passing through the South Gate of Heaven in the early hours of the morning, witness the special aim of their journey – the spectacular rising of the sun over the surrounding mountains.

Located in the homeland of Confucius, the sacred Taoist mountain of T'ai Shan rises to a height of 1,524m (5,067ft) above the plain of the Yellow River in China's eastern province of Shantung. Time and again, Taoist rebels have swept out of Shantung's hills; it was at the foot of T'ai Shan that the Boxers killed a foreign missionary in 1899 and so began an uprising that shook the world.

T'AI SHAN: A SACRED CHINESE MOUNTAIN

Worshipping a multitude of gods

When climbing the 7,000 steps of T'ai Shan, from the town of T'ai-an to the Temple of the Jade Emperor at its peak, the visitor encounters temples, groves of cypress and pine, waterfalls and cascades. In the 1930s, a Western traveller reported that at the time of the annual pilgrimage between February and May, 10,000 people climbed T'ai Shan daily, some making the six-hour ascent on their knees.

At the foot of T'ai Shan is the Temple of the Peak, dedicated to the God of the Mountain, where a magnificently painted Main Hall depicts a procession in his honour. After the coming of Buddhism in the 4th century AD, this god came to be identified with the 'Judge of the Dead'.

Two temples passed on the ascent are dedicated to female deities: the Empress of the West, Wang Mu Chi, and the Goddess of the North Star, Tai Mu. Tai Mu has a third eye, many arms and perhaps originated in India. Her palace is the constellation, Ursa Major, which eternally circles the Pole Star. Further evidence of the strong link with Buddhism of this essentially Taoist holy place is the huge flat rock upon which is carved the Diamond Sutra. Most honoured among the Chinese of all the Buddhist scriptures, this sutra teaches that everything is illusion.

The last steep ascent to the summit brings the pilgrim through the South Gate of Heaven to the temple dedicated to the Daughter of the Mountain, Pi Hsia Yuan Chun, the Goddess of the Dawn. She is said to be the lady to whom T'ai Shan first belonged. The most important temple on the summit is dedicated to the Jade Emperor, Yu Huang, who was honoured as the supreme deity by the Sung Emperor Chen Tsung about 1,000 years ago. The Jade Emperor has maintained first place in the Taoist pantheon ever since and is Lord of Time Present.

A centre of living energy

From the summit of T'ai Shan the view is spectacular, encompassing to the north the course of the Yellow River and to the south the province where the great philosopher Confucius was born in 551 BC. Together with his disciple Mencius, who was also born in the province, Confucius taught the philosophy that was to guide the government of China for 2,000 years.

The ethics of Taoism may not have been needed to help with government, but the services of Taoist experts were required to fulfil correct obligations to people's ancestors. *Feng-Shui*, the understanding of 'wind and water', was needed to determine the most favourable location for ancestral graves. The Taoists, recognizing the earth as a living organism filled with living energy, were skilled in such matters.

The sacred places of Taoism were all chosen as centres of living energy, and T'ai Shan, the most exceptional and mysterious of such centres, draws all powers to itself. Dozens of other temples, where prayers may be offered for fertility, good fortune in business, long life or knowledge of the future, line the path up T'ai Shan. The deities honoured in the temples represent every traditional religion in China, even back to the mountain god of earliest times. But to the Taoist, this is not strange, merely natural. No single answer to the deepest questions will be true, for truth must be found in the variety of nature and human experience. No one god will suffice for all petitions.

Today, in Communist China, the gods have departed from T'ai Shan. There are few pilgrims. Tourists come to marvel at the great ascent, the gates, temples, carvings, murals and the jade and bronze, the wood, water and stone, the winds themselves bent to the mysterious purposes of men and women.

18

The ancient ritual of burning special paper 'money' is still observed by some pilgrims today, in wayside shrines on the slopes of T'ai Shan. The Qing Ming festival in spring is traditionally the best time for such sacrifices, made to 'placate', or bribe, the officials believed to manage the underworld. Since China has been (and still is) much concerned with bureaucracy, it was thought wise to make such offerings in order to gain a smoother final journey.

According to legend, Lao Tzu was the mystical founder of Taoism and traditionally credited with the writing of the sacred text of *Tao Te Ching*, meaning 'The Way and Its Power'. Historically, not much is known of this sage: it is thought he was born in *c.* 604 BC as Li Erh and became librarian to the Chou court. A contemporary of Confucius, he taught the acquiring of effortless action through following the path of natural events with no striving. By the 5th century, Taoism was a fully developed religion, with many of its features adopted from Mahayana Buddhism.

THE SYMBOLISM OF CHARTRES

Chartres Cathedral is one of the most enigmatic in the world. Who built it and why? What is so special about the site? Where and how did the architects find the knowledge to construct it?

The town of Chartres stands beside the River Eure in a fertile plain about 90km (56mi) southwest of Paris. Its cathedral is one of the most venerated and mysterious of all, not least because of the site on which it stands. Even before the Gauls and Celts thrived in this part of Europe, builders who constructed the megalithic circles such as Stonehenge had been at work here, constructing a dolmen and a well within a mound.

The dolmen, two or three sturdy unhewn stones supporting a large flattish boulder, created a sheltered chamber tall enough for a man to pass through. This chamber is thought to house a point of power, an important and fertile source of energy emanating from the earth. Such telluric currents ebbed and flowed with the seasons, revitalizing all who came into contact with them. Thus the mound, the well and the dolmen became revered as holy ground.

Later the Druids, Celtic priests of Gaul and Britain, established a college at Chartres and the site became a centre for Druidic teaching. The mound and dolmen took on a new significance. For when a prophetic vision informed the Druids that a virgin would give birth to a child, they carved from a pear tree an image of this virgin, with the infant seated on her knee. The Druids placed this statue beside the well and the power point within the dolmen and called her The Virgin Under The Earth. The inscription was later changed to *Virgini pariturae*, the Virgin who will give birth to a child.

When the first Christians came to Chartres in the 3rd century AD they saw the carving of the Virgin, by now blackened with age and placed in a grotto, and worshipped her as the Black Virgin. The church they built on the site was dedicated to Our Lady, as were all the succeeding churches and cathedrals. They called her resting place 'The Druid's Grotto' and set it in the church crypt, and for no known reason they called the well beside her the Well of the Strong.

There were six churches in all; the first five were destroyed by fire but each time a new one arose to celebrate the faith and boundless energy of pilgrims, townsfolk, builders and architects. Yet the construction of the sixth and final Chartres, the Gothic cathedral that stands today, is shrouded in mystery. No coherent account exists of the planning or erection of one of the world's greatest architectural masterpieces.

Where was the knowledge found to build it?

From various fragments of information a remarkable story emerges. It begins with Bernard of Clairvaux, founder of the Cistercian Order of monks, who inspired nine knights of France to abandon their worldly possessions and make a quest for secrets believed buried in the Holy of Holies beneath the ruins of Solomon's Temple in Jerusalem. They became known as the Knights Templar and spent nearly ten years in the Holy Land,

A church or cathedral has stood on the hill of Chartres for nearly 1,500 years. The present cathedral is the sixth building to be erected there. The Duke of Aquitania set fire to the first church in AD 743, and the Danes burned the second in 858. The third and fourth churches were also engulfed by flames in 962 and 1020 respectively; and the first cathedral was destroyed by fire in 1194.

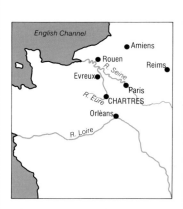

Chartres is one of 80 huge Gothic monuments built in France in the hundred years after the Knights Templar returned from the Holy Land in 1128. It is also one of several cathedrals of that period dedicated to the Virgin and bearing the name Notre-Dame. The others include Rouen, Amiens, Reims, Bayeux, Evreux and Laon.

returning to France in 1128 as mysteriously as they had left.

Gothic architecture began to flower at this time, yet no one knows where and when the seed was sown. Did the Knights Templar discover the key to some arcane knowledge? Did they return to France with secrets which they then put into practice with the help of the Cistercians? Was the Gothic style, of which Chartres is among the finest blooms, the direct result of the Templars' quest?

Controversial claims have been made for and against, but the truth is elusive. Is it possible the Knights unearthed the remains of Moses' Ark of the Covenant or the secrets stored within it – namely, the Divine Law governing Number, Weight and Measure? Many years of decipherment by the Cistercian Order's best scholars would have been needed to understand such secrets and distil the principles of sacred geometry encoded within them. Whatever the nature of their discovery it seems certain that when the fire destroyed most of the first Chartres cathedral in 1194 (but not the Virgin's tunic), the Cistercians were informed enough to put the principles of sacred engineering into practice.

Within 30 years masons, glaziers, sculptors, geometers, astronomers and others had created a sacred shrine so incredible that few people entering it fail to be moved. For its proportions, orientation, position and symbolism have all been designed to alert the psyche and refresh the spirit. The sacred centre of the cathedral lies between the second and third bays of the choir and is the position of the original altar until the latter was moved in the 16th century. Lying some 37m (131ft) below this point is the level of water in the well. Towering the same distance above it is the pinnacle of the Gothic vault where the crossed ogives, the pointed arches characteristic of Gothic architecture, are so perfectly proportioned they seem to bear no weight at all.

Why was Chartres a centre for pilgrims?

The cathedral is a place of spiritual action. It is said to possess the power to transform men, to transmute them into a higher spiritual state, just as the alchemists would transmute base metal into gold. Pilgrims arriving at the Great West Door, the threshold of the cathedral, found they stood more upright with their heads upraised. For the interior design of the cathedral seems to create a definite uplifting effect on the body, as if to prepare it for the telluric emanations from below and divine inspiration from above. As Louis Charpentier, the French investigator of Chartres' mysteries, says: '. . . physiologically, telluric and other currents can only enter man *via* a vertebral column that is straight and vertical. Man can only move to a higher state by standing upright.'

The pilgrim would progress shoeless up the nave to the labyrinth, a maze 13m (42.5ft) across and set out in the flagstones of the floor. Dancing around and around until reaching the centre, a ritual commonly seen at each of the four annual Virgin fairs, the pilgrim became more and more sensitive to the power accumulated in the vast cathedral chamber.

Moving to the middle point where the transepts cross the nave, the pilgrim was supposed to receive the full alchemical force from the luminous light emanating from the three stained glass rose windows. If the pilgrim experienced the entire sensuousness of the cathedral, it would be because the body's senses had apprehended all the musical and geometrical proportions, and all the numbers and lines expressed in the building's interior. For the pilgrim came not to worship Our Lady the Virgin, nor to kneel in obedience, but rather to find awareness through her, to replenish spiritual energy and refresh the soul.

Chartres Cathedral has many small mysteries, not least the purpose of the large rectangular flagstone, set aslant to the other stones in the west aisle of the south transept. At midday on the summer solstice, a ray of sunshine streams through a clear pane of glass in the stained glass window of St Apollinaire and illuminates exactly the conspicuous tenon on the flagstone. The arrangement is evidently a deliberate collaboration between astronomer, geometer, glazier and stonemason.

The groundplan of Chartres (*below*) has probably been designed according to proportions which obey the law of the Golden Number, 1.618. Distances between pillars, and the lengths of the nave, transepts and the choir, are all multiples of the Golden Number.

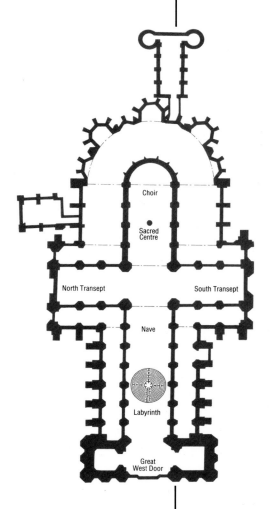

Choir

Sacred Centre

North Transept

South Transept

Nave

Labyrinth

Great West Door

THE POWERS BEHIND CHARTRES

THE SACRED VIRGIN

Chartres Cathedral is renowned for its stained glass windows and for its veneration of the Virgin Mary. The two reputations come together in a remarkable 12th-century figure window, the *Notre-Dame-de-la-Belle-Verrière*, Our Lady of the Beautiful Glass. Today the centrepiece of a large window in the choir, the larger-than-life Virgin sits on a throne with the young Jesus on her lap. Together with the tunic worn by Mary at Jesus' birth, which had been donated by Charlemagne's grandson in 876, the window miraculously escaped the fire of 1194 which destroyed the first cathedral.

THE KNIGHTS TEMPLAR

A religious order whose members took vows of chastity, obedience and poverty, the Knights Templar consisted of a group of noblemen governed by a Grand Master. Founded in 1118, the order held communal prayers and services in the churches and hospices built all over Europe. But the Knights' chief role was to defend the kingdom of Christ, especially Jerusalem. They soon became one of Europe's most powerful secret societies, a fact which caused Philip the Fair of France to eradicate them some 200 years after their foundation.

THE APPLE OF THE VIRGIN'S EYE

St Bernard of Clairvaux (1090–1153), shown preaching to his fellow Cistercians in Jean Fouquet's 15th-century painting, epitomizes the religious climate in Christian Europe during the first half of the 12th century. He co-founded the Cistercian Order of monks with Stephen Harding, the English abbot of the Citeaux monastery that he had joined in 1113. Bernard adored the Virgin Mary for her humility and obedience. Tradition relates that, while praying to her statue, he received three drops of milk from the Virgin's breast.

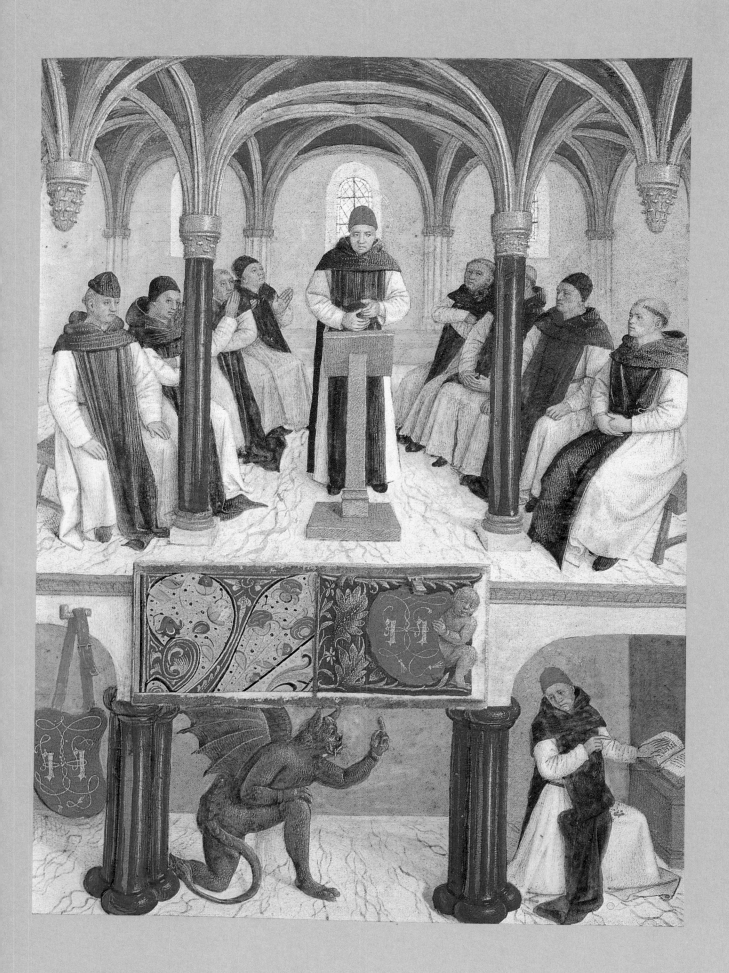

THE MYSTIC TEMPLE OF STONEHENGE

The most famous megalithic monument in the world may once have been an observatory for predicting important astronomical events. Who built it, when and how? What was the extent of the architect's knowledge? Was it a centre for religious ritual?

Stonehenge is a powerful magnet. People of all kinds are drawn into the aura of its huge and ancient stones, from archaeologists with specialist knowledge seeking to probe its mysteries to ordinary citizens wishing simply to visit this magical place. Yet Stonehenge is an astonishing enigma, for even the best brains in the world have failed to reveal the secret of its purpose. Lord Byron, in his poem *Don Juan*, echoed the question many have sought to answer: 'The Druid's groves are gone – so much the better. Stonehenge is not, but what the devil is it?'

The Saxons called the group of standing stones 'Stonehenge' or the 'Hanging Stones', while medieval writers referred to it as the 'Giant's Dance'. Inigo Jones, the renowned 17th-century architect who made the first serious study of Stonehenge, considered it to be a Roman temple. And William Stukeley, an 18th-century antiquary and freemason, convinced many that Stonehenge was once a temple of the British Druids. Only in the 20th century have archaeologists established the true age of the monument and arrived at more realistic conclusions about its purpose.

The building of Stonehenge

The open Wiltshire countryside surrounding Stonehenge in the heart of southern England is rich in prehistoric remains. Woodhenge, Durrington Walls, the Cursus and more than 350 barrows are a testament to the intense communal activity of the semi-nomadic pastoralists who grazed animals, grew wheat and worshipped their gods in and around Salisbury Plain. Around 3500 BC they started to build Stonehenge.

British archaeologists, notably Richard Atkinson, established in the 1950s that the first Stonehenge was a circular bank and ditch with 56 holes, known now as the Aubrey Holes, in a ring around the perimeter. The first standing stone was the Heel Stone, erected outside the earthwork's single entrance. The second Stonehenge was started 200 or more years later. New builders constructed an avenue of parallel banks linking the henge with the River Avon about 3.2km (2mi) away. They brought 80 blocks of bluestone from the Prescelly Mountains 320km (200mi) away in southwest Wales. These large stones were probably carried by raft around the Welsh coast and into a different River Avon at Bristol. Transported up local rivers and overland, they were finally dragged on rollers up the avenue to Stonehenge where they were erected in two circles.

The bluestone circles were soon dismantled and replaced by the gigantic stones that still dominate the site today. Since some of these megaliths weigh around 26 tons, their transport from north Wiltshire must have been a major undertaking involving a large workforce. The men responsible for erecting them were obviously skilled craftsmen: they shaped and carefully fitted into place the lintels covering each of the two vertical stones by the

What remains of Stonehenge today is but a shadow, though an impressive one, of its former glory. The original shape can be discerned, though more than half the stones are either fallen, missing or buried beneath the turf.

Had an aerial view been seen of this megalithic monument some 4,000 years ago, the 'Giant's Dance' would have been complete, after more than 1,500 years of construction in three phases. The four components from the outside to the centre were: a ring of sarsen sandstone monoliths linked by continuous lintels and standing some 5m (16ft) tall; a circle of bluestones; a horseshoe of five sarsen trilithons; and a horseshoe of bluestones, in the middle of which was the great Altar Stone itself. To the northeast, and beyond the outer ditch of the earthwork, stood the bulky Heel Stone (*left* in photograph), guarding the avenue to this sacred site.

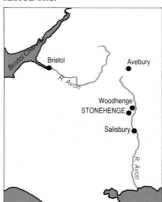

Stonehenge is found on the rolling chalk downland of Salisbury Plain, in the county of Wiltshire at the heart of southern England. The great bluestones, hewn from the rocks of southwest Wales, were probably transported by sea and then along both the rivers Avon to the Stonehenge site.

use of ball and socket joints. Called trilithons because three stones were fitted together, they were erected in the circle and horseshoe shape still visible today.

The dismantled bluestones were later re-erected inside the circle of megaliths and can be seen as the small pillar stones that are dwarfed by the trilithons. Holes were dug outside the main circle for the erection of a double circle of bluestones, but for some reason this construction was never started. Around 1,500 years after the beginning of Stonehenge, the final changes took place: the bluestones were dismantled yet again and re-erected in their present positions inside the circle. At the same time, the stone now known as the Altar Stone, a large block of green sandstone also from south Wales, was set up in front of one of the trilithons.

What was Stonehenge's purpose?

The elaborate planning and workmanship, as well as the many thousands of man-hours that went into its construction, demonstrate how important Stonehenge was. And the fact that the architects needed the Welsh bluestones and green sandstone suggest that these megaliths were a vital ingredient in the correct working of the site. Evidently, Stonehenge was not designed to be a simple meeting place for the local people. But what was it designed for? A few tantalizing clues point to its possible function. The midsummer sun rises between the Heel Stone and another stone no longer present – could the earliest Stonehenge have been used to expose ancestral remains to the life-giving sun at this significant time of year? The cremation burials discovered in the 56 Aubrey Holes show that funerary rites were performed here, and these holes may have symbolized places of entry into the Underworld.

American astronomer Gerald Hawkins has used a computer to decode many of the stone alignments, and concluded that Stonehenge was a sophisticated means of observing the heavens. But it is doubtful if the observations were precise and, indeed, if the ancients were engaged in the same quest for discovery as scientists are today. Their most likely concerns would have been to establish a basic calendar, and to chart the movements of the heavenly bodies for religious purposes.

The builders who constructed Stonehenge were not primitive people living the lives of country peasants. Even though they left no written record, it is almost certain they had remarkable knowledge and skills. Perhaps no one has yet dreamed of Stonehenge's true function. It may be that John Michell, British author and esoteric researcher, is right when he suggests that Stonehenge was 'a cosmic temple dedicated to all twelve gods of the zodiac. It represents the ideal cosmology, the perfect and complete image of the universe.'

Stonehenge retains its power

Although the mystic temple of Stonehenge was abandoned around 3,000 years ago, much of it has survived and its magic has never disappeared. Merlin the magician was credited with erecting the stones, while local people have long believed the stones had healing powers which, when transferred to water, could cure all manner of ailments. Rural gatherings have been held here for centuries and for the last 80 years, modern Druids (who have no connection with the original Celtic priesthood) have celebrated the summer solstice at Stonehenge. For 20 years or so, thousands of people have gathered here each June to hold a festival. But in 1985, the authorities banned both the Druids and the festival for fear the stones and the surrounding land would be damaged.

The size of the monument, the origin of the stones, the orientation of the 'building' (from northeast to southwest), the man-hours of construction time, the centuries over which it was built – all these things point to Stonehenge being more than a neolithic farmers' meeting place. Explanations abound, most archaeologists agreeing a religious function. But anyone who has witnessed the sun rise over the great sarsen stones at the time of the midwinter solstice can hardly doubt the additional astronomical function of Stonehenge.

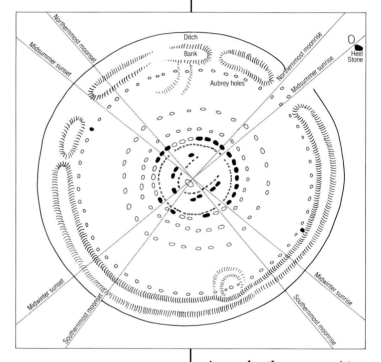

A popular theory to explain the purpose of Stonehenge involves the relatively new science of 'astro'-archaeology', originated for Stonehenge by the American astronomer Gerald Hawkins. According to this theory, Stonehenge is a vast prehistoric observatory, the alignment of whose stones provides precise sightlines for the rising and setting of the sun and moon on key dates, such as the summer and winter solstices. The movements of the sun, moon and stars could be tracked, eclipses predicted and the gods of the zodiac worshipped at appropriate times.

The diagram shows some of the key astronomical directions centred on the great circle of Stonehenge (after Alexander Thom). Black circles represent existing stones, open circles the sites of former stones.

STONEHENGE REVISITED

The association between Stonehenge and the Druids has been fixed in the public mind by the officially sanctioned midsummer ceremony that, until 1985, took place among the stones. The ritual was performed by the white-robed descendants of the United Ancient Order of Druids founded by freemasons in London in 1833. However, they have no connection with the Druids of old. At dawn on the morning of the summer solstice, these latterday 'Druids' played harps and trumpets, saluted the Heel Stone and the sarsen stones, intoned a murmuring chant and raised oak leaves or incense into the air.

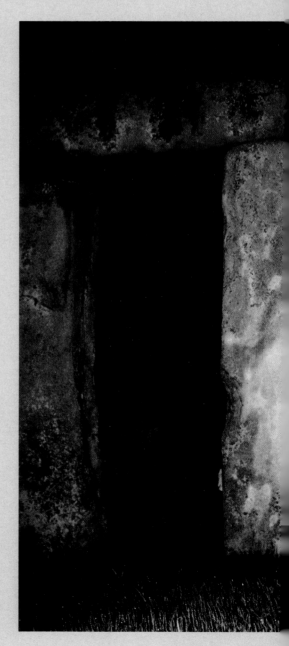

THE ARCHITECT TURNED ARCHAEOLOGIST

A king initiated the first serious study of Stonehenge. In 1620 when James I was staying at the home of the Earl of Pembroke, his curiosity was aroused by the group of standing stones nearby. The king sent for the architect Inigo Jones and instructed him to find out all he could. Jones studied architecture in Italy and later designed several major buildings in London, among them St Paul's Church in Covent Garden and the Banqueting House in Whitehall. He studied Stonehenge extensively and became the first person to take measurements there. He concluded that Stonehenge was the ruin of a Roman temple dedicated to Coelus and built soon after AD 79.

FAMOUS VISITORS

Royal interest in Stonehenge's ancient ruins brought many notable figures to view the site. The renowned diarist Samuel Pepys was one of the first. After his visit in June 1668 he wrote: 'Come thither and find them as prodigious as any tales I ever heard about them, and worthy this journey to see. God knows what their use was! They are hard to tell and yet may be told.'

THE RADICAL PROFESSOR OF ASTRONOMY

The interpretation of Stonehenge took a new turn in the 1960s when Gerald Hawkins, Professor of Astronomy at the University of Boston, claimed the stones could be used as an observatory and a computer. Using a modern computer to 'decode' the positions of the sun, moon and stars as they would have been in 1500 BC, he revealed specific alignments between certain stones and important events in the solar and lunar calendars, such as the midwinter sunrise and the northernmost setting of the moon. He also showed how Stonehenge could be used as a computer to predict solar and lunar eclipses.

31

AVEBURY: AN ANCIENT FERTILITY CENTRE

In the heart of the English countryside stand the remains of a grand megalithic temple. Who built it and when? What religious rituals were performed there? Did the standing stones form a kind of prehistoric power centre?

Britain's most important group of neolithic monuments is clustered around the village of Avebury in the undulating landscape of north Wiltshire. Within sight of one another lie the largest prehistoric tomb in England, the highest manmade hill in Europe and the world's most extensive henge enclosure. This Avebury complex is situated beside one of the country's ancient roads, the Ridgeway, which linked the trade routes running from Dorset to the Norfolk flint mines.

The scale of the henge at Avebury is breathtaking. One of its earliest investigators, the 17th-century antiquary John Aubrey wrote that it 'did as much excell of Stonehenge as a Cathedral does a Parish Church'. Covering 11.3 hectares (28 acres), the henge is formed by a boundary ditch 15m (50ft) deep which runs between two high banks – the outer bank has a perimeter of more than 1km (0.6mi). The henge originally held a large circle of about 100 standing stones – only 27 remain – enclosing two smaller circles represented today by random stones.

In the 14th century, Christians wishing to 'deconsecrate' what they saw as a pagan temple systematically toppled many stones in and around the henge. More destruction followed in the 17th and 18th centuries when stones were broken into pieces using fire, cold water and hammers. Many stones were used for building houses, particularly in the village of Avebury which has grown up inside the henge. The records of extensive work by the 18th-century antiquary Dr William Stukeley have enabled archaeologists to piece together the henge and its surroundings. In his book *Abury Described*, Stukeley wrote that Avebury showed 'a notorious grandeur of taste, a justness of plan, an apparent symmetry, and a sufficient niceness in the execution . . .'

Was Avebury part of a large religious complex?

The Wiltshire countryside surrounding the henge at Avebury is scattered with prehistoric remains. Close to Avebury there is an especially rich concentration, as if the area was of major religious importance. There are four entrances in the henge's bank and ditch. From the southern entrance a double avenue of standing stones, the Kennet Avenue, originally ran for 2.4km (1.5mi) and ended in two small stone circles and several circular wooden buildings. From another entrance ran the Beckhampton Avenue, 2km (1.25mi) long. It contained around 200 stones, of which only one is left standing today.

Other important sites close by are Windmill Hill, a causewayed camp built in 3350 BC before Avebury was conceived; Silbury Hill, Europe's tallest artificial mound, whose purpose is unknown; and England's largest prehistoric tomb, the 104m (340ft)-long West Kennet long barrow. Avebury was almost certainly the centre of religious activity in this area. But the form of this activity has tantalized antiquaries and archaeologists for generations.

The neolithic monument in the village of Avebury has been called the largest henge in the world. The roughly circular earthwork is bounded by a deep ditch with a huge bank outside it and encloses two stone circles. On the inner perimeter of the henge once stood 100 standing stones, but only 27 remain. Red deer antler picks and ox shoulder-blade shovels were used by the henge's Stone Age builders to raise the outer bank more than 15m (50ft) above the bottom of the ditch.

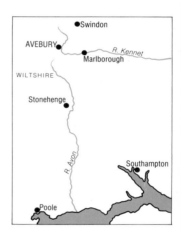

Avebury henge and its associated religious sites lie within sight of one another among the undulating downs near Marlborough in the county of Wiltshire, England. The other major neolithic monument in the area – Stonehenge – lies 26km (16mi) to the south on Salisbury Plain.

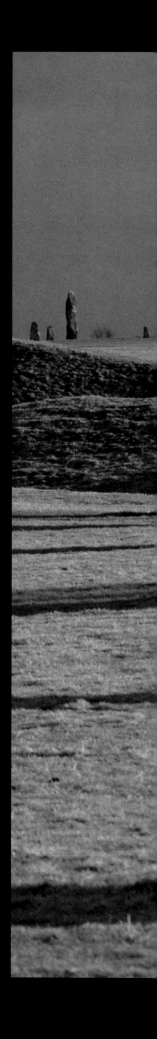

AVEBURY: AN ANCIENT FERTILITY CENTRE

As with Stonehenge, many different theories have been put forward since the 18th century regarding Avebury's purpose. Suggestions include a Roman temple, a Druid college, a representation of the sacred egg and serpent, an astronomical calculator, a planetarium, an amphitheatre. Archaeologists have proved the henge was in use between 2600 and 1600 BC – long before the Romans came to Britain and predating the Celtic priests known as Druids. And while there is much evidence that Stonehenge may have served as an observatory, no significant astronomical alignments have been found at Avebury.

One explanation for this remarkable group of monuments is that proposed by British archaeologist Michael Dames in his book *The Avebury Cycle.* They were, he suggests, 'created as a coherent ensemble to stage a religious drama which took one year to perform, with each edifice offering in turn a special setting for the celebration of a particular event in the farming year, matched to the corresponding event in the human life cycle'.

Ritual celebrations at Avebury

In the absence of written records about prehistoric rituals, clues to Avebury's purpose must be sought in the fragmentary remains of this once mighty sacred site. At significant dates in the farming calendar, festivals were held which involved dancing, processions along the avenues and the offering of objects to the fertility spirits and gods. There may have been ritual animal sacrifice, possibly even human sacrifice. Broken pots, hazel nuts, twigs from fruit trees and damaged flints found buried in the Kennet Avenue could all have been ritual offerings. Various finds from the henge itself, such as knives and human bones, could also have had ritual significance. The proximity of important long barrows has prompted the suggestion that ancestral remains may have been carried from them into Avebury along the avenues. The aid of the ancestors may have been invoked in rituals to ensure the fertility of cattle, crops and people.

Sexual activity may have featured in these rituals, since such imitative magic was often used to encourage fertility. Some surviving traditional customs of Britain, and many no longer practised, contain sexual symbolism. Could these customs be watered down versions of prehistoric rituals? Dancing around the maypole, for example, has sexual and fertility associations. The fact that 19th-century children still danced around a maypole erected inside the Avebury henge may provide a direct link to the rituals of 4,000 years ago.

Why did Avebury's builders go to so much trouble to prepare such a grand theatre as the henge? That they would need a clearly defined stage for their rituals is reasonable, but why erect such huge standing stones? Besides symbolizing the male and female elements, the stones may have had an even greater role to play in the ritual celebrations at Avebury. Modern research is investigating the possibility that standing stones can accumulate and transmit natural earth energies. Such energies have already been detected by scientific instruments and dowsing rods. Some sensitive people can even sense this energy with their bare hands.

Prehistoric people, who lived in harmony with nature, were probably far more sensitive than people are today to the subtle influences emanating from the earth. It is an intriguing idea that the stones had a positive role to play in the ceremonies at Avebury by making accessible earth energy for use by the participants. Should modern research show that standing stones were able to do this, it would be a small yet logical step to conclude that Avebury was not only a fertility centre but also a prehistoric powerhouse.

The enigmatic Silbury Hill rises from the landscape no more than 1.6km (1mi) from the Avebury henge. Although legend relates that a certain King Sil was buried here on horseback, no burial has been found in this, the biggest of Europe's manmade mounds. Covering an area of 2 hectares (5.25 acres) and standing 40m (130ft) high, Silbury Hill was constructed about 2750 BC. But its true purpose remains unknown.

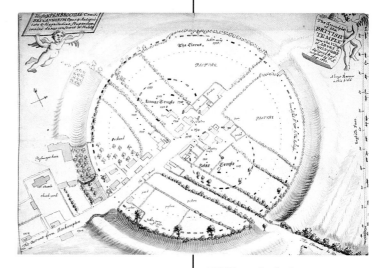

William Stukeley, an 18th-century English antiquary, made a detailed manuscript plan of Avebury and its monument in 1721. He called the northern stone circle the 'Lunar Temple' and the southern stone circle the 'Solar Temple'.

The Devil's Chair is one of the few megaliths to survive the near-destruction of Avebury by Puritans. This huge stone is 4.3m (14ft) wide and 4m (13ft) high and can be found where the West Kennet Avenue joins the great circle. A natural ledge in the stone makes a comfortable seat and, as late as 1900, girls from the village would sit here on the eve of May Day to make a wish.

SANTIAGO DE COMPOSTELA: SHRINE OF ST JAMES

The discovery of the body of one of Christ's disciples led to the foundation of a sacred city. How did this happen? Why do pilgrims visit his shrine? Are the bones under the cathedral's High Altar indeed those of St James?

For more than 1,000 years, pilgrims have travelled the roads and footpaths of Europe to the city of Santiago de Compostela in northwest Spain. Many devote months of their lives to an arduous journey on foot or by bicycle, stopping at shrines, hospices and churches along the route. Even today, their arrival in Santiago's great cathedral square is celebrated with laughter and tears.

The magnificent cathedral is reputed to contain the mortal remains of James, the son of Zebedee, apostle and cousin of Christ, and subsequently patron saint of Spain. Together with Peter and John, James had a special place among the apostles, for only these three had witnessed the transfiguration of Christ. A tradition, based on legend rather than fact, tells how James travelled to Spain after Christ died to preach the gospel.

How did the apostle come to be buried in Santiago? When James was beheaded by Herod Agrippa I in Jerusalem in AD 44, he became the first apostle to be martyred. Legend relates that, after his death, his body was placed in a boat by his disciples at Jaffa in Palestine. Seven days later, guided by the hand of God and by favourable winds, the boat reached the shores of Iria Flavia on the Atlantic coast of Spain, 32km (20mi) from what is now Santiago. After a journey by ox-cart, James was finally buried at the precise spot where the oxen miraculously stopped of their own accord.

The discovery of James' tomb

Early in the 9th century, the hermit Pelagius, who lived near Iria Flavia, was guided by mysterious lights in the sky to a marble tomb. The local bishop identified it as the tomb of St James and summoned King Alphonso II who wasted no time in proclaiming James as the patron saint of the kingdom.

King Alphonso had made a shrewd political decision, for Christian Spain was in danger of being overrun again by the Moors whose Moslem kingdom had stretched from Morocco and Spain to Mesopotamia. Who better than St James to be the new and inspiring champion of the Christians? In 844, at the battle of Clavijo in Castille, St James is said to have appeared on a white horse at the head of the Christian army which, inspired by his intervention, routed the enemy with ease.

News of the discovery of St James' tomb soon spread through Christendom. In 950, the first recorded foreign pilgrim, Bishop Godescalc from Le Puy in the Auvergne in France, made his way with a number of followers to the distant but rapidly growing town of Santiago. The tradition of the pilgrimage to Santiago prospered, due mainly to the patronage of the powerful Benedictine abbey at Cluny in France which built hospitals and priories along the route. Other shrines soon sprang up both in Spain and in France, where four main routes from Tours, Vézelay, Le Puy and Arles were developing.

The ultimate goal of the pilgrims of St James is Santiago's magnificent cathedral, an architectural treasure replete with altars, chapels, paintings and sculptures. The first of the great medieval Spanish cathedrals, Santiago – the Spanish for St James – was begun around 1074 under the direction of Bishop Gelmirez.

Astonishingly ornate, the High Altar of Santiago Cathedral is constructed of silver, jasper and alabaster. Dating from 1672, the altar has as its centrepiece a painted wooden statue of St James which, in 1765, was cloaked in a silver cape and adorned with glittering jewels.

The well-travelled road to Compostela brings pilgrims from all over Europe to the hallowed shrine of St James. Four main routes begin in France – at Tours, Vézelay, Le Puy and Arles – converging on a single route that leads to Santiago across northern Spain.

The cathedral and the relics

The first sanctuary erected by King Alphonso was built on the site of a Roman altar dedicated to Jupiter. An ever-growing number of pilgrims meant the church had to be expanded from time to time. The present cathedral, whose interior epitomizes the Romanesque pilgrim church, was started in 1078. According to Frenchman Aimery Picaud, probable author of a 12th-century pilgrim's guidebook, the cathedral 'had no fault, being admirably constructed, large, spacious, of harmonious dimensions and well proportioned in length, breadth and height'.

The incomparable Portico de la Gloria, carved at the end of the 12th century, lies behind the flamboyant 18th-century Baroque facade. Entering by a side door, the pilgrim is greeted by three richly sculpted portals, made up of ranks of angels, apostles, prophets and elders. Many have musical instruments and all are headed by a seated figure of Christ in Majesty. Immediately below, the genial and gentle figure of St James himself is seated above the tree of Jesse. This is the genealogical tree of Christ, showing his descent from Jesse, the father of David. In the tree, five indentations show where pilgrims have placed their fingers in homage before entering the body of the cathedral.

The gilded statue of St James shines out like a beacon above the High Altar. On either side is a staircase which pilgrims mount before embracing the apostle from behind – it is a disconcerting sight to see a pair of living arms suddenly appear around his neck during a service. The pilgrim's final duty is to descend beneath the altar and gaze upon the silver casket containing the bones of the saint. Pilgrims are then entitled to wear the scallop shell, traditional emblem of their journey to Santiago.

Late 19th-century excavations of a tomb behind the High Altar brought to light the bones of three men – but which ones, if any, belonged to the saint? The matter seemed to be resolved when a fragment of bone, in the ownership of the cathedral of Pistoia in Italy and long held to be part of the skull of St James, fitted one of the three skulls at Santiago. In 1884, Pope Leo III confirmed the existence of the relics, but whether they are truly those of St James – other evidence suggests they may belong to a martyred Spanish bishop – is unlikely to be definitively answered.

Celebrating St James' Day

The citizens of Santiago, and the people of the surrounding villages of Galicia, celebrate St James' Day with great fervour. On 25 July itself and on the preceding day, both the city streets and the Plaza de l'Obradoiro, Spain's most majestic square, are packed with local people and foreign pilgrims. While the town band plays, colourful giant figures called the Xigantes parade in the narrow streets, followed by religious processions and Galician folk music and dancing. At midnight on 24 July comes the first climax: the burning of a wooden mosque in front of the cathedral which provokes wild clapping, the lighting of fireworks and more singing and dancing. On the feast day itself, Mass in the cathedral is the setting for the second climax when the giant censer, the Botafumeiro, is lit. Hauled by 8 men and exuding fire and smoke, the censer is swung across the transepts in a great arc stretching from floor to ceiling.

Celebrations reach their peak in Holy Years when St James' Day falls on a Sunday. Only two such days remain in this century – in 1993 and 1999, when Santiago can expect to receive more pilgrims than ever before. Like their countless predecessors, the pilgrims will have followed the most historical route in western Europe to reach their destination, even if the truth behind the founding of the city and the pilgrimage remains elusive.

The Plaza de l'Obradoiro in front of Santiago Cathedral echoes with the sound of Galician bagpipes and drums during the feast day of St James. Richly dressed in national costume, folklore groups re-enact traditional dances in front of crowds of eager pilgrims and local people. The celebrations end with a spectacular display of fireworks that illuminates the cathedral in a climax of incandescent splendour.

The distinctive emblem of the pilgrimage to Santiago is the scallop shell, traditionally a symbol of Venus, the goddess of love. No one knows how this shell came to be the pilgrims' badge, but ever since the 12th century it has been carved on many church walls along the pilgrims' route. This relief on the wall of St Jacques shows St James' body arriving in Spain by boat from Palestine.

NEWGRANGE: A WEALTH OF PREHISTORIC SYMBOLS

The entrance to the finest passage-grave in Europe opens to the southeast in exact line with the midwinter sunrise. What links does the grave have with astronomy? What is the meaning of the spiral rock carvings? What can the grave's symbols reveal about the religious beliefs in Ireland 5,000 years ago?

Beside the River Boyne in Ireland, where the waters make a wide curve, a prehistoric cemetery harbours more than 25 passage-graves. Known as the Bend of the Boyne, the cemetery appears to be deliberately located on a hill so that its three finest tombs – Newgrange, Knowth and Dowth – can dominate the fertile valley below. Newgrange passage-grave is the finest prehistoric site in Ireland, for apart from the extraordinary structure itself, it is endowed with outstanding rock carvings. But was Newgrange just a sepulchre or did it have some further purpose?

The ruined and plundered tomb was rediscovered in 1699 and the Welsh antiquary Edward Lhuyd (1660–1708) was one of the first to enter it. He wrote:'At the first entering we were forced to creep; but still as we went on the pillars on each side of us were higher and higher; and coming into the cave we found it about 20 foot high. In this cave, on each hand of us was a cell or apartment, and another went straight forward to the entry.' The passage along which Lhuyd entered is more than 18m (60ft) long, and ends in three small chambers containing massive stone basins. In the high corbelled roof, the hundred or so stones are perfectly balanced and remain in place without the aid of mortar. In 5,000 years only two of the stones have broken. This perfection of design and execution shows how the builders of Newgrange around 3250 BC were superb craftsmen.

The meaning of the carvings

The eye of the discerning visitor to Newgrange is caught by a wealth of fine rock carvings. The entrance is guarded by a stone covered with spirals and over a dozen of the upright stones inside the passage are decorated. Several roof-slabs and corbels are also carved, sometimes on the upper surfaces which cannot be seen from below. The finest interior carving is a triple spiral low down on one of the uprights. Outside, many of the kerbstones are decorated, again sometimes on their hidden inner surfaces. Apart from the spirals, the other most popular designs used at Newgrange were lozenges, zigzags and circles. But strangely these do not coincide with the most-used symbols at other passage-graves in Ireland. What then do they signify?

Early antiquaries were somewhat dismissive of these decorations. Thomas Molyneux, an 18th-century Professor of Physic at Dublin's Trinity College, called them 'a Barbarous kind of carving', and many people have since believed them to be simply ornamental. More recently, serious efforts have been made to discover some meaning beyond their decorative effect. One notable researcher in this field is Martin Brennan whose book, *The Boyne Valley Vision*, is an analysis of the 700 or more carved stones in the Boyne valley. He concluded that most of the carvings recorded astronomical and cosmological observations, and

Inside the mound the chamber is cruciform in shape, ending in three small recesses containing large stone basins. The brilliantly conceived corbelled roof rises to a height of 6m (20ft) at a point above the recesses. Many of the stones on the walls exhibit the same rich variety of symbolic carvings as are found outside.

Prehistoric earthworks, mounds, standing stones and passage-graves are concentrated on a hill above the River Boyne in County Meath, Ireland, about 45km (28mi) north of Dublin. The passage-graves at Newgrange, Knowth and Dowth are part of the Bend of the Boyne site, one of Europe's greatest prehistoric cemeteries.

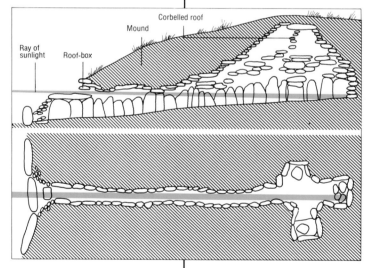

The inner sanctuary of the passage-grave is illuminated only by the rays of the sun around the midwinter solstice. For about 20 minutes every morning, on the few days prior to and following the shortest day, a thin pencil of sunlight enters the roof-box above the entrance and touches the stone basin at the end of the passage.

that Newgrange was, among other things, the largest and oldest sundial in the world. 'To the people of the Boyne Valley,' wrote Brennan, 'the study of the sun's movements was very important. They were the master diallers of the New Stone Age.'

Scientific discovery was not the only motivation of the men who built such magnificent structures as Newgrange and Stonehenge – where astronomical observations were also made. Perhaps they were learning, too, about the universe and relating it to their own lives in a direct and meaningful way. Newgrange is not just a sundial or an observatory. It appears to be a symbol of the life-force itself. In its original form the mound covering the passage-grave was egg-shaped, and into this life-bearing egg penetrated a long passage ending in a cavelike chamber, possibly symbolizing the womb. Inside stands a tall pillar of phallic shape, and the pairs of chalk balls found at Newgrange may also have been male sexual symbols.

The rays of the midwinter sun

Newgrange was constructed to take advantage of the most life-giving element of all – the sun. Above the entrance, which would originally have been sealed by a stone slab, is a small aperture whose roof bears carvings of double spirals and lozenges. It had stone doors which could be opened and closed. The structure is so orientated that at dawn on the midwinter solstice, the rising sun shines into the tomb through this 'roof-box' – its door would have been opened in readiness. The shaft of sunlight penetrates down the passage and into the heart of the chamber.

Newgrange was recently excavated by Michael O'Kelly, Professor of Archaeology at Cork University, and on 21 December 1969 he stood inside the passage-grave at dawn to record the events. 'At exactly 09.54 hours BST', he wrote, 'the top edge of the ball of the sun appeared above the local horizon and at 09.58 hours the first pencil of direct sunlight shone through the roof-box and right along the passage to reach across the tomb chamber floor as far as the front edge of the basin stone in the end chamber. As the thin line of light widened to a 17cm [6.8in] band and swung across the chamber floor, the tomb was dramatically illuminated and various details of the side- and end-chambers as well as the corbelled roof could be clearly seen from the light reflected from the floor. At 10.04 hours the 17cm band of light began to narrow again and at exactly 10.15 hours the direct beam was cut off from the tomb.'

The winter solstice is the shortest day of the year, the time when the new year begins and when the life-force starts to revitalize a dormant earth. Of all the carvings does the triple spiral inside the chamber encapsulate what the builders of Newgrange were attempting to achieve in constructing this misnamed 'tomb'? Does the ingoing spiral symbolize the journey taken by the dead while at the same time the outgoing spiral depict rebirth? If so, it may be that, in Newgrange, is performed a symbolic fertilization of the cosmic egg which would ensure the continuation of the eternal cycle of death and rebirth. The priests may have placed the cremated remains of some of their most revered ancestors inside the stone basins in the chambers where they could be touched by the sunlight at midwinter in a symbolic affirmation that their line would continue.

Newgrange is only part of the complex site at the Bend of the Boyne, although it is the finest part. All the major tombs together may contain a scientific record which is now, 5,000 years later, beginning to be deciphered. The findings show yet again how prehistoric man was neither simple nor barbaric, but was endowed with knowledge and skills far beyond our imaginings.

Spirals, chevrons, lozenges and other symbolic forms are engraved on many of the 97 kerbstones surrounding the exterior of the mound. The symbols on this kerbstone, known as K52 and positioned exactly opposite the entrance, have been interpreted as records of astronomical and cosmological observations.

Magnificently carved spirals decorate the huge stone, 3.2m (10.5ft) long and 1.6m (4.5ft) high, in front of the entrance to the passage-grave. The spirals may represent the labyrinthine journey of the soul to the realms of the dead. The roof-box opening above the entrance admits sunlight only on the mornings of the days around midwinter.

Newgrange passage-grave was originally covered by a huge egg-shaped mound which stood around 14m (46ft) high – it is now 9m (30ft) high – and 76m (250ft) in diameter. Covering more than 0.5 hectare (1 acre), the mound was made of around 200,000 pebbles brought from the nearby riverbed and overlaid by sparkling white quartz.

Set into the outer edge of the mound are 97 kerbstones lying on their sides. Around the tomb is a freestanding stone circle, of which 12 of the original 35 stones remain.

THE MEGALITHIC AVENUES OF CARNAC

Around 3,000 standing stones arranged into avenues represent the most extraordinary megalithic monument in Europe. When were they erected? Was their purpose astronomical or religious or both? What is the significance of the Fairy Stone?

Huge standing stones and earth mounds erected in prehistory bear witness to the great sanctity of the area around Carnac in France. Some of the world's oldest manmade structures are to be found here, at the greatest of all megalithic centres, in the countryside of Brittany. Nowhere can the ancient reverence of neolithic people be felt better than at Kercado, near Carnac, where a large grass-covered mound is topped by an upright stone. This tumulus, whose entrance faces the midwinter sunrise, contains a stone-lined passage leading to a square stone chamber. Once a tomb where successive generations were laid to rest, its most remarkable characteristic is its great age. Dated around 4700 BC, it is the most ancient structure in Europe, nearly 2,000 years older than Stonehenge or the pyramids of Egypt.

Astonishing avenues of stones

Carnac's main claim to fame is the largest grouping of ancient megaliths anywhere in the world. Thousands still stand despite centuries of neglect and active demolition by farmers. Four impressive alignments stretch for nearly 8km (5mi) through pinewoods and heathland, a remarkable testimony to the organizational skills of the ancient inhabitants of the region.

The largest assembly lies beside the hamlet of Le Ménec near Carnac where a group of cottages is surrounded by an ellipse of stones standing shoulder to shoulder. Composed of 70 megaliths, each averaging 1.2m (4ft) in height, this enclosure is 100m (330ft) across but pales into insignificance when compared with its associated megalithic avenues.

Eastward from the enclosure at Le Ménec stand 1,099 stones arranged in 11 avenues that stretch to the horizon. The stones are also arranged by size. Starting from the enclosure, the largest are 3.7m (12ft) high but diminish in height until at the end of the avenues they are 0.9m (3ft) high. The stone rows are not straight but follow a gentle curve toward the northeast and terminate at another stone enclosure over 0.8km (0.5mi) away.

The stunning sight of these avenues was aptly described in 1827 by a French antiquary, the Chevalier de Fréminville, when he called them '. . . that regiment of stones, the startling array of shapeless rocks aligned so symmetrically'. Like any unsuspecting visitor, de Fréminville had been 'filled with astonishment . . . The numbers of these stones in their bizarre arrangements, the height reached by their long, grey, mossy outlines rising from the black heather in which they are rooted, and finally the total stillness that surrounds them, all astound the imagination and fill the soul with a melancholy veneration for these ancient witnesses to so many centuries.'

The alignments at Le Ménec are impressive enough for their length, but a short distance to the east are the even bigger stones of the avenues at Kermario, 'the place of the dead'. The largest of

The little hamlet of Le Ménec, 0.8km (0.5mi) north of Carnac, marks the beginning of four multiple avenues of standing stones. Eleven rows of megaliths known as menhirs stand roughly parallel to one another and leave the hamlet in an east-northeast direction. It was once thought that each row contained 1,000 stones and that all four groups of stone avenues – at Le Ménec, Kermario, Kerlescan and Le Petit Ménec – were joined in one superb array.

The large number of artificial mounds, stone avenues, dolmens, circles and standing stones located around Carnac make it the world's centre of megalithic monuments. Several of them make significant astronomical alignments with each other, while the purpose of the rest remains a mystery.

these megaliths are more than 7m (23ft) high, and like the former array rapidly diminish in size toward the end of the alignment 1.2km (0.75mi) away where three huge stones stand at right angles to the avenues.

The third alignment of stones stands farther east still, near Kerlescan, 'the place of the burning'. Here, an almost square enclosure lies close to 13 parallel rows composed of 540 stones. Eastward yet again are about 100 stones of the Petit Ménec alignment which may once have linked up with the Kerlescan array.

Was Carnac the centre of a cattle cult?

Local folklore explains the ranks of standing stones as Roman soldiers petrified by Cornély, Carnac's own saint and a former Pope who was chased from Rome to his native Brittany. In his flight Cornély used oxen to carry his baggage, and because of this has become the patron saint of cattle. The centre of his veneration at the parish church of Carnac contains an image of Cornély surrounded by standing stones and blessing two bulls. On 13 September each year, local farmers bring their cattle to the church to be blessed. Could this saint's day ceremony be a continuation of an old pagan ceremony in which the magic power of stones was used to heal sick cattle? The answer could be affirmative because some evidence of an old cattle cult has been found in the vicinity. Excavations of a Gallo-Roman villa at Bosseno near Carnac have uncovered the ceremonial statue of a bull, and remains of cattle have been found in local prehistoric burial sites.

Did prehistoric skywatchers erect the stones?

The alignments of stones, earth mounds and single megaliths may have been erected to chart and measure the apparent movements of the sun, moon and stars. The best evidence for this comes from Alexander Thom, former Professor of Engineering at Oxford University, who accurately surveyed the megaliths from 1970–75. He concluded the megalithic complex around Carnac had been designed to make astronomical observations, particularly of the moon. If true, the observations would have been carried out at the avenues, where four of the larger stones, including the 6m (20ft)-high Giant of Manio, produce astronomically significant lines of sight with one another.

The most important stone in this observatory would have been the now-broken megalith known as *Er Grah* (The Fairy Stone) or as *Le Grand Menhir Brisé*. This lies in four huge pieces at the end of a former earth mound near Locmariaquer where it fell during an earthquake in 1722. Originally over 20m (65ft) high, the moving and erecting of a stone weighing more than 350 tons was a fantastic feat of engineering. Thom's survey showed the relationship of this Fairy Stone with other major features. From mounds and stones up to 13km (8mi) from the Fairy Stone, important moon rises and moonsets could be observed using the great megalith as a marker.

The myriad stones of the alignments and the avenues may not have been employed directly for observing astronomical events such as these lunar movements. According to Professor Thom, they could easily have been used for astronomical calculations because they form what he calls a sort of 'megalithic graph paper'. Despite the present irregularities in the alignments and positions of the stones, produced by the wear and tear of the ages and by the more recent re-erection of fallen stones, Thom concluded the layouts were planned by skywatchers as a series of straight lines or regular geometric forms. In other words, the megalithic avenues and associated stones that can be seen today are the remains of a great neolithic astronomical instrument.

The Tumulus St Michel to the northeast of Carnac is one of many large burial mounds in the region. More than 122m (400ft) long and 12m (40ft) high, the mound contains a number of small graves dated around 4000 BC. The pagan site has been christianized by the erection of a chapel dedicated to St Michel (St Michael) the dragon slayer.

The largest megalith in Europe lies broken on the outskirts of Locmariaquer in Brittany. Called the Fairy Stone, this monolith was originally 20m (65ft) high and was thought to have been felled by lightning or an earth tremor. Recent surveys by astro-archaeologists have concluded it was a focal point for studying the movements of the moon. The fact that the pieces of the Fairy Stone lie at the end of an enormous neolithic burial mound suggest it had more to do with guarding the dead.

CUMAE: AN ANCIENT CAVE OF PROPHECY

Temple ruins beside the Bay of Naples pinpoint the place where a mysterious woman delivered her oracles. Who was the Sibyl? Why was Cumae chosen as a sacred site? What was the power of the cave at Cumae?

Greek settlers coming to Italy in the 8th century BC chose a spectacular site for their colony at Cumae. At the northwest tip of the Bay of Naples, a volcanic outcrop commanding a wide view offered the perfect place to build their acropolis, defended as it was on all sides by the sea, lakes, woods and mountains.

Remains of the walls of this acropolis can still be seen, on its highest point the Temple of Jupiter, once a landmark for seafarers. The ruins visible today are those of a building of the 5th century BC, reconstructed under the Roman Emperor Augustus (27 BC–AD 14) and in the 6th century AD converted into a Christian church. Lower down the hill is the base and outline of the Temple of Apollo, of uncertain origins. Lower yet is the cave of the world's most famous oracle, the Cumaean Sibyl.

Oracles of the ancient world

The wise woman who can foretell the future appears in the traditions of many lands – none more celebrated in antiquity than the Sibyl of Cumae. At an early date, people in western Asia knew verses believed to be the oracular utterances of prophetesses known as *Sibyllai*. What the word *sibyl* means is unknown, though legend says it was the name of a seeress at Marpessus, near Troy, who spoke her oracles in riddles and wrote them down on leaves of plants. What is certain is that the tradition concerning Sibyls came to be shared by the Greeks, and thence the Romans, and localized in various places. Eventually *sibyl* became a generic name and was given to a number of different prophetesses – the Roman author Varro (116–27 BC) lists 10 – throughout the ancient world, most notably at Cumae.

Whether there was an actual person known as the Sibyl at Cumae is uncertain, though in the days of the Roman Empire her tomb was shown to people visiting the Temple of Apollo. In Greek tradition, the Sibyls had been associated with Apollo, as god of prophecy: the Delphic Oracle in Greece, known as the Pythia, was a priestess of his shrine at Delphi. She either chewed leaves of laurel – Apollo's tree – in order to fall into a prophetic trance, or sat on her tripod over a fissure in the ground and inhaled intoxicating volcanic fumes. Whichever means she used, she was thought to be directly inspired by the god, who spoke through her in notoriously ambiguous oracles.

Cumae, like Delphi, lies in an area of volcanic activity – the Campi Flegri, or Flegrean Fields, west of Naples, in Roman times favoured by the rich for residential purposes and for the spa developed around the thermal springs at Baia. Like the Delphic Oracle, the Cumaean Sibyl was connected with Apollo. The story the Roman poets told was that she came from the East and Apollo had offered her anything she asked for if she would accept him as her lover. She asked for as many years of life as there were grains in a handful of dust, which proved to be a thousand. But

A branch of mistletoe raised in her left hand, the Sibyl of Cumae leads Aeneas to the entrance of the Underworld in J.M.W. Turner's painting of 'Aeneas and the Sibyl, Lake Avernus'. The mistletoe, known as the Golden Bough, was sacred to Proserpina, the Roman queen of the Underworld.

The Roman poet Virgil described the entrance as a cavern that was 'profound, wide-mouthed, and huge, Rough underfoot, defended by dark pool/And gloomy forest'.

The ruins of Cumae, the oldest Greek colony in mainland Italy, lie about 20km (12mi) northwest of Naples. Naturally defended by local topography, Cumae came to control one of the most fruitful parts of the Campanian plain.

The Cumaean Sibyl was the most famous oracle of the ancient world but she was not the only *sibyl*. Others include the Sibyls of Libica (Libya) and Delphica (Delphi).

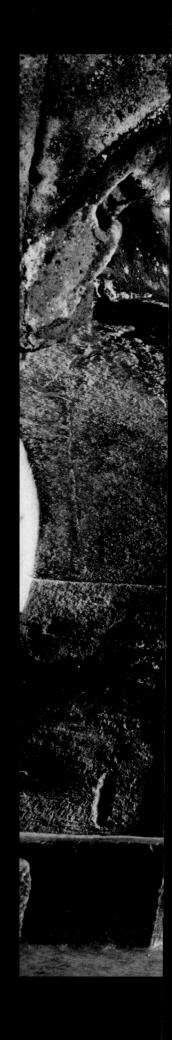

she forgot to ask also for perpetual youth, so she grew older and smaller until she was so shrivelled with age she was shut up in a bottle which hung at Cumae. When children asked her in Greek what she wanted, all she would answer was: 'I want to die'.

The entrance to the Underworld

The cult of Apollo was both necromantic and chthonic – concerned with the dead and the Underworld. It is as a guide to the Underworld that the Cumaean Sibyl appears in the sixth book of the *Aeneid* by the Roman poet Virgil, written between 29 and 19 BC. The Trojan hero Aeneas comes to consult her in her sanctum, a 'dark enormous cave' below the Temple of Apollo. She instructs him first to arm himself with the magical Golden Bough as his passport through the Underworld, before leading him and his men to its gateway at Lake Avernus.

This mysterious lake, only 4km (2.5mi) from Pozzuoli, is still called Lago Averno. In antiquity overhung by dark brooding woods, magically evoked by the painter Turner, it is today much changed by volcanic eruptions and building development. It is none the less a dramatic place. Deep and sulphurous, it fills the crater of an old volcano whose deadly fumes, said tradition, prevented birds flying over it. Hence, it was thought, came its name, supposed to derive from Greek *a-ornos*, 'birdless'.

Where is the cave of the Sibyl?

On the acropolis at Cumae was a cave known by tradition as that of the Sibyl. When excavated in the 1920s, however, it turned out to be bigger than expected, a huge gallery 183m (600ft) long, with light shafts and water cisterns leading off it. This gallery drove straight through the hill to the other side and was soon identified as a military work engineered on the orders of the Roman general Agrippa (*ca.* 63–12 BC). In 1932, a second cave was discovered nearby, which archaeologists were satisfied was the Sibyl's. The approach is a gallery 107m (350ft) long, with 12 short side galleries opening on to the hillside to form light shafts.

The main gallery ends in a vestibule with a pair of built-in stone benches and beyond it, a vaulted chamber. People may once have sat on the seats while waiting to consult the Sibyl, hidden on the other side of the door originally separating the vestibule from the inner sanctum. They were, perhaps, in a state of heightened anticipation for, in daytime, the alternate bands of light and dark created by the shafts along the gallery meant that anyone coming from the inner end to conduct newcomers to the sanctum would seem to appear and disappear.

The light shafts may also have served to overawe visitors to the sanctuary in another fashion. Like apertures remarked elsewhere in oracular chambers, such as those in Malta, these openings in the rock could produce the calculated 'special effect' described by Virgil: 'The cliff's huge flank is honeycombed, cut out/In a cavern perforated a hundred times,/Having a hundred mouths, with rushing voices/Carrying the responses of the Sibyl.'

In 1932, it seemed as if this cavern had certainly been found and it is the one still shown at Cumae as the Sibyl's. But is it? The sanctuary of the Cumaean Sibyl was revered throughout the Greek world from the 6th or 5th century BC, but most of what is now visible belongs to a slightly later period. There were virtually no associated finds to confirm or deny a religious use for the cave and some archaeologists think further investigation is needed. Yet it is easy, standing at the entrance to this cavern, to imagine Virgil's hero Aeneas and his Trojans, seasoned warriors all, yet chill with dread, as the Sibyl 'from her shrine/Sang out her riddles, echoing in the cave . . .'

Petitioners seeking advice from the Cumaean Sibyl would be ushered along the gallery of alternating light and dark to the vestibule outside the Oracle's inner room. Set into the hill at Cumae, the gallery is illuminated by a series of light shafts that open on to the hillside. The disturbing sight of a dim priestly figure intermittently vanishing as he approaches would have unsettled the stoutest of petitioners.

The oracles of the Cumaean Sibyl were gathered into nine books of prophecies and she offered them at a huge price to Tarquin the Proud, the last of the seven kings of Rome. When he refused she burned three and later offered him the remaining six, still at the original price. Again he refused, so she burned another three. But when she offered him the last three, his nerve broke and he bought them. These famous Sibylline Books were kept in the Capitoline Temple in Rome and consulted in emergencies by the Senate. But they were burned along with the Temple in 83 BC.

THE ORACLE AT DELPHI

APOLLO'S MOST SACRED PLACE

By virtue of its location beneath the cliffs of Mount Parnassus and above the valley of the Plistus River, Delphi ranks among the most impressive of the Greek holy places. Known as the navel of the world, Delphi thrived from around 700 BC to 200 BC. At 570m (1,870ft) above sea level, the Temple of Apollo, located beneath the well-preserved theatre, was the site of the Delphic Oracle. Here, a prophetess called the Pythia would enter a trance and communicate with the god Apollo. Her relatively incoherent utterances were turned into intelligible responses – often in verse – by male priests who relayed them to the petitioners. One such response was given to Alexander the Great who was told 'My son, none can resist thee'.

THE CENTRE OF THE EARTH

The marble *omphalos*, dated to the 4th century BC, was placed between two statues of golden eagles in the Temple of Apollo at Delphi. The *omphalos* (the word means 'navel' in Greek) stood at the spot marking the centre of the earth. The two eagles had located this spot after the god Zeus had made them fly toward each other at the same speed from the western and eastern edges of the world.

APOLLO, THE GREEK GOD OF PROPHECY

When he was young, the god Apollo killed Python, the huge serpent of Mount Parnassus, with an arrow. In honour of this deed, the Pythian Games were established in the 6th century BC at Delphi. The Temple of Apollo was built over the serpent's lair and a priestess, the Pythia, was bestowed with the gift of prophecy by Apollo himself. Before consulting the Pythia, visitors would make substantial offerings to Apollo in the hope of a satisfactory response from the oracle.

THE EXTERNSTEINE: A GERMAN SANCTUARY

The enigmatic rock pillars in Germany's northern forests hold many ancient mysteries. Who made the caves and the carvings? What are they for? Why does the chapel face the midsummer sunrise? What is the significance of the world-pillar carving?

The Teutoburger Wald holds an important place in German history. It was here, near Detmold in Lower Saxony, that Hermann, leader of the Cherusci tribe, decisively defeated the Roman legions in AD 9 and so prevented the Roman conquest of all the Germanic tribes. Not far away from this famous battle site lies the Externsteine, a towering outcrop of five enormous weathered limestone pillars rising 30m (100ft) above the forest.

The German Stonehenge

A natural place of power, the Externsteine has since ancient times been recognized as a sacred site. It holds in German tradition a place similar to that of Stonehenge in the mysteries of Britain. Frequented by nomadic hunters in the Stone Age, the Externsteine has been a major ceremonial centre of German pagan worship since the earliest times. Because of this, it is redolent with mystical and mythological associations.

Charlemagne, King of the Franks and Holy Roman Emperor, set about a systematic suppression of paganism and, in AD 772, forbade worship at the Externsteine. Later, monks from the nearby abbey of Paderborn used the rock-cut chambers for their Christian devotions. During the religious wars of the 17th century, the rocks became a military stronghold, while in more peaceful times they proved an irresistible subject for romantic artists and writers. Today, the Externsteine is a major tourist attraction, equipped with an artificial lake to enhance its picturesque qualities.

The natural crags of the Externsteine are riddled with man-made caves and apertures which seem to have been enlarged by successive generations. While some, such as the chapel, have obvious uses, others are a complete mystery. There are steps that lead nowhere, as well as platforms, slots, niches, small drilled holes and larger openings in the rock faces. In the widest rock pillar, a chamber of irregular shape is accessible via two entrances. The northeastern entrance and both the chamber's windows face the midsummer sunrise, but the other entrance gives entry via a narrow passage which has been carefully carved into a bizarre shape.

The main chamber was used in initiation and purification rituals by a pre-Christian priesthood. Many of its features, such as the various niches, the carving of a grotesque face, the circular depression in the floor and ancient graffiti, parallel other subterranean religious structures found elsewhere in Europe.

Was the chapel an ancient solar observatory?

Carved into the living rock near the top of one of the pillars is the chapel, perhaps the most mysterious place among the Externsteine. Accessible only by rock-cut steps and a precarious footbridge, the chapel is roofless and, at its easterly end, has a

The medieval rock relief which Cistercian monks carved on to the side of the Externsteine symbolizes the domination of Christianity over the former pagan religion. To reach Jesus and remove his body from the Cross, Nicodemus stands on the bent form of the pagan world-pillar, *Irminsul*, the backbone of the universe. Below ground lies the World Serpent, symbol of the earth energies accumulated at the site.

The Externsteine rises up from the forests of the Teutoburger Wald, 11km (7.5mi) from Detmold and 80km (50mi) from Hannover in Lower Saxony. The country all around, known as the sacred heartland of Germany, is thick with standing stones, hermitages, mark stones, churches and other sites which form a network of straight lines called *Heilige Linien*.

The Externsteine has been a sanctuary and a place of pilgrimage since prehistoric times. In the base of the rocks, caves provided monks and hermits with chambers of tranquillity for their devotions.

rounded niche with a pillar-altar of a type unknown in church architecture. Directly above this altar is a circular window 50cm (20in) in diameter.

In 1823, the prehistorian Otto von Bennigsen saw from the chapel the sunrise at the midsummer solstice and also the most northerly rising point of the moon. These are two important astronomical events marked at many prehistoric stone circles and other megalithic sites. The location of the chapel, high above the ground, had been chosen specifically to look out over the forest canopy to view these events over landmarks on the horizon 6.5km (4mi) away. In addition, the Externsteine lies at virtually the same latitude as Stonehenge, and so the direction of midsummer sunrise is identical in both places – an important factor to Europe's astronomer-priests. Von Bennigsen suggested the chapel was of pre-Christian origin built by the priesthood of an ancient 'light cult'.

An evangelical parson, William Teudt, expanded upon the ideas of von Bennigsen, and in the 1920s conducted detailed archaeological and astronomical research at the Externsteine. He found that the site lay on his network of *Heilige Linien* across northern Germany. These 'holy lines', a rough equivalent to the English leys, linked the Externsteine to the megalithic stone circle at Bad Meinberg not far away. Teudt believed that above the chapel there had been other chambers and wooden structures for use in observing sunrises other than midsummer, as well as the cycles of the moon and stars.

Teudt's discoveries convinced him and many others that the roofless and ruined state of the chapel was the result of the deliberate mutilation of an earlier shrine by Christian monks attempting to destroy a pagan observatory. Teudt showed that a 50-ton slab lying at the bottom of the rocks had fallen away from the chapel's side. This work of destruction had, he claimed, been carried out to make the pagan sanctuary a viable place of worship for Christians.

The carving of the world-pillar

When Christian monks supplanted the pagan priesthood, they often, as a matter of policy, took over existing sacred sites for the new worship. The Externsteine is a remarkable instance of this. In about AD 1120, Cistercian monks made a carving of the *Deposition from the Cross* which included a symbolic reference to the religion formerly practised there. The bas-relief shows the pagan world-pillar, *Irminsul*, which upheld the universe and was associated with the cult of the supreme sky-god. But the *Irminsul* is bent double to form a kind of chair upon which Nicodemus stands to remove Christ's body from the Cross. This subjection of *Irminsul* symbolizes the submission of the elder faith to the later creed. An interesting feature of the carving is that the feet of Nicodemus have been deliberately hacked away. Such vandalism is explained locally as the pagans' revenge on the confiscators of their sacred place.

Below the carving lies the World Serpent, believed by some to be the work of a different carver, possibly an Anglo-Saxon. It is also thought to be symbolic of the telluric energies felt beneath the site. These energies run through the earth and are accessible only to people who enter the caves or holes in the rocks. The creation of artificial crypts, chambers and grottoes is a means of gaining entry into the bones of the earth. Throughout the world there are rock-cut sacred places, either completely subterranean or else carved into the side of rock outcrops, as at the Externsteine, where men have deliberately sought to move closer to the energies of mother earth.

An ancient chamber stands at the top of one of the rock pillars of the Externsteine and is reached by a curved footbridge. It was for a long time used as a chapel. A round window, 37.5cm (15in) across, looks northeast over the forest. From a niche in the wall opposite, an observer can witness through the window not only the midsummer sunrise but also the most northerly rising of the moon.

MALTA: SHRINES TO AN EARTH MOTHER

The temple complex of Tarxien found beneath a field in Malta is one of the largest ancient monuments in Europe. Who built it, when and why? How is it linked to other sacred sites in Malta? Is it part of a megalithic culture found elsewhere in Europe?

In 1902, a new housing development was underway in Paola, a suburb of Malta's capital of Valletta. Workmen, cutting through the rock to make water cisterns, suddenly broke into the top of a great subterranean chamber. Descending into the bowels of the earth, they found a series of interconnecting caverns containing a multitude of human bones. Fearing delays, the building contractor hushed up the discovery until the houses were finished.

By the time the find was reported, much damage had been done: the upper levels of the site had been disturbed by building works and the underground chambers used as waste dumps. To make matters worse, the first official investigator of the site died without leaving written records. Yet what had been discovered turned out to be one of the most ancient and mysterious structures in western Europe, if not in the world.

The Hypogeum of Hal Saflieni

Between 1905 and 1911, the father of Maltese archaeology, Sir Themistocles Zammit, explored the Paola site and revealed to the world the Hypogeum (from the Greek for 'underground chamber') of Hal Saflieni. It consists of a series of more than 20 caverns, both natural and manmade, which lead off one another. A main sequence of large chambers running north–south has, at its southern end, a 'Holy of Holies' where a temple facade carved out of the living rock gives access to an inner sanctum.

To one side of the north–south sequence is the Oracle Room. A small oval niche in one of its walls produces a high echoing sound when someone with a deep low voice speaks into it. In the later classical world, oracles were associated with the dead, as at Cumae in Italy. Anyone hearing the echoing voice issuing from the hole could easily believe that the Oracle was a medium through whom a dead ancestor spoke. A statuette of a so-called 'Sleeping Lady' was found at the Hypogeum in a votive pit into which thank-offerings were thrown, either after a consultation with the Oracle or following the cure of an illness. The Sleeping Lady shows, according to some authorities, the practice of 'incubation': the act of sleeping in a shrine in the expectation of prophetic dreams or of dreams effecting a cure.

In accordance with this idea, two sets of rock-cut niches, placed one above the other in a side wall of the Main Hall, are sometimes interpreted as cubicles for sleepers awaiting dreams, in ancient times thought to be communications from the dead. However, others share the more prosaic belief that the dead themselves occupied these niches, as in a mortuary.

Many small side-chambers lead off the large series of caverns and it was in these that most of the bones were found. Whatever else it may have been, the Hypogeum was plainly a collective tomb. It belonged, in principle, to the same tradition as the communal rock-cut burial chambers of Sardinia, Italy, southern Spain

The high altar of the south temple at Tarxien is decorated with spiral designs which are thought to represent the eyes of the Earth Mother goddess. Excavators discovered a stone drawer in the altar where there was evidence of animal sacrifice – a flint knife and the horn of a goat left by a sacrificial priest or priestess.

The island of Malta lies in the Mediterranean, 112km (70mi) to the southeast of Sicily. Malta's most important sites – Tarxien and Hal Saflieni – are found close together in the suburbs of Valletta. Similar pairings of temples and tombs are found elsewhere in Malta and its close neighbour, Gozo.

and Portugal. Like the surface-built megalithic passage-graves also found in Spain and Portugal, these burial chambers in the west Mediterranean were in use in the first half of the third millennium BC, though they may have been constructed somewhat before. But Malta's Hypogeum differs from what is normally meant by 'megalithic' building, in which the surfaces of the great stone blocks were usually left rough, for its doorways and facades were carefully shaped. Who had done this and why?

The temples of Tarxien

More of Malta's past was discovered after a local farmer told Zammit what he had found in his wheatfield at nearby Tarxien (pronounced Tarshen). Encouraged by the potsherds thrown up by the farmer's plough, Zammit began work in 1915 and soon realized he was uncovering a prehistoric temple.

The site of Tarxien stands amid the modern housing blocks of suburban Valletta, but in its original form it must have been considerably more impressive. The three temples whose remains can be seen today were built here consecutively to meet the changing needs of the local worshippers. From the evidence of potsherds, they were thereafter used at the same time. In 1929, Zammit dated their construction to the end of the Stone Age, about 3000 BC. Radiocarbon tests have since pushed back by 500 years the construction date of the first temple.

At Tarxien, Malta's inhabitants worshipped a deity represented by a 'fat lady'. They sacrificed cattle and sheep to her and may have consulted an Oracle. Vivid testimony to animal sacrifice is a panel carved in realistic relief showing sheep, pigs and bulls. The goddess in whose name these beasts were slaughtered is still present in replica form – the original is in Valletta Museum. She must have stood 2.4m (8ft) high, judging from what remains – the lower part of a pleated skirt and two bulbous legs.

The cult of the Earth Mother

Statuettes and figurines of enormously fat women have been found elsewhere in Malta. In his book *The Search for Lost Cities,* British writer James Wellard suggests that, in view of Malta's rocky terrain, the dread of hunger must have been uppermost in the minds of the island's ancient inhabitants. He proposes that this was the inspiration for the 'fat ladies' of Malta: 'In other words, are we not seeing here the glorification of obesity, so distasteful to well-fed Westerners, so admired by all under-nourished races?' Wellard also takes the view that the statuettes may represent, not a goddess, but an earthly Venus, 'beautiful because her plenitude of flesh typified a plenitude of food'. Others, however, agree with British archaeologist Jacquetta Hawkes who, in her *Atlas of Early Man,* concludes that representations of this 'very ample' lady 'prove beyond reasonable doubt that these temples were devoted to the ancient Mediterranean worship of the Mother Goddess'.

The proximity of Tarxien to Hal Saflieni – the sites undoubtedly form a pair – confirms this view. If, at Tarxien, neolithic people honoured the goddess in obese shape signifying the abundance of crops springing from the fruitful Earth Mother, may they not, at Hal Saflieni, in burying their dead in underground chambers, have seen them as returning to her womb?

The Maltese temples flourished for about 800 years but they were abandoned and their users vanished. Drought, plague, famine and invasion are among suggestions as to the cause. Whatever it was that eclipsed this civilization, when Bronze Age settlers arrived at the end of the third millennium BC, they seem to have found Malta empty.

Catacombs and chambers, beautifully shaped and once painted red, dominate the main hall of the Hypogeum at Hal Saflieni. The style of this underground complex imitates the architecture of the above-ground temple at Tarxien. The bones of more than 6,000 people were found here, most of them dated to between 3500 and 3000 BC.

The Earth Mother, or Great Goddess, whom the ancient peoples of Malta worshipped, is represented in many statues, such as this now headless limestone figure, 48cm (19in) high and found in the temple Hagar Qim. The figure shows characteristics of other statues, particularly the wide hips, the bulbous legs and the folded arm.

60

GIZA: THE RIDDLE OF THE GREAT PYRAMID

The tomb of the Pharaoh Cheops is the most extraordinary sepulchre of all time. How was it built and why? Does it have a further, more secret, purpose? What is significant about the dimensions of the Great Pyramid?

The long incline leading to the plateau of Giza, near Cairo, takes the visitor back almost 5,000 years in history. At first, and from a distance, the three main pyramids look like sharp-edged mountains. As one approaches them they seem momentarily less impressive. But close to, their size finally strikes home: they are huge. Half the world is stone, the other half sky.

The largest is the Great Pyramid of King Cheops – Cheops is the Greek form of Khufu, the ruler's Egyptian name. The middle one belongs to King Chephren, or Khafre, and is only slightly smaller. The smallest is the tomb of King Mycerinus, or Menkaure.

Tombs of the living gods

Egypt came into being as a connected series of settlements along the Nile valley. These eventually formed two kingdoms of Upper and Lower Egypt, toward the head and the mouth of the Nile respectively. Between 3100 and 2700 BC, the two kingdoms were made one under a single king whose palace was at Heliopolis, roughly where Cairo is today.

These Egyptian kings thought of themselves as living gods who would one day leave the earth to join the other gods, and particularly the sun god, Ra, who journeyed across the sky each day in his flaming 'Boat of Millions of Years' and then voyaged through the perilous darkness of the Underworld by night. In readiness for the afterlife, the kings built themselves dwellings on the edge of the desert plateau, strategically placed between the life-giving Nile and the western horizon where the sun disappeared each night.

At first, these 'houses of death' were actual palaces, with public rooms and storage chambers. All around were the smaller house-tombs for the courtiers who would continue to serve the king once they, too, had passed on. But in the period after 2700 BC, King Zoser built the Step Pyramid at Saqqara to the south of Giza. Perhaps this first step-shaped pyramid, represented, literally, a staircase to the sky. The following kings developed the smooth-faced shape that Cheops, Chephren and Mycerinus brought to full grandeur. This, the great age of pyramid building, lasted throughout the Old Kingdom (*c.* 2700–2200 BC), and the Great Pyramid was probably completed around 2500 BC.

In later eras, kings would plan great temples, dig tombs in the Valley of the Kings where Tutankhamun was buried, and pile up smaller pyramids of mud bricks faced with stone. But the Great Pyramid of Giza, *Akhet Khufu*, 'The Splendour of Khufu', was the finest of them all.

Extraordinary engineering

How did the ancient Egyptians manage to assemble such a vast aggregation of blocks into a building 5.3 hectares (13 acres) in area, possibly incorporating complex mathematical formulae?

The scale and structure of the Great Pyramid of Cheops at Giza can clearly be seen in this photograph taken in 1895. The massive monument measures just over 230m (756ft) along each side and originally stood about 147m (481ft) high when the topmost stones – which mystics claim were made of gold – were in place. By comparison, the spire of Salisbury Cathedral in England rises 123m (404ft) and the Washington Memorial in Washington, D.C. is 169m (555ft) high.

The pyramid contains about two and a half million blocks of limestone and has a total weight of approximately six million tons. Some of the blocks weigh as much as 15 tons apiece.

The famous site of Giza is to the west of the Nile, less than 16km (10mi) to the southwest of Cairo. The three great pyramids can be seen looming on the horizon as soon as one has passed through the suburbs of the great city. The Shari'a al-Ahram (Avenue of the Pyramids) leads straight to the majestic monuments.

Unlike many other aspects of ancient Egyptian society, there are no contemporary records to help answer the question.

The architects must have been well versed in the study of science, for the proportions and measurements of the pyramid show astonishing accuracy. The four sides of the pyramid are oriented toward the cardinal points of the compass to within less than a tenth of a degree. The lengths of the shortest and longest sides differ by 20cm (8in) in all. The pavement around the Great Pyramid is level to within less than 2.5cm (1in). Such precision must have been achieved with the simplest of measuring rods and cords, aligned by observations of the sun and stars, and perhaps the use of water levels for setting horizontals. But just how it was all brought together is still a matter of conjecture.

All the stone for the core of the pyramid came from the plateau of Giza itself: the Sphinx, a representation of King Chephren, sits in what was one of the limestone quarries. The fine facing stone of Tura limestone came from quarries on the east bank of the Nile. Most of this facing stone has long since been stripped off, vanishing into other ancient projects, probably including some of the buildings of Cairo. Granite for chambers within the pyramid itself came from Aswan, 800km (500mi) farther up the Nile.

From start to finish, the Great Pyramid probably took between 20 and 30 years to build. During that time an estimated 4,000 masons and builders were continually at work, shaping stones and supervising their placement. Almost certainly, tens of thousands more came to join them each year during the months when the Nile flooded and work on the land was impossible. As a result, huge numbers of people had to be organized, fed and housed. Even strikes may have occurred. Indeed, there is a report of workers on later royal tombs laying down their tools when the promised bread and onions did not arrive.

Inside the Great Pyramid

Unlike any of the other ancient Egyptian pyramids, the Great Pyramid has corridors and chambers high within its structure. An entrance just above the base in the centre of the north side leads to a small passageway sloping down into a chamber in the rock beneath the pyramid. From this passageway, another leads upward, first to a small chamber, now called the Queen's Chamber, and then to the Grand Gallery. This is an internal sloping passageway 47.5m (156ft) long and 8.5m (28ft) high. The Grand Gallery in turn leads to the largest chamber, the King's Chamber, that contains a sarcophagus-like coffer.

For 3,000 years the inside of the pyramid remained untouched. And when Abdullah al Mamun and his men discovered an entrance in AD 820, they found the ascending passage had been made impassable by large granite plugs. After forcing their way around, they reached the King's Chamber only to find the king's sarcophagus empty.

To this day, no one knows for sure what the Great Pyramid was intended to be. If it was not a tomb to house the body of King Cheops, what was it for? Who blocked the passageway, how and why? Because such questions seem impossible to answer with any degree of certainty, all those inclined to mystical speculation have tried their hand at explanation.

The Great Pyramid is, in a sense, a monument to the fact that an effective bureaucracy could flourish more than 4,500 years ago. Accountants, farmers, builders, politicians and all kinds of practical people can look on the Great Pyramid with just as much awe as mystics. It is, after all, the only one of the Seven Wonders of the Ancient World to survive to the present day.

Giza is probably the most systematically excavated site in Egypt. This illustration shows an expedition party in 1890, just one of the many exploratory groups to visit Giza during the 19th century. In the background can be seen the pyramids of (from left to right) Mycerinus, Chephren and Cheops, with the Great Sphinx in the middle distance.

A 19th-century drawing by Luigi Mayer of the interior of the Great Pyramid shows the precision with which the massive blocks fit together. The steep ascent of the Grand Gallery leads to the King's Chamber of burial, although to this day only Cheops' empty sarcophagus has been found. Great granite blocks would have slid down this slope to seal the tomb forever. The level passage below leads to the Queen's Chamber.

Two rows of men pulling a sled over wet timbers and up a spiralling side ramp (**1**) might have been the way the Egyptians transported stones to the top of the growing pyramid. Another way might have been to build a ramp against one face (**2**), but this would mean that to maintain a gradient of 1 in 10, a ramp to the top would start 1,830m (6,000ft) away. Once the top stones were in place, the ramp would be gradually removed and the white casing stones put in place (**3**).

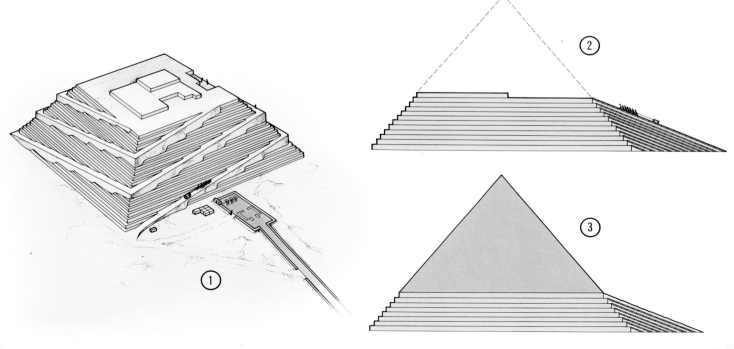

CHAMPIONS OF PYRAMIDOLOGY

WILLIAM FLINDERS PETRIE

In 1880, British archaeologist William Flinders Petrie began to measure the dimensions of the three pyramids of Giza with the greatest possible accuracy. To him, the layout of the Great Pyramid was 'a triumph of skill. Its errors, both in length and in angles, could be covered by placing one's thumb on them.' Petrie spent 50 years digging at more than 39 sites in Egypt, and founded the British School of Archaeology there.

CHARLES PIAZZI SMYTH

A 19th-century Astronomer Royal for Scotland, Charles Piazzi Smyth was an able scientist but also a religious fanatic. Together with his pyramidology mentor, London publisher John Taylor, Smyth believed that the Divine Geometer had designed the Great Pyramid. Smyth reckoned that the pyramid's dimensions incorporated the true value of *pi*, the length of the year, the circumference of the earth and the distance of the sun. From his measurements of the internal passages of the Great Pyramid, Smyth detected God's plans for the world, even the date of the Second Coming.

NORMAN LOCKYER

In 1894, British astronomer Sir Norman Lockyer published *The Dawn of Astronomy*, a book that made him the father of the 20th-century science of astro-archaeology. For Lockyer proved that the Egyptians had built their solar temples as astronomical observatories: when the sun rose or set at the midsummer solstice, a ray of sunlight shone through a contrived opening into the darkness of each temple's interior. Lockyer also discovered that Stonehenge had been aligned toward the sunrise on midsummer's day.

RICHARD ANTHONY PROCTOR

The founder of the popular scientific magazine *Knowledge,* 19th-century British astronomer Richard Proctor evolved the theory that the Great Pyramid was used as an observatory by astronomer-priests before its completion. Using the Grand Gallery as a sighting line before it was built over, priests could have established a true meridian for detecting the movements of the sun, planets, stars and moon as they appear to cross the heavens.

PALENQUE: A MAYAN CEREMONIAL CENTRE

The temple-city of Palenque was once a major seat of power in the Mayan society which flourished more than 1,000 years ago. What lies within the Temple of Inscriptions? Who was Lord Pacal? Why did the Mayan astronomer-priests manipulate their history?

Tall rain forest cloaks the beautiful ruins of Palenque that nestle on the edge of low hills in the Mexican state of Chiapas. The brilliant plumage of parrots and macaws brightens the dense green of the trees and only the curious shouts of howler monkeys disturb the serene setting of an ancient Mayan ceremonial centre.

In 1841, the American author and traveller John Lloyd Stephens published a book which brought Palenque and the whole of the vanished world of the Maya to the attention of the public. He wrote: 'In the romance of the world's history nothing ever impressed me more forcibly than the spectacle of this once great and lovely city, overturned, desolate and lost.'

The Palace and the Temples

The labyrinth of the Palace at Palenque lures the visitor into a series of galleries and rooms which lead eventually to the base of a four-storey tower. From the top of the tower the Maya once studied the stars and watched over the green plain of the River Usumacinta that stretches 128km (80mi) to the Gulf of Mexico.

From the tower the visitor can survey the religious buildings of Palenque. Arranged around a plaza are three similar temple-pyramids: the Temples of the Sun, the Cross and the Foliated Cross. Each temple is built on top of a stepped pyramid, has a mansard roof surmounted by a curious vertical 'comb' structure, and has two vaulted rooms inside.

The innermost room of each temple has a sanctuary where a tablet of stone is beautifully carved with hieroglyphs and two Mayan men. Between the men is a ceremonial object. In the Temple of the Sun, said by many to be the most perfect of all Mayan buildings, this object is the mask of the Jaguar God of the Underworld. In the other two temples, it is a tree in the form of a cross upon which sits a bird.

The most remarkable of all the buildings at Palenque is the Temple of Inscriptions. To reach it, the visitor must climb 19.8m (65ft) up the steep stairway at the front of the pyramid. On each of the four supporting pillars of the temple are life-size stucco figures, each holding either a baby or a small child.

The crypt in the pyramid's heart

Little was known of the Temple of Inscriptions until 1949 when Mexican archaeologist Alberto Ruz Lhuiller found a huge stone slab in the floor of the temple. He removed it to find the beginnings of a staircase blocked by a mass of rubble which took him and his workforce three years to clear. At the foot of the stairs, which was exactly at ground level, Lhuiller discovered an upright triangular slab of stone and the skeletons of six young people who were probably sacrificial victims.

When he removed the slab, Lhuiller opened a tomb which had remained untouched for more than 1,000 years. He described it

The ceremonial centre of Palenque, one of the most impressive of all Mayan sites, lies on the edge of the Mexican rain forest. On the right is the Palace, on the left is the Temple of the Sun and at the back is the Temple of Inscriptions. A small stream, the Otulum, flows through the site and under the Palace via an aqueduct with a corbelled roof.

Mayan culture thrived in southern Mexico, Belize, Guatemala and the western fringes of Honduras and El Salvador. Palenque was one of several major Mayan sites, including Chichen Itza in the Yucatan and Tikal in Guatemala.

The Temple of Inscriptions is a funerary monument that rivals the best of the Egyptian pyramids. In the middle of the nine-stepped pyramid is the funerary crypt of Lord Pacal, a 7th-century ruler of Palenque. The whole temple-pyramid was probably raised above the tomb during his lifetime. Steps lead from the temple at the top to the tomb below and, following the course of the steps, is a stone tube of square cross-section. This tube is thought to have been a channel of communication with the dead man or else a means of releasing his spiritual energy.

as '. . . an enormous empty room that appeared to be graven in ice, a kind of grotto whose walls and roof seemed to have been planed in perfect surfaces, or an abandoned chapel whose cupola was draped with curtains of stalactites, and from whose floor arose thick stalagmites like the dripping of a candle . . .'

In this funerary crypt was a five-ton slab of richly carved stone lying on top of a sarcophagus; all around the walls were sculptured reliefs of the nine Mayan Lords of the Night. Within the sarcophagus, Lhuiller found the remains of a tall man who had been about 40 years of age when he died. His body and face were covered with green jade jewellery that contrasted sharply with the cinnabar-red lining of his tomb. Most remarkable of all was the death mask of jade mosaic whose eyes were eerily inlaid with obsidian and shell.

The carvings on the lid of the sarcophagus are not, as Erich von Daniken claimed in his book *Chariots of the Gods?*, depictions of an astronaut in a space capsule. Rather, they represent in rich symbolism the transition of one man's living soul to the realms of the dead. Moreover, they show the transformation of a particular Mayan leader into a god.

The Mayan cult of ancestors

In the 1970s, Mayan scholars, such as the Americans Floyd Lounsbury and Linda Schele, deciphered many of the inscriptions found on the walls of Palenque's temples. These revealed that the skeleton in the funerary crypt belonged to Lord Pacal, which means 'Hand-shield'. His mother, Lady Zac-Kuk, was ruler before him and may have acted as regent when Pacal ascended the throne at the tender age of 12.

The inscriptions relate that Pacal died when he was 80 years old, in the year AD 683, which is strange since the skeleton belongs to a man half this age. During his rule, the great Palace was built and Palenque reached the height of its power and dominated many of the Mayan settlements in the land. Lord Pacal turned Palenque into a ceremonial centre of great significance, where age-old rituals based on the seasonal cycle of agriculture were combined with an extraordinary ancestor cult.

Lord Pacal was the epitome of the élite class which ruled the Mayan people and was obsessed with the cult of honouring the dead. Pacal's ancestors are carved on the side of his sarcophagus and Pacal's successors all left inscriptions emphasizing their special relationship with him.

Mayan astronomer-priests were also instrumental in this ancestor cult, for it seems they played an intricate numbers game which matched the needs of religion and power with that of history and genealogy. The Temple of Inscriptions is so called because it contains a series of 620 hieroglyphs – the longest in Mayan culture. While not all of these have been decoded, some evidently refer to people and gods who played a part in a history stretching back thousands of years.

Lounsbury found from inscriptions that the Temple of the Cross was dedicated to Pacal's son on exactly the same day as an ancestral mother figure had been born 1,359,540 days (3,724 years) previously. This vast number of days is important because it can be divided by seven significant Mayan cycles, either planetary or calendar. This numerological coincidence, one of many, suggests that Mayan history was contrived to suit the activities of the ruling élite in linking themselves with their ancestors. The last deciphered date found at Palenque is AD 835. After that time, this sacred centre of the Maya was mysteriously abandoned. Only the inscriptions and undiscovered tombs can reveal more of its ceremonial lords.

Lord Pacal's funerary crypt lies behind the pyramid's front stairway, about 24m (80ft) below the temple. The crypt, 9m (30ft) long and 7m (23ft) high, contains Pacal's sarcophagus and is surrounded on the walls by relief carvings of the guardians of the Underworld.

The elaborately carved lid of Pacal's sarcophagus describes in rich symbolism the voyage of his spirit to the realms of the dead. The central figure reclines in front of and below the sacred tree which the Maya believed links the earth with the Underworld and the heavens. All around are images of dragons and symbols of ancestry which, taken together, ensure Pacal's supreme place in Mayan history.

THE UNIQUE FACE OF THE MAYA

ANCIENT AND MODERN MAYA

The Maya form the largest single group of American Indians north of Peru. Today, around two million Maya live in the same area of Mexico, Guatemala, Belize and the western fringes of Honduras and El Salvador, as did their ancestors when their civilization was at its height. Despite a changing world, the Maya have maintained their cultural identity. Even their physical features remain little changed from the images of the ancient Maya elaborately carved on temple walls, such as this relief from Bonampak in the Mexican jungle.

THE JADE LORD OF PALENQUE

The lifesize death mask of Lord Pacal was made from 200 fragments of jade fixed to a wooden mould. The staring eyes were fashioned from shell and obsidian. This astonishing mask was found covering the face of Pacal's skeleton in the sarcophagus in Palenque's Temple of Inscriptions. The skeleton was adorned with jade – earspools, a necklace and rings on his fingers were all made from the green stone. A large jade had been placed in his mouth, a jade stone in each hand, while at his side stood two jade figures.

MECCA: THE MAGNETIC CITY

The holiest Moslem site in the world lies in the heart of the city of Mecca. Why was Mecca chosen as the holy city? What is the Black Stone in the sacred Ka'ba enclosure? What rituals do the pilgrims perform? What is the importance of the holy Well of Zemzem?

No other city in the world has quite the mystique and magic, nor is as highly venerated, as Mecca. Located midway between Suez and Aden on the Arabian peninsula, Mecca attracts more than a million pilgrims every year. And each day, millions more devout Moslems prostrate themselves in the direction of this magnetic city, like compass needles swinging toward a lodestone. A place of glittering domes and javelin-slim minarets, it is also a centre of industry and commerce, for Islam permeates every activity of a Moslem's life, from art to science, from washing to eating.

Mecca is the birthplace of the prophet Mohammed. Born around 570 AD, he brought his people out of the darkness of paganism and showed them the way to the one God, Allah. Only followers of the teachings of Mohammed may enter the precincts of Mecca. And only those in a state of ritual purity may set foot inside the Great Mosque and approach the sacred Ka'ba and the nearby Well of Zemzem to perform the expected rites. Every pilgrim dresses simply and without adornment, for within the open square Al-Haram mosque all worshippers are deemed equal.

What is the Ka'ba and why is it holy?

The most sacred structure of all Islamic architecture, the Ka'ba was traditionally built by Abraham and his son Ishmael. The word Ka'ba simply means 'square building'. This beating heart of the Moslem world is 12m (39ft) long, 10m (33ft) wide and 15m (49ft) high, raised on a platform and covered in black brocade. The curtain over its door and the band running around its outer dimensions bear inscriptions in gold. The grey stone and marble building is orientated so that the four corners roughly correspond to the points of the compass.

Inside the Ka'ba gold and silver lamps are suspended, but the most important feature is the Black Stone, which pilgrims have to circle and kiss seven times after completing the *Hajj* – the journey to Mecca. The origins of this Black Stone are obscured by the mists of legend and the sanctity bestowed upon it by Mohammed. Geologists believe it to be of meteoric origin, but tradition says that it fell from Heaven into the Garden of Eden and was given to Adam to absorb his sins after God had expelled him from Paradise. In the legend, the Stone was initially white, but has been turned black by the accumulated sins of men. Traditionally the Stone was passed to Abraham by the angel Gabriel – it is said to bear Abraham's footprint – to use as the cornerstone of his temple.

The power of the Ka'ba before Mohammed

Before Islam came to the Arab people, they lived in the Time of Ignorance when they practised a naturalistic and animistic religion, worshipping stones, trees and the sun. Their spirit world was peopled with good and bad demons. The Ka'ba was a

Arms raised in rapt worship at the birthplace of their faith, crowds of devout Moslems pray at the great brass doors of God's house, the Ka'ba, set in the centre of the immense courtyard of Islam's holiest shrine, the Great Mosque of Mecca. Half draping the doors hangs a rich tapestry, emblazoned with verses from the sacred Koran. To the left of these doors, and out of the photograph, the Black Stone that Mohammed raised and purified in the name of Allah during the 6th century is set in silver into the eastern wall.

The sacred Islamic city of Mecca is situated in the Arabian peninsula some 64km (40mi) from the Red Sea and Jeddah, and about 320km (200mi) south of Medina. Despite a harsh desert climate, God did not forsake this land – the Prophet Mohammed was born in Mecca and he established it as the centre of the Moslem world.

pagan sanctuary and the Black Stone a cult object, attracting pilgrims from all over Arabia. Worshippers of the pagan gods and idols stroked and kissed the Stone to imbibe its power, a custom Mohammed endorsed after purifying it in the name of Allah.

Several stories attest to the magic of the Black Stone. In one, the Abyssinian warrior Abaha swore to destroy the pagan Ka'ba. But as he arrived with his army outside the gates of Mecca, his elephant knelt down and refused to carry him inside. Whereupon birds arrived in great flocks and dropped stones on his troops with deadly accuracy, causing Abaha and his men to flee.

In the Time of Ignorance, the Ka'ba was stocked with idols to such deities as Venus and Fortune, but there was one among them, a Semitic god called Allah, who would see all the others swept away. When Mohammed was about 40 years old, he was visited in his sleep by the angel Gabriel, who commanded him to 'Recite in the name of your Lord, the Creator, who created man from clots of blood'. When Mohammed awoke the Koran – the Recital – was inscribed upon the prophet's heart and he knew that all the false gods had to be destroyed, leaving Allah alone to reign supreme and uncontested. But although paganism was already declining in its power, Mohammed did not find it easy to convert the people of Mecca to monotheism. His act of legitimizing the Ka'ba and the Black Stone was just one of many politically inspired moves.

In the Old Testament, the story is told of Hagar, the mother of Abraham's first-born son Ishmael, who was driven out into the wilderness by Sarah, Abraham's barren and jealous wife. It was Sarah's hope that Hagar and her baby would die of thirst in the desert. However, God guided Hagar to a place where a spring of fresh water bubbled miraculously from the sand and so saved mother and child. Moslems believe that when Hagar saw the flood of water gushing on to the sand, she cried out: 'Zem! Zem!', meaning 'Stop! Stop!' They also believe that this life-giving spring is the same as the well located only a few yards from Adam's Black Stone in Mecca.

In earlier times, the Well of Zemzem was the only source of water in the city of Mecca. Covered by a dome on teak columns, it was used for washing, drinking and cleaning out the Ka'ba. Water from the Well is still used to wash and clean the Ka'ba three times a year.

Violations of Mecca's sacred precincts

Although unbelievers are forbidden to enter the Great Mosque, for the last 200 years adventurers disguised as Moslem pilgrims have violated this Islamic law. Johann Ludwig Burckhardt, the Anglo-Swiss explorer who rediscovered Petra, was the first to record his visit in 1814. Perhaps the most famous unbeliever to visit Mecca was the English adventurer Sir Richard Burton who entered the city in 1830 and later wrote: 'I may truly say that, of all the worshippers who clung weeping to the curtain, or who pressed their beating hearts to the stone, none felt for the moment a deeper emotion than did the Haji from the far-north.'

Islam is a religion that conquers by the sword rather than persuasion, so disagreements are often settled by violent action. Mecca has not been spared such conflict. In 1802, for example, the sons of the puritan Muhammad Abdul Wahhab entered Mecca after a terrible slaughter outside its gates, smashed every shrine and image in the city, and accused its inhabitants of idolatry. In 1979, there was a bloody battle in the precincts of the mosque. The city of Mecca is steeped in mystery and intrigue. It is the birthplace of Mohammed and Islam. It has seen much violence and yet is a place of perfect peace.

Every year, over a million pilgrims, all in a state of ritual purity, humility and fervent piety, gather within the sacred precincts of the Great Mosque in Mecca to worship the one God, Allah. For some, the *hajj*, or journey to Mecca, is made but once in a lifetime – it is a compulsory journey for a devout Moslem. The object of the pilgrims' worship is the stark, cube-shaped Ka'ba, draped in black brocade and looming high above the crowds. Seven times they circle Islam's holiest of holies, accompanied by a ritual chanting of devotions. An integral part of this *umra* ceremony is the kissing of the Black Stone itself. Its powers are thus imbibed by believers, who are given the strength to continue their holy lives.

The lodestone of the Islamic world, the Ka'ba features in the centre of this seemingly abstract design on an 18th-century Turkish tile. A plan of the courtyard is depicted, enclosed by the colonnades of the Great Mosque. Wherever they are in the world, millions of Mohammed's followers turn to Mecca's holy shrine five times each day in prayer.

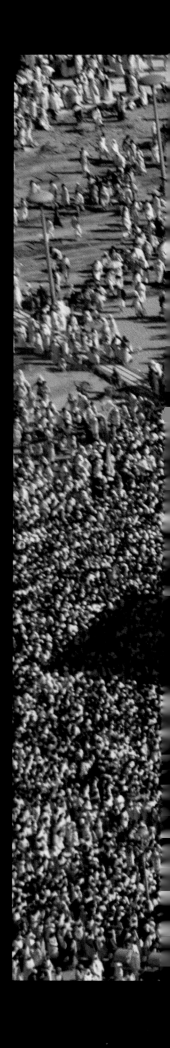

THE BEATING HEART OF ISLAM

A SACRED TILE
The religious duties of every devout Moslem are written down in the Koran and constitute the Five Pillars of Islam. These are prayer, pilgrimage to Mecca, fasting, almsgiving and reciting the creed of Islam which is written and uttered throughout the Moslem world. This medieval pulpit tile from Turkey bears that creed: 'There is no god but Allah, and Mohammed is his prophet.'

THE INTREPID UNBELIEVER
Dressed in the clothes of a Persian *dervish,* or wandering holy man, and going by the name of Mirza Abdullah, Richard Burton became one of the first unbelievers to enter the Moslem heart of Mecca. He furtively sketched the Great Mosque, the Ka'ba and other sacred places and, in 1855, published them in his book *Pilgrimage to Al-Medinah and Meccah.* The year before, Burton had become the first European to enter the forbidden Moslem city of Harar in East Africa, and live to tell the tale.

BOWING TO MECCA

Five times a day Moslems the world over face Mecca and prostrate themselves in prayer. At dawn, at noon, in the middle of the afternoon, at sunset and at the onset of darkness, they pray to Allah. Even soldiers fighting the *jihad*, or holy war, perform this simple but essential act of prayer. The Prophet Mohammed originally commanded his disciples to face Jerusalem, but pressure from the Jews persuaded him against this and so instead he used Mecca as the Islamic focus of prayer.

JERUSALEM: THE HOLY CITY OF GOD

On the site where Abraham prepared to sacrifice his son Isaac, Moslems built the great mosque of the Dome of the Rock. Why is the Rock holy? Why is the Wailing Wall so called? Does the Church of the Holy Sepulchre truly mark the burial place of Christ?

The holiest of all the world's holy cities should be Jerusalem, for within its Old City walls, built four centuries ago by Sulaiman the Magnificent, lie three pre-eminent shrines of the great monotheistic religions: the Western or Wailing Wall, the Church of the Holy Sepulchre, and the Dome of the Rock.

Judaism, Christianity and Islam meet and mingle in this ancient city, which is a testimony to their common heritage. But they are a family divided. Voices that should be raised in unison proclaiming the One God are too often heard bickering over their inheritance. Jerusalem is at once their glory and their shame.

The Dome of the Rock

The most beautiful building in Jerusalem is the mosque at the heart of the Old City. This, the Dome of the Rock, gets its name from the great rock – still exposed inside the mosque – which is literally the foundation of Jerusalem's claim to be a holy city.

The ancient rock is Mount Moriah where Abraham prepared to sacrifice his son Isaac to Jehovah, and where, 1,000 years before Christ, King Solomon built the first Temple. This was destroyed in 588 BC, and the one that Jesus knew was Herod the Great's, much larger than Solomon's. Built on the platform on which the Dome of the Rock now stands, Herod's Temple was the scene of the Purification of Mary, when the aged Simeon took the infant Jesus in his arms and uttered the *Nunc dimittis.*

The Romans destroyed Herod's Temple in AD 70, but the Moslems, when they conquered Jerusalem in the 7th century, proved more tolerant. Mohammed regarded himself as the successor of the Old Testament prophets and of Jesus, whom the Moslems revere as the Prophet Isa. They accept the Virgin Birth and Mary is honoured both in the Koran and in Islamic practice. Just outside Jerusalem, in the church of Mary's Tomb, a mark in one wall shows the direction of Mecca for pilgrims.

The great rock was the scene of the Prophet Mohammed's ascension into Paradise on his celebrated 'Night Journey' related in the Koran. It was at first more venerated by Moslems than Medina or Mecca. The Dome of the Rock was built in AD 691 by the Caliph of Damascus who covered the outside with gold mosaics, the Ottoman Turks later replacing these with 45,000 Persian tiles. The Dome today is of gold-plated aluminium embellished with verses from the Koran.

Fundamentalists of all three religions see the rock as the setting for the 'last things': Jews and Christians as the site of Armageddon, the final struggle before the Second Coming of the Messiah; Moslems as the place where Jesus and the Mahdi – Messiah – will together bring about the destruction of evil and the conversion to Islam of the Jews and Christians. Unbelievers are not barred from the Dome – as, in the 300 years of Crusader rule, Jews and Moslems were barred from Jerusalem – though

The Dome of the Rock ranks third among the four wonders of the Islamic world, after the mosques at Mecca and Medina, but before the mosque at Damascus. Built between AD 687 and AD 691 by the Ommayad caliph Abd al-Malik, the Dome stands on the rock that was once the primary site of Moslem pilgrimage.

Jerusalem's Old City is perched amid the hills of Judea about 64km (40mi) from the Mediterranean Sea. The divided city stands in the middle of Israel, halfway between the Gulf of Aqaba to the south and the Lebanese border to the north, but on the border with Jordan.

The huge sacred rock lying beneath the golden dome has a perimeter of about 61m (200ft). Scents, such as ambergris and musk, were sprinkled on the rock so that worshippers would be recognized later by their holy fragrance.

the fundamentalists vie, often violently, for sole possession. The 1980s have seen a series of attempts to blow up the mosque foiled by Israeli authorities.

The Western or Wailing Wall

Dispossessed by the Moslems of the Temple Rock, the Jews needed another focus of devotion and found it in the massive wall along the western edge of the Old City. Although the huge blocks of stone at its base are traditionally said to be from Solomon's first Temple, they are in fact part of the retaining wall of the restored and enlarged temple built by Herod.

It received its popular name of the Wailing Wall because Jews traditionally come here to bewail the destruction of the Temple and the Jewish Exile. They write prayers, or the names of those they are praying for, on scraps of paper which they thrust into cracks between the stones. Perhaps a quarter of a million Jews visit the Wall at the annual pilgrim festivals of Passover, Succoth and Shavuot.

Guidebook photographs of the Wall are often misleading, showing only picturesque Hasidic Jews, all of them men, in their sombre garments. But the Western Wall is a lodestone for pilgrims of a great community of the spirit, and Jews – men, women and children – come from all over the world to pray there. The only restrictions are that men may not pray at the Wall bareheaded and women are segregated according to Orthodox Jewish custom. After praying they recombine in family groups in the great plaza in front of the Wall to meet friends and acquaintances – it is a joyful as well as a solemn occasion.

The Church of the Holy Sepulchre

For more than 1,600 years, the most revered of all Christian holy places has been the Church of the Holy Sepulchre. Outside the confines of the Old City, the church marks the spot where Joseph of Arimathea buried Jesus in a tomb that he had made for himself 'in a garden'. This was near to Golgotha, or Calvary, where Jesus was crucified.

When the Roman Emperor Hadrian razed Jerusalem in the 2nd century AD, he built on this venerated site a temple to Venus. This at least marked the spot so that when St Helena, mother of the first Christian Emperor, Constantine, came to the Holy Land in AD 326, she knew where to look for the burial place of Christ.

The Madaba Map, a 6th-century mosaic in the church at Madaba, Jordan, shows Roman Jerusalem with the Basilica of Constantine, the original church on this site. Nearby is the Tomb Rotunda covering the rock-cut tomb of Christ, by now separated from the hill out of which it was carved so that processions could walk around it. To one side of the Tomb is an open space marked by a cross – the site of Calvary. The Crusaders brought the Basilica, the Tomb and Calvary under a single roof in their Romanesque cathedral, restored in 1959.

Many visitors to the Holy Sepulchre are disappointed – it is cluttered with a multitude of chapels and shrines with their accompanying paraphernalia. Following a division made in 1757 by the ruling Turks, the holy place is uneasily shared between the Greek Orthodox, Roman Catholic, Armenian, Syrian and Coptic Churches. The Ethiopian Church once had rights within it, but has now been relegated to the roof of St Helena's chapel.

Echoes of a religion more archaic than Judaism, Christianity or Islam haunt Mount Moriah. As to the Holy Places of these three great monotheisms, opinions differ. For some, Jerusalem is still the City of God. Others wonder if, above the wrangling of factions, the still, small voice will be heard.

The Western Wall in Jerusalem has listened for more than 1,000 years to the countless tears, laments, hopes and prayers of the Jewish people. Like an open roofless synagogue this wall remains a sacred place of worship and pilgrimage for Jews the world over. Male and female worshippers are segregated by a wooden fence and lockers along the Wall hold sacred scrolls.

TAKHT-I SULAIMAN: CITY OF THE ROYAL FIRE

Iran's holiest pre-Islamic site lies on the shore of a bottomless lake. Who built it and why? What connection does it have with the Towers of Silence?

In the mountains of northwest Iran lies a deep blue lake, 100m (328ft) across and traditionally said to be bottomless. It is fed by thermal springs and the steady outpouring of its waters has gradually built up a basin of mineral deposit with sheer sides over 40m (131ft) high. Known today as Takht-i Sulaiman, 'Throne of Solomon', this mysterious and beautiful lake in its chalice of stone was revered as Iran's most sacred site until the coming of Islam.

The combination of fire and water drew Iran's ancient founders, the Aryans, to the site, which lies in a region of vulcanism and seismic activity. The sacred lake replaced an earlier one close by, which had been drained in an earthquake. The Aryans venerated fire and water as the elements of their chief god, Ahuramazda, and the water-goddess, Anahita.

Their third most revered deity was Mithra, the god of heavenly light, who as Mithras became the subject of an austere mystery cult which seriously challenged Christianity as the official religion of the late Roman Empire.

The Aryans considered the pollution of the elements – earth, fire and water – a great evil. This principle and the ritual use of fire-altars they handed on to the Zoroastrians.

Who are the Zoroastrians?

For over 2,000 years, the fortunes of the Zoroastrians have waxed and waned. In 1976, there were only about 130,000 in the world, most living in Bombay, India, where they fled when Moslems invaded Iran and where they are known as Parsees.

Said to be the oldest of the world's revealed religions, Zoroastrianism represents the teachings of the sage Zarathustra, known to the Greeks as Zoroaster. A priest of the Aryan faith in eastern Iran soon after 600 BC, he broke away from the orthodoxy and declared himself the chosen prophet of Ahuramazda.

Zoroastrianism was a reformed version of the Aryan faith, stressing the principle of dualism – the eternal conflict between the creator Ahuramazda and his adversary Ahriman, between Good and Evil, Truth and Lie.

The Magi, originally members of a tribe who lived in northwest Iran, were widely regarded throughout the ancient world as the privileged priests of Zoroastrianism. The Three Wise Men, who were said to have travelled from Saveh in Iran to witness the birth of Jesus in Bethlehem, were Magi. From this word comes the word 'magic', once used to denote the rites of Zoroastrianism. Later, when that faith was supplanted by other religions, it simply came to mean 'sorcery'.

Fire remained the central feature of Zoroastrianism as the symbol of Ahuramazda. Modern Parsees maintain, as their ancestors did, a perpetual fire in their temples. The priests still wear veils to prevent their breath from contaminating the purity of the fire and only clean, dry wood is burned.

The ancient ruins of the Zoroastrians' holiest place at Takht-i Sulaiman stand timelessly around the blue and inexhaustible lake. Known later as Shiz to the Arabs and Saturiq to the Mongols, the city was built solely for religious purposes. Central to its function is the fire-temple, the tower seen beside the shore of the lake, where the most sacred of all Zoroastrian fires, Atur Gushnasp, burned perpetually.

The three sacred fires of Zoroastrianism were located in different regions in ancient Iran. The Royal Fire, Atur Gushnasp, burned at Takht-i Sulaiman in Media in the northwest. The fire of priests, Atur Farnbog, burned in Persia in the south. And the fire of herdsmen and farmers, Atur Burzen-Mihr, burned in Parthia in the northeast.

TAKHT-I SULAIMAN: CITY OF THE ROYAL FIRE

Pollution or defilement of the three elements continued to be a sin. Rubbish could not be burned because it would contaminate the fire: it had to be destroyed with acid. The most spectacular demonstration of this reverence for purity was the practice of building *dakhmes*, large round stone-surfaced towers at the top of which corpses were laid out naked. In this rite of exposure, the corpses lost their flesh to the devouring vultures while their spirits travelled upward on the sun's rays. Later, their stripped and bleached bones were either buried or thrown down a central well in the *dakhme*.

The Royal Fire

Under Iran's flamboyant Sasanian dynasty which ruled from the 3rd to the 7th century AD, Zoroastrianism was proclaimed the state religion and its writings were brought together as the *Avesta*. Fire-altars with perpetually burning fires were set up all over Iran. Some, crowning rocky heights, burned in the open air and were visible for long distances. Others were enclosed in fire-temples known as *chahar taq*, 'four arches', because their basic plan was a square consisting of four pillars joined by arches and supporting a dome.

Nearly every town and village had its sacred fire, as did each province. The social classes likewise had their own fires: Atur Gushnasp, the fire of warriors and kings; Atur Burzen-Mihr, the fire of the peasants; and Atur Farnbog, the fire of the priests. These three great sacred fires were probably consecrated in early Parthian times, around 150 BC, and were said to have been created by Ahuramazda for the protection of the world. Today, only the location of Atur Gushnasp, the Royal Fire, is precisely known. Its divine flames burned in the fire-temple at the ancient site of Takht-i Sulaiman.

The unique site of Takht-i Sulaiman was rediscovered in 1819 by British explorer Sir Robert Ker Porter. But it was not until 1959, when excavations by the German Archaeological Institute found stamped clay impressions, that the site was proved to be the city where the Royal Fire had once burned. They also discovered that Takht-i Sulaiman had been a holy place long before its temple had been refurbished and a city built by the Sasanian king Khusrau I (AD 513–79). It was Khusrau who made Takht-i Sulaiman into Iran's primary place of pilgrimage and worship. He had already built the fantastic palace at Ctesiphon on the River Tigris, a palace so huge that people later thought it had been built by genies.

Takht-i Sulaiman was bisected by the Processional Way which ran straight from the spectacular entrance at the north gate, through to the fire-temple and its altar with the Royal Fire, and finally to the lake. After their glorious coronation at Ctesiphon, the Sasanian kings would make a pilgrimage on foot to receive a divine investiture at the altar of the Royal Fire. This ritual had its symbolic counterpart in sculpture, in the great bas-reliefs which were cut, in the first 150 years of the dynasty, into cliff faces all over Iran, but mostly in the province of Fars. These reliefs were placed above spring-fed pools or the banks of rivers and were advertisements for the monarchy: they showed the Sasanian kings receiving their diadems from the gods Ahuramazda, Anahita or Mithra.

Sacked by the Byzantines in AD 624, Khusrau's holy city was later rebuilt and remained in use under the Mongols, including the notorious Abaqa Khan who, in the 13th century, drank himself to death here. But the Royal Fire had been extinguished, and eventually this most spectacular of sacred sites became the desolate mass of ruins visible today.

The Zoroastrians built Towers of Silence or *dakhmes* where they disposed of their dead, such as this *dakhme* outside Yazd in central Iran. The bodies could not be cremated as they would contaminate the fire, nor buried lest they pollute the earth. So they were exposed instead to vultures, eagles and the sun on top of the towers.

Great rock reliefs, sometimes larger than life, commemorated the divine investiture of the early Sasanian kings. Carved into the cliff wall at Naqsh-i Rustam in Iran, the god Ahuramazda invests Ardashir I in AD 224 with the right to rule by handing him the symbolic diadem.

The Zoroastrian fire-temple at Naqsh-i Rustam is one of many that burned with perpetual fires throughout Iran. Standing 11m (36ft) high, the basalt and limestone tower was probably erected by Darius I. The fire was only allowed to go out when a king died and was then rekindled by his successor.

THE FIRE OF THE ZOROASTRIAN FAITH

PERSIA'S GREAT PROPHET
Zoroaster, the founding father of
Zoroastrianism, lived on the Central
Asian steppes north and east of Persia
from about 628 to 551 BC (although
some researchers suggest he lived
between 1400 and 1200 BC). A major
theme in his teachings, which were
passed down through generations as
17 hymns, was that each person must
choose for themselves between the
forces of good and evil. Few images of
Persia's great prophet remain – this
3rd-century wall painting was found in
the Syrian town of Dura-Europos, an
outpost of the Parthian Empire.

THE INITIATION OF A CHILD

A young boy from the Parsee community in Bombay is initiated into the Zoroastrian faith. The boy receives the white *sudra*, or sacred shirt, and the symbolic belt, the *kusti*. The belt is repeatedly tied and untied during prayer, an age-old ritual designed to help the wearer concentrate his thoughts on the practice of his faith.

THE PARSEES OF INDIA

The centre of Zoroastrianism today is in Bombay, India, where a population of some 90,000 adherents – the smallest racial minority in India – continue the faith of Zoroaster. Their forefathers fled from Persia in the 10th century and settled in the state of Gujarat where they became known as Parsees, the people of Pars, a region in the south of Persia. When the British colonized India the Parsees moved to Bombay and became prominent in trade, politics and education. Although their numbers are declining, Zoroastrians are spread over the world, from America to Hong Kong.

THE FABULOUS TOWER OF BABEL

The splendid city of the ancient Babylonians was renowned for the temple in its midst. What was the Tower of Babel? Who built it? What was the purpose of the temple-towers called ziggurats? How did Babylon finally meet its end?

'And the whole earth was of one language, and of one speech. And it came to pass, as they journeyed from the east, that they found a plain in the land of Shinar; and they dwelt there . . . And they said, Go to, let us build up a city and a tower, whose top may reach unto heaven . . .' So in the Book of Genesis, begins the story of the Tower of Babel, built by the descendants of Noah.

'And the Lord came down to see the city and the tower . . .' and perceiving that, so long as the people all spoke the same language they would not give up what they planned to do, visited on them 'the confusion of tongues' so they could not understand one another, and scattered them over the face of the earth.

This curious tale combines two quite separate myths. One tells how humankind built a tower to reach heaven and was punished for its presumption, while the other accounts for the multiplicity of languages. The second was attached to the first perhaps only because of the similarity between the name Babel, from the Babylonian *Bab-ili* meaning the Gate of God, and *balal*, a Hebrew word meaning confusion. But of all the ziggurats in Mesopotamia ('the land of Shinar') that could have inspired the tower story why was that at Babylon singled out? The answer is undoubtedly because the Book of Genesis took shape during the Babylonian captivity of the Hebrews, beginning in 597 BC.

The rise of Babylon

Babylon, near modern Hilla, south of Baghdad in the middle reaches of the River Euphrates, was already old before the Hebrews sat down by its waters and remembered Zion. It is first referred to in the third millennium BC, though only when Semitic invaders from the west made it their capital did Babylon become prominent.

The sixth king of this new Semitic dynasty, Hammurabi (1792–1750 BC), built Babylon's first ziggurat. He brought the whole of Mesopotamia under his rule and in his reign Babylon enjoyed a great flowering of culture. Literature, mathematics, astronomy and astrology flourished, as also did law. Found at Susa where it had been taken in about 1600 BC by the conquering Elamites was a black diorite stele. Now in the Louvre, Paris, it is inscribed with the Code of Hammurabi, promulgated early in his reign. It was this law code that inspired the famous Hebrew law of retaliation: an eye for an eye and a tooth for a tooth.

A German expedition led by the architect Robert Koldewey excavated Babylon between 1899 and 1917. As a guide to the mounds which covered its ruins, the team had several classical accounts of the fabled city, especially those of the Greek historian Herodotus who visited Babylon in about 460 BC, and of Ctesias, the physician of the Persian king Artaxerxes II.

'It surpasses in splendour any city in the known world,' said Herodotus, and for the Bible writers it was the last word in

The story of the tower constructed by the descendants of Noah so that it may reach heaven has inspired many artists. Perhaps the most detailed is the 'Building of the Tower of Babel' as imagined by the Flemish painter Pieter Brueghel the Elder in the 16th century.

The splendid city of Babylon was situated on the original course of the River Euphrates, near modern Hilla and south of Baghdad. The city lay in the Mesopotamian land of ziggurats, such as those at Ur, Aqar Quf and, to the east, at Choga Zanbil, near Susa.

luxury and decadence. But the Babylon viewed by Herodotus and whose ruins can be seen today was not the city of Hammurabi. For, following his death in 1750 BC, Babylon fell into decline and languished for a thousand years in the grip of one or other great power, notably the Hittites and the Assyrians. Then, in 604 BC, a new Babylonian Empire was founded. It was its second king, Nebuchadnezzar, who made Babylon the most magnificent city in the world.

The House of the Foundations of Heaven and Earth

Nebuchadnezzar's city was enormous by ancient standards; it covered 2.6sq.km (1sq.mi) and was divided in two by the River Euphrates. Its chief marvel, according to Herodotus, was its city wall which was broad enough for two chariots, each drawn by four horses, to meet and pass. Walls fitting this description were uncovered by Koldewey. He also exposed a broad avenue called Procession Street – 19m (63ft) wide and paved with slabs of white limestone and red breccia. On each side of the street a wall, faced with blue ceramic, boasted 60 reliefs of lions – the emblem of the goddess Ishtar.

Procession Street passed through the Ishtar Gate to Nebuchadnezzar's rebuilt temple of Marduk, Babylon's chief god, inside which was a large hall entirely lined with gold. Beyond the temple stood the colossal ziggurat which the king restored to eight or nine storeys – about 100m (328ft). A triple flight of steps led to the second storey, while the rest of the tower was ascended by ramps. Herodotus reported that on top was a shrine, empty except for a large couch with a golden table beside it. 'The Chaldeans say – but I do not believe it – that the god himself is wont to visit the shrine and rest upon the couch . . .'

Herodotus may have thought this was where the Sacred Marriage between the city-god and city-goddess – perhaps represented by the king and a priestess – was annually consummated at the New Year festival. However, this was more likely to have taken place in one of the temples.

Only the stump remains of this greatest of ziggurats which the Babylonians knew as Etemenanki, 'the House of the Foundations of Heaven and Earth', but which the Hebrews, made captive by Nebuchadnezzar, called the Tower of Babel.

The fall of Babylon

After the death of Nebuchadnezzar, Babylon's power rapidly declined. Its last king, Nabonidus (556–539 BC) lived in the desert while his son Belshazzar ruled as regent. At a banquet in one of Babylon's great palaces, Belshazzar dared to use the gold and silver vessels taken from the Temple in Jerusalem. A hand appeared and wrote mysterious words on the wall that no soothsayer could interpret. The prophet Daniel was sent for. He read the writing as *mene, mene, tekel upharsin*, 'Numbered, numbered, weighed and divided' – a warning that Belshazzar was about to lose his kingdom. And indeed for the Babylonians the writing was on the wall. In 539 BC, Cyrus the Great took the city and Babylon became part of the Persian Empire.

Cyrus and his immediate successors continued to maintain Babylon's religious buildings, but later kings shunned the duty. More serious for the city than even its partial destruction in 482 BC as a reprisal by Xerxes were decades of neglect. Gradually the buildings crumbled and fell. By the time Alexander the Great (*d.* 323 BC) thought of making it his capital, even his indomitable will could not rebuild the huge ziggurat. When Septimus Severus, Roman Emperor from AD 193 to 211, came to visit the once fabulous city he found it deserted.

Greek historian Herodotus claimed in the 5th century BC that the city of Babylon surpassed any in the world. But 700 years later it was deserted. When architect Robert Koldewey came to Babylon in the 19th century, all he found was a mass of mudbrick rubble. But somewhere under it, he knew, lay not only the Tower of Babel but the Hanging Gardens of Babylon, one of the Seven Wonders of the World. Built on terraces and consisting of flowers and fruit trees, the gardens were supposedly made by Nebuchadnezzar to please his wife by reminding her of the mountains of her native land.

A facing of sculptured and brightly coloured glazed brick disguises the mudbrick construction of Babylon's magnificent Ishtar Gate. The double gateway is adorned with an estimated 557 sacred animals. It is not decorated with the lion, symbol of the goddess Ishtar, but with the bull of the storm god Adad, and the Babylonian dragon. This horned and snake-headed monster, called Sirrush, was sacred to Marduk, chief god of Babylon.

TEMPLE-TOWERS OF THE NEAR EAST

THE ZIGGURAT OF AQAR QUF

The core of the ancient ziggurat at Dur Kurigalzu (Aqar Quf), standing at a height of 57m (187ft), is made of sun-dried brick reinforced with layers of reed matting. The ziggurat is part of the ancient administrative capital founded by the Kassite king Kurigalzu in the 15th century BC and lies 15km (9mi) west of Baghdad. The Kassites came from ancient Iran, conquered the Babylonian region and ruled there until around the 12th century BC.

THE ZIGGURAT OF UR

The best preserved ziggurat in Mesopotamia stands at Ur in southern Iraq. Dedicated to the moon-god Nanna, the temple-tower was built by King Ur-Nammu of the Sumerians around 2100 BC. The four corners of the ziggurat were oriented to the points of the compass, and its base measured 58m (190ft) by 40m (130ft). The main body of the tower was made of sun-baked brick reinforced by reed matting.

THE ZIGGURAT OF CHOGA ZANBIL
Within a walled enclosure in the royal
city of Dur-Untashi (Choga Zanbil), built
by King Untash-Gal around 1250 BC,
stood a great ziggurat, 53m (174ft) high.
Dedicated to the Elamite god
Inshushinak, the ziggurat is the largest of
the 20 or so whose remains have been
found. Originally faced with kiln-fired
bricks glazed with a blue and green
metallic sheen, it must have shimmered
with ethereal beauty in the arid summer,
as the blue-tiled domes of Iranian
mosques do today.

SYMBOLIC LANDSCAPES

BOWING TO MECCA

Five times a day Moslems the world over face Mecca and prostrate themselves in prayer. At dawn, at noon, in the middle of the afternoon, at sunset and at the onset of darkness, they pray to Allah. Even soldiers fighting the *jihad*, or holy war, perform this simple but essential act of prayer. The Prophet Mohammed originally commanded his disciples to face Jerusalem, but pressure from the Jews persuaded him against this and so instead he used Mecca as the Islamic focus of prayer.

JERUSALEM: THE HOLY CITY OF GOD

On the site where Abraham prepared to sacrifice his son Isaac, Moslems built the great mosque of the Dome of the Rock. Why is the Rock holy? Why is the Wailing Wall so called? Does the Church of the Holy Sepulchre truly mark the burial place of Christ?

The holiest of all the world's holy cities should be Jerusalem, for within its Old City walls, built four centuries ago by Sulaiman the Magnificent, lie three pre-eminent shrines of the great monotheistic religions: the Western or Wailing Wall, the Church of the Holy Sepulchre, and the Dome of the Rock.

Judaism, Christianity and Islam meet and mingle in this ancient city, which is a testimony to their common heritage. But they are a family divided. Voices that should be raised in unison proclaiming the One God are too often heard bickering over their inheritance. Jerusalem is at once their glory and their shame.

The Dome of the Rock

The most beautiful building in Jerusalem is the mosque at the heart of the Old City. This, the Dome of the Rock, gets its name from the great rock – still exposed inside the mosque – which is literally the foundation of Jerusalem's claim to be a holy city.

The ancient rock is Mount Moriah where Abraham prepared to sacrifice his son Isaac to Jehovah, and where, 1,000 years before Christ, King Solomon built the first Temple. This was destroyed in 588 BC, and the one that Jesus knew was Herod the Great's, much larger than Solomon's. Built on the platform on which the Dome of the Rock now stands, Herod's Temple was the scene of the Purification of Mary, when the aged Simeon took the infant Jesus in his arms and uttered the *Nunc dimittis*.

The Romans destroyed Herod's Temple in AD 70, but the Moslems, when they conquered Jerusalem in the 7th century, proved more tolerant. Mohammed regarded himself as the successor of the Old Testament prophets and of Jesus, whom the Moslems revere as the Prophet Isa. They accept the Virgin Birth and Mary is honoured both in the Koran and in Islamic practice. Just outside Jerusalem, in the church of Mary's Tomb, a mark in one wall shows the direction of Mecca for pilgrims.

The great rock was the scene of the Prophet Mohammed's ascension into Paradise on his celebrated 'Night Journey' related in the Koran. It was at first more venerated by Moslems than Medina or Mecca. The Dome of the Rock was built in AD 691 by the Caliph of Damascus who covered the outside with gold mosaics, the Ottoman Turks later replacing these with 45,000 Persian tiles. The Dome today is of gold-plated aluminium embellished with verses from the Koran.

Fundamentalists of all three religions see the rock as the setting for the 'last things': Jews and Christians as the site of Armageddon, the final struggle before the Second Coming of the Messiah; Moslems as the place where Jesus and the Mahdi – Messiah – will together bring about the destruction of evil and the conversion to Islam of the Jews and Christians. Unbelievers are not barred from the Dome – as, in the 300 years of Crusader rule, Jews and Moslems were barred from Jerusalem – though

The Dome of the Rock ranks third among the four wonders of the Islamic world, after the mosques at Mecca and Medina, but before the mosque at Damascus. Built between AD 687 and AD 691 by the Ommayad caliph Abd al-Malik, the Dome stands on the rock that was once the primary site of Moslem pilgrimage.

Jerusalem's Old City is perched amid the hills of Judea about 64km (40mi) from the Mediterranean Sea. The divided city stands in the middle of Israel, halfway between the Gulf of Aqaba to the south and the Lebanese border to the north, but on the border with Jordan.

The huge sacred rock lying beneath the golden dome has a perimeter of about 61m (200ft). Scents, such as ambergris and musk, were sprinkled on the rock so that worshippers would be recognized later by their holy fragrance.

'We are symbols, and inhabit symbols.'

Ralph Waldo Emerson

The natural urge of our ancestors to transform their environment for ritual purposes means that today's world is endowed with a rich assortment of figures and graphic images in the landscape. These range from enigmatic mazes to curious 'effigy' mounds, from etchings on the land to carvings in the earth, from statues on the skyline to panoramas shaped by the hand of geomancy.

This chapter brings together the wealth and variety of such landscapes available to the discerning traveller. A review of the mazes and labyrinths adorning sacred rocks, pagan ground, churches and ornamental gardens illustrates the different ways of expressing the journey of the soul. Surveys of the earth mounds of North America and the picturesque landscapes created by the Chinese geomants show some of the diversity of environmental transformations.

The need to live in the shadow of dominant ritual figures, and to feel their power on important occasions, is a feature shared by many societies. Nowhere is this more dramatically illustrated than in the huge statues of Easter Island, the fertility giant of Cerne Abbas or the sacred shapes and markings on the face of Ayers Rock.

NASCA: THE PATTERNS OF PERU

The world's most impressive and ambiguous inscriptions are etched on to the desert in a remote part of southern Peru. What are these inscriptions? Who drew them, when, how and why?

Between the Pacific Ocean and the Andes Mountains, covering an area of about 520sq.km (200sq.mi), hundreds of immaculately straight lines, gigantic geometric patterns and huge animal drawings are sprawled over 'the greatest scratch pad in the world'. Most of the desert designs lie on the surface of pampa colorado near Nasca beneath violet-black mountains. The bare grassless mesa constantly shimmers in the heat of one of the driest places on earth.

In the last 10,000 years, very little rain has fallen on the light yellow soil, a mixture of sand, clay and calcite. If anyone walked upon it now, their footprints would remain for many years. The surface is sprinkled with angular fragments of reddish rock, turned black with a coat of desert varnish brought regularly by fierce winds.

Except for some references by the Spanish chroniclers in the 16th and 17th centuries, the Nasca lines remained virtually unnoticed until about 50 years ago. The founder of Peruvian archaeology, Julio Tello, and two friends first recorded the designs in 1926 which, in the early 1930s, became familiar landmarks to airline pilots. But the patterns of Peru only received serious attention after the American archaeologist Dr Paul Kosok, and his wife, had visited Nasca in 1941.

What are the inscriptions?

All the Nasca lines and figures have been shaped by scraping away the rocks to reveal the yellow soil beneath. This was probably done by hand as no evidence of draught animals has been found. Countless lines of varying width and length – some more than 8km (5mi) long, one even as long as 65km (40mi) – fan out in all directions and often cross over one another in a seemingly random fashion. Gigantic rectangles, triangles and trapezoids conjure up images of airports and runways, while enormous drawings and other abstract shapes, together with huge sketches of animal figures, are scattered throughout the elaborate crisscross of lines.

A variety of figures is depicted on the desert floor. They include a spider, several birds, a monkey, a whale, a snake, a llama and a lizard, as well as a flower and a man with a halo. Some of these figures are larger than two soccer fields – the lizard, for example, is more than 180m (590ft) long. There are 18 bird shapes, notably the hummingbird and the condor, of which some measure about 25m (82ft) long while others are up to 275m (902ft) in length.

Throughout the whole area are thousands of Nasca pottery fragments and deliberately placed piles of stones, like the cairns so familiar in Europe. Beside some of these piles are the remains of wooden posts – thought to have been used in surveying the patterns – while on others there is trace evidence of animal sacrifice. At the end of the mesa, beside the fertile Nasca valley, is a

The huge spider, about 45m (148ft) long, is one of the most curious of the desert figures. It is a member of the genus *Ricinulei*, one of the rarest genera of spiders in the world and one whose species are found only in the inaccessible places of the Amazon jungle. The ground drawing is so accurate that the creature even has one leg extended with the distinctive reproductive organ on its tip – a copulatory mechanism normally only visible under a microscope.

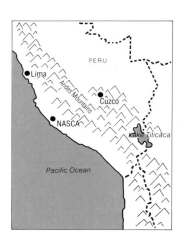

The largest work of graphic art in the world lies on the desert landscape among the valleys of several rivers that flow from the Andes to the Pacific Ocean. Roughly equidistant from Peru's capital, Lima, ancient Machu Picchu and Lake Titicaca (the world's highest lake), Nasca has a 12,000-year history of settlement.

collection of statues and rock carvings. One is a 25m (82ft)-high double rock, shaped like a human head and covered with drawings some have interpreted as showing the four races of man. And many of the carvings in the rock wall can only be seen when sunlight illuminates them – at a certain time of day or during a particular period of the year.

Who constructed the patterns and when?

Many of the animal drawings at Nasca preceded the lines. This is obvious since many of the lines cross over many of the animal designs and suggest that the desert was inscribed in two stages, first with animals and other figures, second with lines. The patterns overall were almost certainly made by the Nasca Indians during the thousand-year period between 500 BC and AD 500. The Nascans preceded the Incas and lived in a large part of the southern coastal region of Peru. None of them now survive and they have left no evidence of a written language. They were simple agriculturalists dedicated to nature and all living things. And the style of the paintings on their pottery indicates they were a happy and carefree people.

Much of what we know about the Nascans comes from their graves. They buried their dead in a crouched-up position, like a fetus in a womb, together with pottery and other artefacts. They interred them in burial grounds along the walls of the valley where the fertile ground rises up to meet the desert. One such cemetery contains an estimated 5,000 graves but nearly all of them have been stripped and desecrated by the local grave-robbers, the *huaqueros.*

Why were there so many lines and figures?

One of the few early references to the Nasca lines is found in the writings of Luis de Monzon, a magistrate with the Spanish conquistadors of the late 16th century. In referring to traces of some ancient tracks, worked stones and other archaeological finds, de Monzon records how the old Indians talked of the Viracochas, a small group of people from another country who preceded the Incas. The Indians who came after them apparently listened to the word of the Viracochas and treated them as saintly and built paths to them which can be seen today.

No one really knows why so many lines and figures were drawn, nor why the figures were so large and the lines so straight. What is certain is that the soil is far too soft for the rectangles and lines to be landing strips for the spaceships of extraterrestrial creatures. (This presumes, of course, that such craft would have been of a weight and form similar to those built in modern times.) Neither are the lines ancient roadways, for some end abruptly at the tops of mountains while others lead nowhere. Nor is it likely that the lines are skyline markers, since no more than would be expected by chance point to a distant peak, hill or detectable target.

Dr Paul Kosok, one of the first investigators of the lines, felt they represented 'the largest astronomy book in the world'. His theory that the lines were designed and used as an astronomical calendar has been taken up by Dr Maria Reiche, a German astronomer and mathematician who has been studying the patterns since the mid-1940s.

Dr Reiche believes that the lines predict the positions of celestial bodies – the sun, moon, planets and stars – and that they were used to determine the correct time of year for planting seeds, the annual appearance of water in the rivers and the right times to harvest the crops. They may also have been used to predict the summer and winter solstices, the spring and autumn

A hummingbird with outspread wings is caught for all time on the desert floor, but it has been drawn so large that it can only truly be appreciated from the air. Like all the other Nasca figures, the hummingbird's outline is delineated by a single uninterrupted line. The fact that its long nectar-seeking beak terminates neatly on one of Nasca's many straight lines suggests the bird and the line were designed and drawn at the same time.

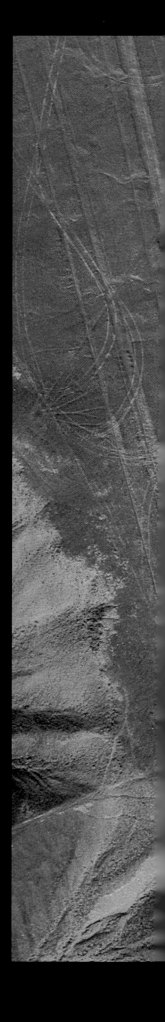

equinoxes and the eclipses of the sun and moon. However, computer studies carried out in detail by American astronomer Gerald Hawkins in 1968 do not substantiate Dr Reiche's theory, to which she counters that the statistical sample used was not sufficiently large to give significant results.

A more religious explanation has emerged from the theories and hypotheses of various investigators, including the Peruvian historian Dr Hans Horkheimer, and Tony Morrison, a British filmmaker and writer who has tried to decipher the patterns. They suggest that each line or pathway may have belonged to, or have been cared for by, an individual family or group of families with kinship ties, who regularly kept the lines clear and clean. At these sites, especially at the spirit places which are often marked by piles of stones, a spring or a sacred hill, the memory of their ancestors may have been worshipped. Large lines, rectangles and trapezoids could have belonged to an entire community – the figures of animals acting as their religious icons – where the whole population would gather to worship or give thanks on days sacred to all Nascans.

How were the lines and figures drawn up?
The great size of the figures coupled with their perfect proportions, plus the incredible straightness of the lines, led to intense speculation as to how the Nascans achieved such precise surveying. Straight lines can be drawn simply enough using three wooden poles aligned by eye: the first is a starting mark, while the middle one some 100m (328ft) away is moved from side to side until it aligns with a more distant third pole and the eye of the observer at the first. The mystery is how the Nascans were able to retain their accuracy over large distances – some lines deviate less than 2m (6.5ft) in each kilometre (0.6mi).

A challenging if far-fetched idea is that the Nascans were able to fly through the air in some sort of balloon. If the Nascan surveyors were able to do this, it would go a long way toward explaining how they were able to check that the engineers on the ground were keeping the lines straight and not veering erratically off course. Besides, the sheer size of the figures leads to the thought that to appreciate the patterns fully they had to be seen from the air at some time.

Evidence that the Nascans might have flown comes from two sources. First, paintings on the abundant pottery found in the area reveal images of what may have been balloons and kites. Second, wide circular 'burn-pits' containing blackened rocks have been found at the end of many of the lines and may have been launch sites for hot-air balloons.

To test out the theory that the Nascans may have flown, Bill Spohrer, an American resident of Peru, assembled a balloon using only materials and technology which he felt the Nascans would have had available to them. Nascan tombs, for instance, had revealed fabric that had a weave finer than present-day parachute material and tighter than that used in the manufacture of hot-air balloons.

In November 1975, Spohrer's Condor I was launched by lighting a fire in a 'burn-pit' beneath it. The balloon flew some distance carrying two experienced balloonists – Jim Woodman and Julian Knott – inside its reed gondola. After prematurely but safely discarding its passengers when a gust of wind brought it close to the ground, Condor I soared up to a height of about 350m (1,150ft) and flew for a further 3km (1.8mi). It seems possible, therefore, that the Nascan surveyors and engineers could have organized the drawing up of the lines and figures from the air. Whether they did or not has yet to be proved.

The dead straight line stretching across the desert to the mountains looks like an airport runway. Intersected today by the tarmac of the Pan-American highway, the line was precisely etched on to the desert by the painstaking removal of many tons of angular rock. The Nascan Indians must have hauled the rocks by hand for no evidence of any draught animals has been found. This line and others only become apparent when viewed from above or at least lengthways. In other words, if an observer stands a short distance to one side of a line, its clarity is lost.

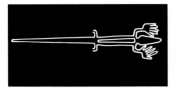

The Nasca desert is like a huge scrapbook, containing more than 100 giant designs of animals, plants, mazes and abstract figures. Some are remarkably clear, such as this lizard, flower and monkey. Covering an area of around 520sq.km (200sq.mi), many of the figures extend over narrow hilltops and into ancient dried-up riverbeds.

THE PEOPLE BEHIND THE LINES

THE LADY OF THE LINES

'I have always been very curious,' says Maria Reiche, the German mathematician who has spent more than half her life investigating the mystery of the Nasca lines. 'We will never know all the answers,' she says, 'and that is what a good mystery is all about.' After World War II she began her study of the lines and has since documented and mapped many hundreds of them, together with numerous geometrical shapes and 30 huge animal and plant figures.

Maria's poor health has not diminished her determination to keep visiting the Nasca lines. One of her assistants finds that his most important task is to carry her on his back, knowing a single misplaced step could damage evidence which has waited centuries for discovery.

THE BATTLE TO SAVE THE LINES

Maria Reiche has almost single-handedly fought the battle to protect the lines from the hordes of visitors attracted to the site by von Daniken's book, *Chariots of the Gods?* Knowing her contribution to solving the Nasca mystery was coming to an end, she has sought a successor. When Phyllis Pitluga, senior astronomer at Chicago's Adler Planetarium, came to Nasca in 1985, Maria knew her prayers had been answered. Phyllis, pictured here with Maria, has since pledged to continue Maria's work and admits: 'I feel like I've been handed the golden ring, and I'd be a fool not to accept it.'

COULD THE NASCANS FLY?

Two members of the International Explorers Club of Coral Gables in Florida believed that Nascan engineers were able to build a lighter-than-air craft for surveyors to view the progress of the desert etchings. To substantiate their belief, Jim Woodman and Julian Knott, inspired by the design on a fragment of Nascan pottery, constructed a primitive airship. Using materials which they knew would have been available to the Nascans, they built a simple balloon and called it Condor 1. In 1975, the balloon was launched and even though it jettisoned the two men shortly after take-off, it went on to fly for 20 minutes and 4.8km (3mi), proving it was possible that the Nascans could have flown.

PATHS OF THE AYMARA INDIANS

Clues to the mystery of the Nasca lines may be found in the isolated communities of the Aymara Indians who have lived high up in the Andes around Lake Titicaca since the 16th century BC. Straight lines similar to those found at Nasca are present around many Aymara villages and have been used, within living memory, in rituals of ancestor worship.

The Aymara inhabiting the village at the foot of this smooth-sided hill believe the spirits of their ancestors dwell at its summit. And, forged by the wear of centuries, each straight path ascending the hill leads to an east-facing shrine. The brightly-dressed Aymara celebrate various festivals by dancing together in the village square before proceeding along the paths to the shrines, often stopping on the way to make small animal offerings.

MAZES AND LABYRINTHS: SYMBOLS OF THE SOUL

One of the world's most enduring symbols is to be found in many forms and in many countries. What is the Cretan labyrinth? What is the link between mazes and death? Are mazes used in fertility rituals?

At the Montreal World Fair in 1967 more than a million people visited a pavilion called 'Labyrinthe', inside which cinematic effects recreated the tale of Theseus slaying the Minotaur. The experience was designed to show man's conquest of himself, as the exhibition's director, Roman Kroitor, explained: 'The theatres are life's experiences and the "beast" is the inevitably incomplete realization of one's nature which we hoped would be conquered or dispelled as one moved through the various phases of "Labyrinthe".'

All peoples, however different their lifestyles, have responded to the maze symbol for it reaches into shared experiences and has a significance at an unconscious level that transcends race and culture. This is demonstrated by the use of the same basic symbol in a great variety of ways over many centuries – in fertility rituals, death rites, as a religious aid, as a garden feature, in puzzles and games, and as a decorative design on craftwork.

The origin of the maze symbol

While mazes and labyrinths remain powerful symbols for people the world over, the origin of man's fascination with them is lost. The earliest known examples are clustered around the Mediterranean, particularly in Europe. Of Greek origin, the word 'labyrinth' refers to the myth of the Cretan labyrinth constructed by Daedalus for King Minos to contain the monstrous Minotaur. No one has ever found a definite geographical location for this labyrinth, although some suggest it may be the caves of Gortyna on Crete. Yet the design of the Cretan labyrinth appears again and again at places all round the world.

Early symbolic labyrinths often took the form of rock carvings which are difficult to date precisely. Those at Pontevedra in Spain, for example, may date from 900 to 500 BC and those at Val Camonica in Italy from 750 to 550 BC. A labyrinth carved at the entrance to a rock-cut tomb at Luzzanas in Sardinia, if contemporary with the tomb and not added later, may date as far back as 2500–2000 BC. The labyrinth symbol has also been inscribed on roofing tiles, pottery vessels, clay tablets, coins and seals, as well as mosaic designs – all during the period 1300 BC to AD 250 and all in countries around the Mediterranean. Eventually it appeared in many parts of the world, especially northern Europe, but also India, Africa and the Americas.

The link between mazes and death

The maze as recognized by many people today presents a puzzle – a choice of paths in a hedge maze, for example, offers an exciting and sometimes fearful journey from the entrance to the centre. The earliest labyrinths, however, had only one route to the centre and more often than not they took the form of a design carved on stone or inscribed on pottery. Small labyrinth

The maze epitaph on a tombstone in the village cemetery at Alkborough, England, is a tribute to the interest of the deceased in the local turf maze. Until he died in 1922, village squire J. Goulton-Constable made sure the 12th-century turf maze, 13.5m (44ft) in diameter and called 'Julian's Bower', was well maintained.

Symbols of secrecy adorn the clothes of an anonymous 16th-century gentleman, painted by Italian artist Bartolommeo Veneto around 1510. 'Solomon's Knots' surround the central labyrinth on his chest and are embroidered on the fabric of his coat. These knots are the so-called emblems of divine inscrutability and are a synthesis of the equal-armed cross, swastika and labyrinth.

designs, such as the maze used by the Hopi Indians, and also the Cretan labyrinth, may well have been employed to symbolize larger constructions, either real or mythical. Older still were the Egyptian labyrinths, such as the tomb of King Perabsen of around 3400 BC and designs found on Egyptian seals.

As mazes and labyrinths are thought to have a history of around 5,000 years, great problems arise in piecing together the clues which will reveal their original form and significance. But it is clear that the maze symbol had close connections with death, as Perabsen's tomb and the tomb at Luzzanas in Sardinia bear witness. In addition, the common circular labyrinths are similar to the spirals often carved on prehistoric tombs, such as the fine triple spiral still visible inside the Newgrange passage-grave in Ireland. Mazes and labyrinths – the two are to all intents and purposes indistinguishable – may therefore have been maps of the Underworld which the departing soul must follow. As such they are symbolic of death. They may also have simultaneously symbolized rebirth, for if the soul can wind into the heart of a labyrinth it can also follow the route out again.

The relationship between mazes and death was well summarized by Michael Ayrton (1921–1975), sculptor, writer and artist, who spent two years reconstructing the Cretan labyrinth out of brick and stone at Dry Brook in New York State's Catskill Mountains. In his autobiographical novel, *The Maze Maker*, he wrote: 'Each man's life is a labyrinth at the centre of which lies his death, and even after death it may be that he passes through a final maze before it is all ended for him.'

Were fertility rites performed in mazes?

Certain maze rituals clearly indicate their links with death and rebirth. On the remote Pacific island of Malekula in the New Hebrides, a labyrinth called 'The Path' was traced in the sand. The ghost of every dead man had to travel the same journey to the land of the dead but on the way must encounter the female guardian ghost. She would rub out part of The Path as a ghost approached, forcing the ghost to complete the design before he could continue his journey and so be reborn into a new life.

On the other side of the world in Europe, maze rituals often took the form of dances, though many are now only a folk memory. In England, turf mazes were used during the spring festivals of Easter and May Day, both of which are important celebrations of rebirth. While the exact nature of the turf maze rituals is not known, in Scandinavia some of the games played in the stone mazes are well remembered and they are clearly linked with the return of fertility in the springtime. In Finland and Sweden there are several mazes where the young men had to penetrate into the heart of the maze in order to rescue a girl from her prison. These mazes were sometimes called *Jungfraudanser* or Virgin Dances. A wall painting in Sibbo church in Finland, dating back to the 15th century, shows a maze with a female figure at the centre. This theme, the rescue of a woman from a labyrinthine fortress, has also been found in the Mediterranean and in India, and there can be little doubt that in these areas the labyrinth was closely linked with the springtime fertility rites.

The labyrinth design has been used in some areas as a magical talisman to bring good luck. Fishermen in Scandinavia once walked through stone mazes in the hope of controlling the weather, increasing their catch and ensuring a safe voyage. In other areas such designs were employed as a protection against evil spirits or wolves. Perhaps some of the earlier carved labyrinths, those on seals and roof tiles for example, were intended as protective devices in the same way.

Greek hero Theseus slays the Minotaur in the centre of a mosaic maze discovered on the floor of a Roman villa near Salzburg in Austria. The maze, 4.6m (15ft) wide and 5.5m (18ft) long, is entered on the right, next to the seated figure of Ariadne who waits for the return of her lover.

The Christian route to salvation

The Romans used the labyrinth to illustrate the myth of the Cretan labyrinth – the mosaic in Cremona in Italy shows Theseus slaying the Minotaur at the centre of the design. When the Christians adopted the labyrinth they adapted its significance to the needs of their religion: the path became the route to salvation. Perhaps the earliest use in a Christian context is the pavement maze in a church in Orléansville in Algeria, now in Algiers Cathedral. Dated to the 4th century AD, it contains at the centre the letters of the words SANCTA ECLESIA (the Holy Church) repeated in a large square design. Other church mazes include the small but forceful carving on a pillar in Lucca Cathedral in Italy and several mazes in French cathedrals such as Chartres.

English churches still retain some interesting mazes. The Norman font in Lewannick church in Cornwall is carved with several geometric designs including a spiral and a simple maze, while St Mary Redcliffe church in Bristol has a tiny roof boss with a 15th-century maze. Pavement mazes are found at Bourn church in Cambridgeshire and at Ely Cathedral, although the latter dates only from 1870. The paths of the pavement mazes in Christian churches would have been followed by pilgrims for penitential purposes, often on their knees. These mazes were sometimes named *Chemin de Jérusalem* or Road to Jerusalem, because it was the journey along this road which helped pilgrims meditate on Christian ideals.

Mazes made of turf, stones and hedges

English turf mazes were given intriguing names such as Mizmaze, Julian's Bower, Troy Town, or Shepherd's Race. They were once widespread but only a few now remain – after years of neglect, many have become overgrown. Wherever turf mazes have existed – Denmark and Germany also possess some, though not as many as does England – they were certain to play an important part in the life of the local community, especially in the spring-time festivities.

Scandinavia is rich in stone mazes, perhaps the best known example being the Trojeborg (Troy Castle) near Visby on the Swedish island of Gotland in the Baltic Sea. Often located by the sea where the fishermen once used them in magic rituals, they may be formed of smallish stones or else of large boulders. These mazes are difficult to date: they may be as recent as the 18th or 19th century, but some may be several centuries older. Those labyrinths found in the heart of Sweden, close to prehistoric burial sites, are likely to be older still.

In the 16th century when it was all the rage to plant herbs, flowerbeds and dwarf shrubs in elaborate designs, hedge mazes became popular and the fashion for garden mazes spread throughout Europe and even further afield. But while they are fascinating for their complexity of design they carry no obvious link with the ancient labyrinth. Their main differences are their lack of spiritual significance, plus the indirectness of the route to the centre and a number of dead ends. Nevertheless, a well-designed hedge maze, with narrow paths and tall well-maintained hedges without gaps, can provide an eerie experience for unwary travellers who lose their way.

Britain's oldest surviving hedge maze is at Hampton Court Palace near London. Constructed in 1690, it probably replaced an older maze, and, although it is small compared to other hedge mazes, its paths still extend for 0.8km (0.5mi). The attraction of hedge mazes continues – at Longleat House in England, a maze of yew hedges covering an area of 6,185sq.m (66,500sq.ft) was completed in 1978 and is the largest in the world.

Curious fingers have erased the image of Theseus killing the Minotaur from the centre of a maze carved into a wall in Lucca Cathedral, Italy. The maze measures 49cm (19.5in) across – small for an Italian maze. Beside it, the Latin inscription explains: 'This is the labyrinth which the Cretan Daedalus constructed, out of which nobody could get who was inside, except Theseus. Nor could he have done it unless he had been helped by Ariadne's thread, all for love.'

Typical Cretan labyrinths have been found in many parts of the world. This perfectly carved symbol is one of a pair found on a rock in Rocky Valley gorge near Tintagel, England.

An octagonal pavement maze greets worshippers and visitors as they enter the parish church at St Quentin, France. They must first cross the maze, which is 10.5m (34.5ft) in diameter, before they can walk along the nave of the church.

AYERS ROCK: THE DREAMTIME SANCTUARY

A giant chunk of red sandstone in the centre of the Australian desert is steeped in mystery and legend. What is its significance for Aborigines? Why are the marks left by erosion so important to them? Do visitors to the rock feel any sense of the sacred?

While exploring the arid lands of Australia's Northern Territory in 1873, William Gosse, a deputy surveyor-general, discovered a range of domelike rock mounds south of Alice Springs. The most impressive was a great red monolith which he named Ayers Rock after the Australian Premier, Sir Henry Ayers. What Gosse did not know was that the rock, with its vivid sunset and sunrise colours, already had a name given to it by the Aborigines: Uluru.

The lump of coarse arkose grit, standing 335m (1,100ft) above the surrounding desert and with a girth of 9km (5.5mi), is a crossroad on the Aboriginal Dreamtime trails. Gosse had stumbled on the place of the Sacred Water Python; of Kandju, the benign lizard; of the hare-wallaby and carpet-snake peoples.

Every crack, crevice, indentation, lump and striation had a meaning to the local Aborigines. The water stain down one side was the blood of the venomous-snake people, conquered in a famous Dreamtime battle. The holes in one boulder were the eyes of a long-dead enemy; the lump on another was the nose of an ancestor, now asleep. And each cave around the base of the rock had a purpose in the rituals of the Aborigines.

Who are the people of Ayers Rock?

The Dreamtime was the time when the earth was still malleable and in the process of being formed. During that time, animal-human heroes carried out journeys and quests, setting the pattern for their descendants in tracks and trails across the vastness of the Australian deserts. Waterholes and soaks were formed and found. The survival of the Aborigines living in the wilderness today depends on the knowledge of where to find these watering places along the Dreaming trails, a knowledge passed down to them from their ancestors in the form of songs and ritual ceremonies. But Dreamtime is more complicated than this – its mysteries and magic are locked into the minds and emotions of the Aborigines themselves. Outsiders receive but a mere glimpse of the network of fables and legends.

Uluru is a remote landmark on the Dreaming trails which form intricate patterns across the continent. It was the Dreamtime home of the Pitjantjatjara, the hare-wallaby people who live on its north side, and of the Yankuntjatjara, the carpet-snake people who live on its south side. In the vicinity of Uluru two great battles took place and these are still alive in the songs and ceremonies of today's Aborigines.

From the Dreamtime south came a ferocious tribe of venomous-snake people, intent on slaughtering the carpet-snake people. But Bulari, earth-mother heroine of the carpet-snakes, met the onslaught of the attackers breathing a lethal cloud of disease and death, so vanquishing the invaders. Some bodies of the venomous-snake people are locked into the shape of Uluru. The remnants of their tribe went further south to attack other

A huge domed monolith projecting from a flat plain, Ayers Rock is gradually decreasing in size but is not changing its shape. The continuous spalling of small flakes from its surface means that the rock is shedding skins of equal thickness all the time. The Aborigines, however, believe that their Uluru has remained unchanged since the Dreamtime moment when it emerged from a large flat sandhill.

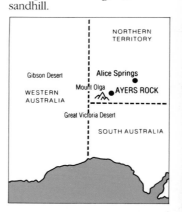

Ayers Rock lies on a flat desert plain in Australia's Northern Territory, some 320km (200mi) southwest of Alice Springs. Mount Olga, another extraordinary rocky outcrop and sister to Ayers Rock, lies about 32km (20mi) to the northwest.

Rock engravings abound in the caves and grottoes of Ayers Rock. Some of the most sacred cave designs are reputed to be of non-human origin. Many engravings have fertility or initiatory meanings, while others, such as this tree design, date back to the mythological Dreamtime era.

non-venomous snake tribes, only to meet a similar fate.

The hare-wallaby people on the north side also had to deal with an aggressive enemy, a terrifying devil dingo. This beast had been sung into existence by a hostile tribe who had filled the creature with savage malice before letting it loose. The hare-wallabies escaped by using their fantastic leaping ability – the footprints of their frantic retreat are visible in a series of caves around the base of Uluru. They were eventually saved when the totem, which had been the source of its power, was snatched from the mouth of the great beast.

The importance of the geophysical markings

The substance of the rust-coloured rock is sedimentary sandstone which flakes away in a process known as 'spalling', just as a snake might shed its skin. As a consequence, it always retains its distinctive shape. All the geophysical markings on the body of Uluru have meanings related in a tale, fable or song. In the overlapping folds of the rock, the Aborigines see the lizard, Kandju, who came there to find his lost boomerang. On the northern face are the famous markings which non-Aborigines call the Skull because the pattern of grooves resembles a human head.

The rock is a natural water trap. Around its base are some 11 soaks and holes which provide vital liquid for the people who live there, for visiting animals and for a skirt of foliage. On the rock face are many sacred cave paintings, some of which are exclusive to women and others to men. Neither sex can so much as look in the direction of the caves of the other and must even avert their eyes when passing forbidden places. In 1978, a European woman who visited a spot taboo to females was threatened with death if she ever repeated the transgression. Ayers Rock was also the scene of the recent and much-publicized Azaria case in which the Chamberlain family claimed a dingo had stolen and killed their baby. Whether this death had anything to do with the mythology of the Aborigines is not clear, but it ranks among the strangest 'murder' cases in the world.

The hare-wallaby cave of Mala, now off-limits to non-Aborigines, is a place where local boys are initiated into the tribe. The walls of this rock tunnel are covered in strange markings and inscriptions said to be the ritual cuts of original Dreamtime and subsequent initiates. On a large flat stone at the entrance to the cave, the boys are painted with ochre, and beside this natural table stands a rock which is the sleeping form of a Dreamtime elder. The cave of Mala is known among the Aborigines as a 'plenteous happy place' where returning initiates – Aborigines who have travelled and come home – weep with joy when they recall their own personal initiation rites.

What do visitors feel about the rock?

Known as 'the dead heart' to the white population of Australia, Ayers Rock is growing into a tourist attraction with all the attendant problems that entails. Many climb the white line painted up the side of the rock to film the remarkable views from the top.

Few visitors fail to be surprised by the strength of emotion they experience when confronted by what is, after all, a giant lump of red rock in the Australian desert. Robyn Davidson, an Australian adventurer who made an epic journey by camel across half the continent, described her feelings in her book *Tracks*: 'The indecipherable power of that rock had my heart racing. I had not expected anything quite so weirdly, primevally beautiful.' For all its wonderment, the rock will remain the Uluru of the Aborigines who see themselves as custodians of a symbolic landscape bequeathed to them by their ancestors.

Motionless and at peace in the sacred home of his forefathers, an Arunta man sits with his hunting equipment and gazes out on the flat plain surrounding Ayers Rock. The evocative contours of the overhanging rock behind him make it easier to see why the Aborigines believe that mythical beings created the topography of the monolith.

A respect for Nature is part of the Aborigines' culture and their art features animals and plants. What better 'canvas' to use than the living rock itself? The Aborigines of Ayers Rock made sacred cave paintings; the people of the far north, near the sea at Darwin, have decorated parts of Nourlangie Rock with decorative images of local fish, found in the East Alligator River: (from left to right) a barramundi, a saratoga and a multitude of small catfish.

THE EARTH MOUNDS OF NORTH AMERICA

More than 100,000 artificial mounds lie scattered over the United States between the Great Lakes and the Gulf of Mexico. Who were the mound builders? What links did they have with ancient Mexico? What did the 'effigy' mounds symbolize?

Thomas Jefferson, who drafted the American Declaration of Independence, was also America's first true archaeologist. In 1781, he wrote: 'I know of no such thing existing as an Indian monument . . . Unless indeed it be the barrows of which many are to be found all over the country.' He went on to describe them as being 'of different sizes, some of them constructed of earth, and some of loose stones. That they were repositories of the dead, has been obvious to all; but on what particular occasion constructed, was a matter of doubt.'

Near his home at Monticello in Virginia, Jefferson himself investigated a barrow which was spheroidal in shape, 12.2m (40ft) across at the base and around 1.5m (5ft) high. His excavations revealed that recent farming had destroyed sizable trees and had removed around 2.1m (7ft) of earth from the height of the mound. Digging down through the various layers of the mound, Jefferson found about 1,000 skeletons, some randomly heaped beneath the earth, while others were in strata, the oldest at the bottom.

Were the builders of this and other mounds the first Americans? Jefferson suspected that they were and suggested that they had originally come from Asia via a northern route – and he would be proved right more than a hundred years after his death. But what Jefferson was never able to ascertain was exactly who built the mounds and when. Nor could he possibly hope to grasp the vast number and extent of the mounds in North America.

The Great Serpent Mound

The earth mounds are chiefly located in the valleys of the Ohio and Mississippi rivers. While many are shaped like pyramids, the most extraordinary are moulded into animal shapes – snakes, eagles, foxes, bears, elks, buffaloes, and occasionally humans. Unique in the world, these 'effigy' mounds are remarkable for a feature which remains a mystery – like the Nasca lines in Peru, they can be seen properly only from the air.

Most celebrated of all 'effigy' mounds is the Great Serpent Mound in Adams County, Ohio. An earthwork nearly 0.9m (3ft) high, its sinuous body follows, at a height of 46m (150ft) above the water level, the bend of a small stream known as Bush Creek. Raised in the 1st century BC, the Serpent is 405m (1,330ft) long. Its mouth is open, apparently in the act of swallowing an egg. No bones or artefacts have been uncovered, only traces of where the Serpent was first outlined in stones and then built up with clay brought from the valley below.

Archaeologists do not yet know why the Serpent was made nor what it meant. But some clues may be drawn from the world's mythologies and cosmologies where the serpent is often linked with the life-giving properties of water. In Amerindian legend, the Horned Serpent represents the fertilizing power of water, while

Amateur archaeologist and physician Dr Montroville Dickenson often made the wild claim that he had excavated more than 1,000 American Indian sites. As if to prove it, he commissioned Irish-American artist John Egan to paint a scene showing him excavating an earth mound. This detail from Egan's painting shows how the mound was stratified and the skeletons arranged, with the artefacts still in place.

North America's artificial earth mounds are congregated especially along the Ohio River valley in the state of Ohio. But they are also found in profusion from Wisconsin to the Gulf of Mexico, along the valleys of the Illinois and Mississippi rivers.

for the Aztecs of Mexico, the Plumed Serpent symbolized not only the sun but also rain and storm. The Great Serpent Mound may well represent the all-important union of earth and water with its power to bring about the germination of crops and the regeneration of the land.

Who were the first mound people?

The Great Serpent Mound is the chief surviving work of the Adena people who flourished in the Ohio River valley and were among the earliest maize growers in America. Much of what is known about them comes from the thousands of burial mounds they built during the last half of the first millennium BC. Inside the mounds rectangular tombs were constructed for the corpses and their accompanying grave goods, which included stone tobacco pipes shaped like people and animals, stone tablets with abstract or animal designs, and hammered copper objects.

The origins of the Adena people are obscure. Many of the bones excavated from their mounds were stained with red ochre, a practice known as early as 2450 BC at Red Lake in New York State. However, the broad-headed Adenas also practised cranial deformation by binding the malleable skulls of their infants to produce unusually high foreheads. Such a practice suggests they had a Central American origin for the nearest comparable skulls come from sites close to modern Mexico City.

The cult of the dead

Many Adena customs were apparently preserved by a second group of mound builders, the Hopewell Indians. These long-headed people, physically distinct from the Adenas, seem to have taken over their territory and in the Ohio and Illinois river valleys practised a more sumptuous version of their culture. They likewise bound the skulls of their infants, but they developed the burial mound tradition in their own way, building much larger and more complex earthworks.

The Hopewell mounds are a testimony to an elaborate cult of the dead. Large wooden mortuary houses were erected on specially levelled sites, the larger ones without roofs and looking much like stockades. Inside the enclosures they cremated roughly threequarters of their dead, having first removed the flesh from the bones. Only a privileged élite were buried intact and their corpses were laid on the mortuary floors, fully extended and surrounded with grave goods for their use in the next world.

The adornments lavished on their nobility suggest the Hopewells operated a wide-ranging trade network. In their mounds have been found hammered ornaments and plate armour made of copper from Lake Superior, sharks' teeth from the Gulf of Mexico and knives made from obsidian found only at Yellowstone. Other ornaments include earspools of polished stones and stone pipes resembling those of the Adenas. Most dramatic of all are the great strings of freshwater pearls found in particular abundance in the Seip Mound, Ross County, Ohio. And while the symbols on the Hopewell grave goods – the serpent and the bird of prey – repeat those of the Adena, there are also new ones, notably swastikas and sun discs.

At the peak of their culture, between 100 BC and AD 200, the influence of the Hopewells was far-reaching, spreading from Ohio and Illinois to Indiana, Michigan, Wisconsin, Iowa and Missouri. But in the course of the next century they, like the Adena before them, declined and disappeared. They were followed, however, by a third group of mound builders – creators of the spectacular temple mounds.

Earth mounds in the shape of animals are common in a rough triangle that covers the woodland areas of southern Wisconsin, northwest Illinois and eastern Iowa. These 'effigy' mounds are also found elsewhere in the USA; the largest of all, the Great Serpent Mound, is in Ohio, and this huge eagle is in Georgia. With their feet pointing downhill, the animals – mammals, birds and reptiles – are usually about 30m (100ft) long and moulded in low earthen forms along the crest of a ridge.

The equal-armed cross features strongly on this Mississippian shell gorget found at Spiro Mound, Leflore County, Oklahoma. Gorgets fashioned from shell and incorporating important symbols in their design were frequently worn around the neck by Adena and Hopewell Indians, as well as by the people of the Mississippian culture.

THE EARTH MOUNDS OF NORTH AMERICA

The Mississippian temple mounds

The builders of North America's great temple mounds, earthen equivalents of the temple pyramids of the Aztecs and the Maya, were the Mississippians. They seldom used their mounds for burial but scaled them with stairways and ramps, and on top built wooden temples to their gods.

The rise of the Mississippian culture from about AD 700 roughly coincided with the Toltec domination of Central America and could conceivably be one of its ripples. The great city of Teotihuacan, situated about 53km (33mi) north of Mexico City and probably sacked by the Toltecs around AD 650, certainly exerted an influence which reached as far north as the Mississippian city of Cahokia. Located across the Mississippi from St Louis, Cahokia reached its final form in the 13th and 14th centuries – its ruins can still be seen in the Cahokia Mounds State Park, Illinois. A population of 5,000 to 10,000 lived in a huge complex of flat-topped mounds arranged around rectangular plazas. These mounds supported not only temples but also the homes of priests and other notables. Beyond the city, farmlands produced beans, maize and squash; and outlying villages, each with its own temple mound, completed a society ruled by a god-king from a ceremonial city – along the lines of Teotihuacan.

Central American ideas of the cosmos seem to have influenced the planning of Cahokia. Of its one hundred or so mounds, the biggest is Monk's Mound – the largest earthwork in the world. Roughly 305m (1,000ft) long, 213m (700ft) wide and 30m (100ft) high, it covers 5.7 hectares (14 acres) – more than the base of the Great Pyramid in Egypt. Built in stages like a Middle Eastern ziggurat, it may likewise have symbolized the cosmic mountain uniting earth and sky. Standing at the centre of Cahokia, Monk's Mound embodies the mythological idea of the quartered cosmos, represented worldwide by the swastika and the equal-armed cross.

The Great Sun of the Natchez Indians

By the time the Europeans arrived in America in the 16th century, the great age of the temple mounds was past and the Mississippians had all but vanished. But something of their culture survived among the local Indian populations which flourished from Alabama and Georgia to Wisconsin.

The most notable inheritors of Mississippian culture were the Natchez Indians who lived along St Catherine's Creek near Natchez in the state of Mississippi. Each of their seven villages had its own mound, but the group as a whole was focussed on the great Emerald Mound, more than 11m (35ft) high.

The Natchez had an absolute ruler known as the Great Sun, a god-man too holy to touch another living person or even to tread upon the ground except on special mats laid down for him. Like the god-kings of the major Central American societies, the Great Sun was believed to be possessed of solar energy.

The days of the Natchez were likewise numbered. To Frenchmen who lived among them in the late 17th and early 18th centuries, they were already a people in decline, perhaps due to imported European diseases such as measles and smallpox. The Frenchman de la Vente wrote of the Natchez in 1704: ' . . . our people in the six years in which they have been descending the river know certainly that the number has diminished a third . . .' The French themselves added the finishing touch by massacring most of the Natchez Indians after they had rebelled. Thus ended the age of the mound builders who, although they had a history of nearly 3,000 years, remain one of North America's archaeological enigmas.

The fantastic showpiece of the North American earth mounds, the Great Serpent Mound, was discovered in 1848 in the heart of Ohio by American archaeologists Ephraim Squier and Edwin Davis. These men had found other large serpent mounds in Ohio as well as in Iowa and Minnesota, concluding that they all had a ceremonial function. In 1885, F.W. Putnam of the Peabody Museum excavated the site and raised money to buy the 'effigy' mound for posterity.

Artistically carved platform pipes, for smoking tobacco were widely used by the Adena and Hopewell Indians. The soapstone pipes were mass-produced – 136 were found in the Trapper Mound, Ohio, for example. The pipe bowl was carved into various shapes – toads, human heads, and even a duck sitting on a fish.

When Spanish conquistador Hernando de Soto landed in Florida in 1539, he travelled northward and discovered many earth mounds which were still in use. This mound in Jefferson County, Arkansas, was named after him.

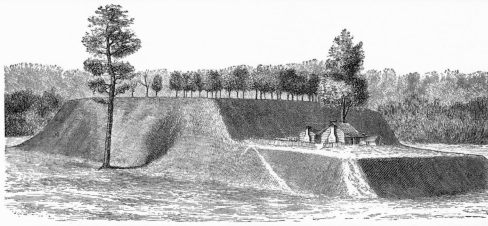

GEOMANCY: MYSTERIOUS ART OF PLACEMENT

The ancient Chinese art of shaping the landscape to harmonize with the earth's vital energy continues today. How does this practice of geomancy work? What part do colour and decoration play? Are astrological influences taken into account?

Bruce Lee, the former king of kung-fu, suffered an untimely death in 1973 because, say informed sources, he lived in an unlucky house in Hong Kong's Kowloon Tong district. Knowing of this negative power, Lee sought to defuse it by installing an eight-sided mirror outside his front door. But when a typhoon dislodged the mirror, Lee's house was left unprotected and he died soon afterward. Coping with such negative powers – and encouraging positive ones – are at the core of geomancy, a complete system of mystical landscaping based on ancient Chinese wisdom and philosophy.

Harmonizing heaven and earth

The picturesque harmony of traditional Chinese landscapes has not come about by chance. Skilled geomants, the practitioners of geomancy, have blended natural forces with manmade forms, reducing bad influences and amplifying good ones. Why did they do this? To bring health, happiness and prosperity to the people living in a specific place. But how does a geomant harmonize a place with the people who have to live there? Literally, geomancy's Chinese name, *Feng-Shui*, means 'wind and water'. *Feng-Shui* represents the powers of nature acting on a place: the wind on the hills and in the trees, and the water in rain, streams, rivers and underground. These forces come from three sources: heaven, which includes astrological and time factors; earth, including geology, terrain and weather; and the human element. Only when these three have been harmonized about a place is the geomant's task complete.

In China, *Feng-Shui* has always been a part of everyday life. In former times, geomants were consulted whenever any building, tomb or other alteration which might affect the landscape was being considered. The placement of a new house, or even the erection of a fence or post, creates an alteration in the environment: it was the task of the geomant to determine what effect such change would bring and, indeed, whether it ought to be effected at all. In *Feng-Shui*, people's fortunes depend on how correctly their dwelling-places are laid out and how favourably their ancestors were buried.

People may overcome their limitations by living harmoniously with all the forces of nature; by uniting these forces with the power of the Supreme Being; and by bringing the opposing principles of *yang* and *yin* into harmony with one another. Balance of *yang* and *yin* manifests itself as *ch'i*, the beneficial 'cosmic breath'. Imbalance manifests itself as *sha ch'i*, the 'breath of ill-fortune' and the opposite of *ch'i*. Geomancy's intention is the promotion of *ch'i* and shielding against or avoidance of *sha ch'i*. To create true harmony, every building and every feature of the landscape, both natural and manmade, has to occupy its correct position and must be placed by the geomant.

Skilled geomants use an instrument called a *Feng-Shui* compass to help them determine the correct situation for building houses, tombs and other places. Concentrically arranged on the face of the compass is information relating to astrology, geographical direction, landscape features and symbols from the ancient *Book of Changes*.

122

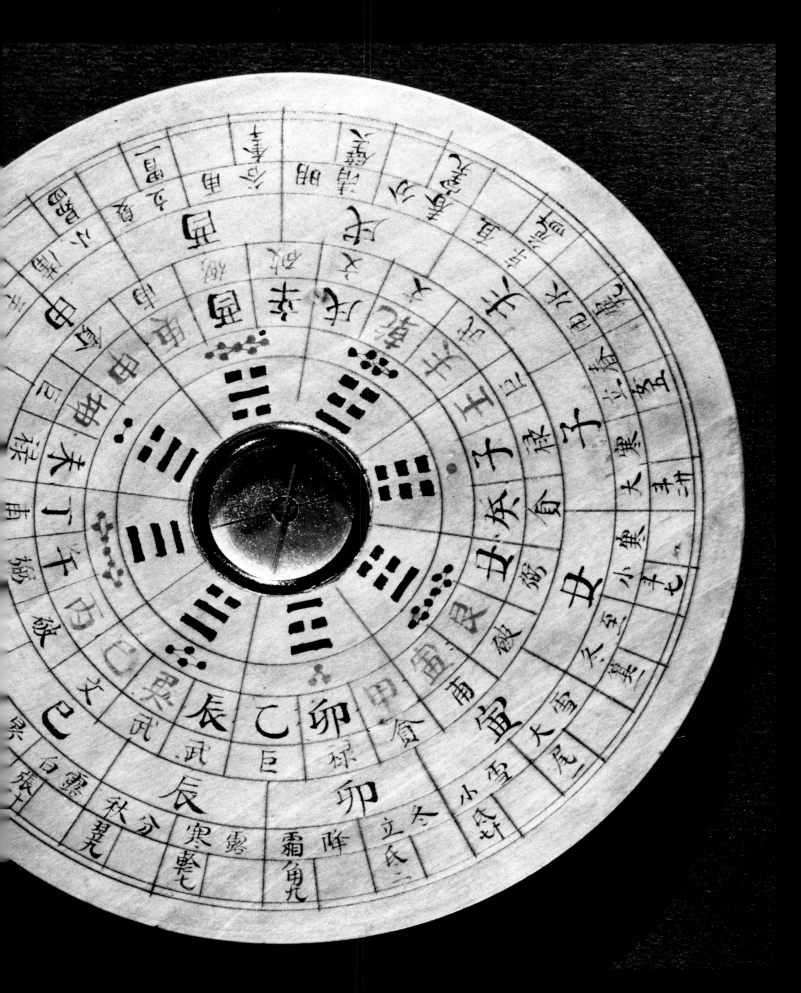

GEOMANCY: MYSTERIOUS ART OF PLACEMENT

The art of placement

Being at the right place, facing the right direction and doing the right thing at the right time, is to be ritually correct and practically efficient. It is being in harmony with the universe. To accomplish this state, *Feng-Shui* uses precise rules of placement – whether it is in siting a tomb, a building, a city or simply a desk in a businessman's office. To the north and at the back of the site there should be mountains or hills to ward off evil influences. To the south, there should always be a view, preferably with running water or the sea.

The choice of the correct site is governed by five factors: *Loong*, the Dragon, is the form of hills or undulations of the ground at the site in question; *Xue*, the Hole, is the foundation, the type of ground and the stability of the soil; *Sha*, the Sand, is the surrounding landscape of the site; *Shui*, the Water, is the form of the streams flowing near or through the site; and *Xiang*, the Orientation, is the direction the site faces.

Long experience, combined with Chinese mystical thought, has determined a complicated set of rules which define how these factors are considered. The geomant, who has gained his position after years of apprenticeship under a master, uses a mixture of knowledge, experience and intuition in determining whether or not to adopt a site under consideration. Such decision-making is of prime importance, for once a site is selected the fortunes of the people who will use it are fixed.

In Chinese mythology, the dragon is symbolic of the powerful and beneficial forces of nature and the Supreme Being. In geomancy, the Dragon is the site's topography, the 'ups and downs' of the hills. Flat land is considered bad, being a 'false Dragon', and may bring disharmony, illness or even destruction. Regular undulations are a 'good Dragon'. A good Dragon profile makes for the picturesque nature of many Chinese landscapes, especially in the famous surroundings of the tombs of the Ming Emperors near Beijing, formerly Peking, which is the most perfect geomantic site of all.

Finding good sites is not easy. In the ancient Chinese *Song of Geomancy* there is a saying that it can take three years to find the Dragon, but ten years to find the Hole. And in *Feng-Shui*, the adage 'To find the Dragon is easy, the *Xue* difficult', stresses this part as the most important and, at the same time, the most taxing. To find the *Xue* is the key task of the geomant, and is still a guarded secret among practitioners. The other factors, Sand, Water and Orientation, are secondary to the Dragon and the site, but these can also be good or bad. There are as many as 27 types of Sand and nine types of Water, all of which interact with other aspects of the site to render it fortunate or unfortunate.

Astrology is the last aspect to be considered. In *Feng-Shui*, a house, business office or a tomb must be orientated to the horoscope of the person occupying it. The date and time of birth of this person is referred to the geomantic compass so that the most auspicious orientation can be found and then incorporated into the structure. Striking examples of this are the traditional Chinese cemeteries on the island in Miro Bay off Hong Kong, where tombs face the various directions determined by their occupants' horoscopes.

The significance of decoration

Every feature in traditional Chinese building is decided by *Feng-Shui*. What appears as mere ornament has in reality a specific meaning and a symbolic function. The roof dragons which are the hallmark of Chinese architecture symbolize the vigour and power of the gods and are a means of warding off evil influences.

Hong Kong Island was called the 'barren rock' by the Chinese because of its bad *Feng-Shui*. It had no beneficial *ch'i* energy and was bedevilled by pirates. When the British took over in 1842, they made the *Feng-Shui* even worse. In building the first business centre, they built roads that were inauspicious, flattened hills and filled in lakes. Only after it was moved to Hong Kong Central, where it looked out over water and was backed by mountains, did the business centre thrive.

124

Fish-dragons on a building are symbols of success. The mythical guardians of good, the white tiger of the west and the blue dragon of the east, are widespread. The white tiger is placed at the right side of a building and the blue dragon on the left. Alternatively, the words *loong yin*, 'the dragon speaks', may be written on the left and *hu xiao*, 'the tiger roars', may be written at the right side of the building.

Colour, too, is important. Each colour has a precise meaning in Chinese tradition and in architecture this is applied to decoration. Colours are chosen with care in order to have a specific effect which counters harmful influences and enhances beneficial ones. Red, the most auspicious colour, reflects the *yang,* or active principle, and as a symbol of virtue and sincerity is used to bring blessings and happiness to the occupants of a house. Yellow, once the Imperial colour, symbolizes earth and is the carrier of the *yin* or passive principle. It is used in the burial of the dead and gaining geomantic blessings, charms against evil influences in dark corridors being written on yellow paper. Green is related to wood and reflects growth, youthfulness and long life. White symbolizes purity, but also penance and mourning; it is considered a bad colour and consequently not used for large surfaces such as the walls of houses.

How is *Feng-Shui* used today?

Originally formulated in China, *Feng-Shui* spread to Japan, southeast Asia and, in the 20th century, to other parts of the world. Although the Communist government of China has discouraged *Feng-Shui*, it is widely followed in Hong Kong, Malaysia and Singapore, where it is regarded as a means of assuring good fortune for businessmen as well as houseowners. Many prominent modern office buildings and hotels in Hong Kong and Singapore were designed along *Feng-Shui* principles.

Finding virgin sites for the erection of houses is not the only role of *Feng-Shui*. In fact its main function today is the remedying of harmful situations. The perfect site is now rare and people have to put up with less than ideal situations. Geomancy sees these imperfect sites as places where the forces of *yin* and *yang* are in imbalance and has the means to remedy the problem. Milton Glaser, for example, a well-known graphic artist in New York, was so exasperated after his office was burgled six times, he sent a detailed plan of the space to a Hong Kong *Feng-Shui* expert. The reply urged him to introduce an aquarium with six black fish and to hang a red clock from the ceiling. Since obeying these instructions he has not been burgled once.

Pagodas are the most familiar of all the remedial structures and objects in the *Feng-Shui* repertoire. These towers have been built at geomantically active sites in order to remedy bad influences such as unfavourably shaped hills. Another device is the geomantic mirror which, when placed along a roof, road or a fence, deflects the 'breath of ill-fortune' that always travels in straight lines. Most commonly, the mirror is circular and surrounded by the eight trigrams taken from the Chinese *Book of Changes,* the *I Ching.*

Demolishing walls, blocking up old windows and making new ones, or simply changing the direction in which a door faces, are other techniques of remedial *Feng-Shui* work. When the front door of the Hyatt Hotel in Singapore was altered along geomantic lines, trade was said to increase dramatically. The effect of geomancy in creating aesthetically pleasing landscapes and buildings is often self-evident. But particularly in Chinese communities all over the world, it is a living tradition which continues to flourish and enrich people's everyday lives.

126

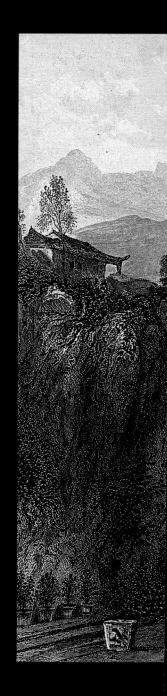

The picturesque landscapes of China were shaped by *Feng-Shui* experts. 'The Imperial Travelling Palace at the Hoo-Kew-Shan' illustrates some of the important geomantic elements – mountains at the back, water in the front and a pagoda on a hill to deflect harmful influences.

The Forbidden City in the heart of Peking was laid out according to *Feng-Shui* principles. In this 18th-century map, the city is shown as a blank square surrounded by ramparts, its boundaries perfectly aligned. Chinese emperors would sit on the dragon throne facing south. In this way, they were protected from the evils from the north, and derived beneficial *ch'i* energy from the sea and the sun to the south.

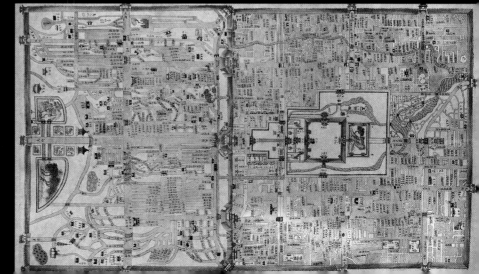

LEYS ON THE ENGLISH LANDSCAPE

LEY HUNTER EXTRAORDINAIRE
British author and esoteric researcher
John Michell took up the gauntlet
thrown down by Alfred Watkins and set
out to discover if leys actually existed.
Using only Neolithic and Bronze Age
sacred sites in a small area around Land's
End in Cornwall, England, Michell
established that there were 22
alignments between 53 sites. His results,
published in *The Old Stones of Land's
End*, showed that this ratio was well
beyond the laws of chance and
convinced him of the reality of leys.

THE MAN WHO UNCOVERED LEYS
While riding over the hills of
Bredwardine in Herefordshire,
65-year-old Alfred Watkins was suddenly
struck by the existence of a ley system
on the English landscape. Amateur
archaeologist, inventor and
photographer, Watkins saw in a flash a
network of lines laid out across the
country connecting churches, old stones
and other sacred sites. He published his
findings in *The Old Straight Track* in
1925, which provoked virulent attacks
from orthodox archaeologists. But since
that time, many ley hunters have
ventured into the English countryside,
equipped with maps and a ruler, and
have discovered for themselves the truth
of Watkins' vision.

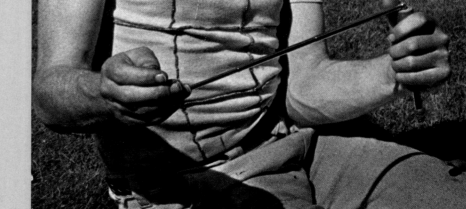

THE SAINTBURY LEY

On the northern edge of the Cotswold Hills in the west of England, a short ley runs 5.5km (3.5mi) through the village of Saintbury in Gloucestershire. The aerial view of the ley looks south, beginning at a cross beside a road junction; it follows a road to Saintbury Church and in the distance a Bronze Age round barrow. Beyond this, the ley passes through a neolithic long barrow and a pagan cemetery, before ending at the ancient farmstead of Seven Wells.

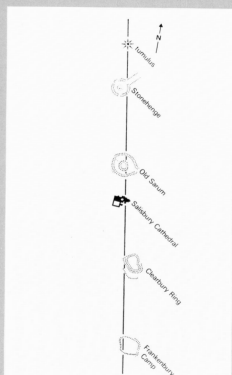

THE OLD SARUM LEY

Passing north by northwest to south by southeast (NNW to SSE) across the Wiltshire–Hampshire countryside in southern England, this ley extends for 30km (18.5mi): starting from a tumulus, it links Stonehenge, an Iron Age fort at Old Sarum, Salisbury Cathedral, an Iron Age camp at Clearbury Ring and the Iron Age hill-fort of Frankenbury Camp.

THE GIANT STATUES OF EASTER ISLAND

Hundreds of calm, still, tall statues lie broken or buried on a bleak volcanic island in the Pacific Ocean. Who made them and why? Are they linked to other Polynesian cultures? Or is there evidence of South American influence?

On Easter Sunday 1722, the crew of a Dutch ship running before the southeast trade winds in the Pacific Ocean unexpectedly sighted land. Closing with the rocky and inhospitable shore, Admiral Jacob Roggeveen saw with astonishment that it was lined with giant statues, their backs to the sea and some crowned with distinctive red topknots. Upon landing, the Admiral found the islanders to be impoverished – they had stone tools and weapons, and possessed only a few canoes which were both small and patched.

The English seafarer Captain Cook visited the island 50 years later. Among his crew was an Hawaiian sailor who could understand the islanders' speech, for it was Polynesian like his own. The islanders revealed that they were indeed the descendants of the statue-carvers. According to their legends, they had been led to the island by the chief Hotu Matu'a and since that time 22 generations had passed.

The coming of people to Easter Island

Around 1000 BC, a race of skilled potters and navigators, called by archaeologists the Lapita, reached Fiji from New Guinea and then made the long and perilous crossing to Tonga and Samoa. Their descendants sailed farther east about 400 years later, looking for new islands 'above the wind', as the Polynesians say. They knew the world was full of islands, and that the islands 'above the wind' were always empty of people.

A Sanskrit text describes the skills of the pilot: 'He knows the course of the stars and can always orient himself.' And again: 'He distinguishes the regions of the ocean by the fish, by the birds, by the colour of the water.' The Lapita added the knowledge of the ocean swells and wave patterns, of cloud formations and of prevailing winds. In their powerful double canoes capable of sailing to windward, they made long voyages to distant islands, and so became the 'people of the many islands' – the Polynesians.

It may be that around AD 380, the younger son of a chieftain of the Tuatomu Islands put to sea with some of his followers after a quarrel, and sailed eastward. They voyaged for many days without sighting land. Driven to leeward into the belt of wild westerly winds far to the south, they despaired of ever finding a haven. Food ran short as all their animals, except a few chickens, were lost. And then, when the wind eased, they turned their canoes north, found the southeast trade winds again and, running before them, came upon the last island: *Te Pito o te Henua*, the Navel of the World.

Or it may have been, as the Norwegian archaeologist Thor Heyerdahl has argued, that the first settlers came from the east, from pre-Inca South America, bringing with them on their rafts the sweet potato, the bulrushes which grow in profusion around the crater lakes on Easter Island and their skill in working stone.

Massive statues gaze across Easter Island to the eternal horizon. Raised on platforms at the inland Akivi *ahu*, this grand group of ceremonial giants is probably the most prestigious on the island. They were re-erected in 1960 by American archaeologist William Mulloy and his team. Each statue weighed six tons – the first took four weeks to set up, the last less than a week.

The remote fastness of Easter Island lies on the southeastern corner of the Polynesian triangle; Hawaii and New Zealand lie on the other two corners. Polynesians navigated their way through a multitude of islands and across uncharted ocean before they reached Easter Island.

Easter Island covers an area of 116sq.km (45sq.mi) and has three main volcanoes, of which Rano Raraku provided all the stone for the statues. Most of the *ahu* funerary platforms are located around the edge of the island, their statues facing inland.

The making of the stone statues

The people of Easter Island became the most skilful sculptors in all the islands of the Pacific. From about AD 400, they built stone funerary platforms, the *ahu*, by the shore and faced some of them with large dressed stones that were expertly shaped and fitted.

The *ahu* became taboo while a dead body was cleaned to a skeleton by birds, wind and weather. All this time, the dead person's family watched by the *ahu*. Then the clan gathered and buried the bones inside the *ahu* and afterwards held a great feast in honour of the dead.

To further honour the ancestors and display the strength and wealth of the clan, the Easter Islanders carved statues from the soft rock of a small volcanic hill, Rano Raraku. At first, the statues were varied in form. Later, from about AD 1100, a single image came to dominate: a male human figure with a stylized head and long earlobes, sometimes with detailed decoration on the body to represent tattooing. The statues were set up on the *ahu* to gaze from their inlaid eyes over the clan's houses and fields. Some authorities suggest these 'long ears' indicate that a new group of settlers came to the island at that time.

Easter Island flourished for 600 years. Yams, sweet potatoes and bananas were cultivated, canoes were built for fishing, chickens were raised. Trees were cut down to build fine houses with stone foundations and reed thatch roofs. Clan chiefs vied with each other to erect the finest, tallest statues.

From about AD 1500, a new cult grew up on the island. This was the cult of the birdman, perhaps the god *Makemake*. From the ceremonial village of Orongo, which clings to the cliffs by the crater of Rano Kau, cult followers annually raced each other to the shore and swam to the island of Motu Nui, to capture the first egg laid by the sooty terns after their annual migration.

The chief of the clan whose servant brought back the first egg became, for a year, a powerful ritual figure to whom gifts were due. The houses, caves and rocks around Orongo are adorned with carvings and relief sculptures of the legend of *Makemake*. And his ritual involved the chanting of prayer inscribed on wooden tablets, *rongorongo*, in a script unique to Easter Island.

The demise of the people of Easter Island

The rise of the cult of *Makemake* may mean that another group of settlers came to the island after AD 1400, but no one knows for certain. What is known is that at some time, after AD 1600, war broke out. Timber became scarce, and without timber life was harsh. Lost canoes could not be replaced, good houses could not be built. Without trees the soil deteriorated and, as crops failed, food was hard to come by. Women and children taken in war were eaten by their captors. The *ahu* were captured by enemies, the ancestral images overturned.

Legends tell of a great battle, only a generation before the European ships came, which ended in the capture and slaughter of the 'long ears' by the 'short ears'. These peoples may have been the last descendants of different cultures, from east and west, driven to war when the trees failed and famine came.

Rare visits by European ships offer glimpses of the continuing warfare and of the hunger and misery. By 1838, few of the great statues were standing. In 1862, Peruvian slave ships carried off every able-bodied man and woman to the mines in Peru where they succumbed to disease. The few who returned brought smallpox and leprosy. In 1877, the island's population was 110 souls. In 1888, it was annexed by Chile. With better food and medical care, the people survived to see their island become the focus of one of the great riddles of the modern world.

Gigantic eyes stare down in sinister fashion from one of the few re-erected statues. More than 600 statues have been found, some by the *ahu* on which they once stood, many around the Rano Raraku quarry. Several statues are 9m (30ft) or more in height. Of the statues left unfinished in the quarry, one is over 20m (66ft) high with an estimated weight of an astonishing 300 tons.

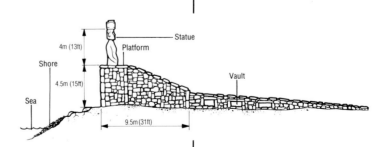

The funerary platforms called *ahu* were usually built of blocks of volcanic rock neatly fitted together. Located on the seashore, the *ahu* had long ramps studded with ordered rows of pebbles on the inland side. The largest *ahu* is at Vinapu on the south coast.

THE CHALK GIANT OF CERNE ABBAS

The gigantic figure of a man has been cut into the surface of a chalk down in Dorset in southern England. Who is the giant and what does he represent? Who carved the figure, when and why?

The largest and best preserved of England's hillside figures is carved into the green turf near the village of Cerne Abbas in the county of Dorset. He is uncompromisingly pagan: 55m (180ft) tall, brazenly naked with an erect phallus, his ribs and nipples delineated. In his raised hand he wields a knobbed club 37m (121ft) long; his left arm is outstretched and he may once have held an object in his left hand.

Letters and numbers may once have been inscribed between the feet of the giant but have not survived, and considerable argument has arisen over their message. The letters may have been the giant's name; or they may have been ANO, standing for *anno*, 'in the year of', the numbers being the date 1748 when the figure was recut. Alternatively, they may have been IHS which represented JESUS, or IAO which referred to Jehovah, or JHD *Jehovah/Jesus hoc destruxit*, meaning 'God has overthrown this'.

Over the centuries, many legends have grown up around the figure. He was said to represent a real giant who created havoc in the area by eating sheep and causing other destruction. One day he lay down on the hillside to digest his latest meal and fell asleep. The local people took the opportunity to kill him and then carve his outline in the chalk.

Ancient god or recent folly?

The first clear written reference to the Cerne Abbas Giant dates only from 1751 in a letter written by the Dorset historian John Hutchins whose *History of Dorset* was published in 1774. Of the giant he said: 'I have heard from the steward of the manor it is a modern thing, cut out in Lord Holles's time', in other words between 1641 and 1666. However, Holles may only have recut the figure and the absence of any earlier reference does not prove the giant was first carved in the mid-17th century.

The Cerne Abbas figure closely resembles a depiction of Hercules, also naked and wielding a club, on a fragment of Romano-British ware found in Norfolk. The giant is also similar to a Bronze Age carving from Bohuslän in Sweden of a naked man with erect phallus, holding a spear in his right hand. Whereas the Swedish carving may represent Tiwaz, a northern sky-god, war-god and fertility figure, Hercules was an athlete-hero from Greek mythology. And there was a Hercules cult in the Roman Empire under Emperor Commodus, who ruled from AD 180 to 193, which probably had devotees in Britain. The giant may have been their emblem, or the Celtic equivalent of Hercules. The name Helith, Helis or Heil was traditionally used for the giant, and this could be a corruption of Hercules.

Similarities between the Cerne Abbas Giant and ancient gods suggest a much older origin than the 17th century. Some English hill figures are very old indeed. The Uffington White Horse in Oxfordshire, for example, may date back to the Iron Age, while the Long Man of Wilmington in Sussex could be neolithic. These

The giant effigy of a naked man may have been nurtured as a fertility symbol for nearly 2,000 years. That the chalk giant could have been maintained by the local people of Cerne Abbas for so long is a testimony to his power. Above him on the hillside is The Trendle, an Iron Age earthwork where May Day festivities – themselves fertility rituals – were regularly held.

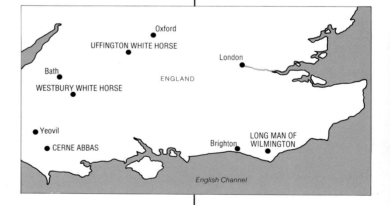

England's chalk hill figures are usually found on the slopes of chalk downs: the Cerne Abbas Giant on the North Dorset Downs in Dorset; the Uffington White Horse on the Berkshire Downs in Oxfordshire; the Westbury White Horse on the Bratton Downs in Wiltshire; the Long Man of Wilmington on the South Downs in East Sussex.

ages are uncertain for there is no sure way of dating such figures. They were originally outlined by cutting away the turf and leaving the white chalk exposed. A number of hill figures have become overgrown and lost. Others thought to date from the 18th and 19th centuries may be recuttings of older figures and may even be inaccurate, such as the Westbury White Horse in Wiltshire.

The close proximity of several surviving hill figures to a prehistoric site also suggests an ancient origin. The Uffington White Horse lies just below the Iron Age hillfort of Uffington Castle; the Westbury White Horse lies below the Iron Age earthwork of Bratton Castle; the Long Man of Wilmington is close to a neolithic long barrow and other burial mounds. Above the head of the Cerne Abbas Giant, with his club pointing directly at it, is The Trendle, a small rectangular Iron Age enclosure outlined by banks and ditches.

Was the giant a fertility symbol?

British folklore is full of memories of fertility rituals. Childless women would visit certain old stones in search of fecundity, and there practise the age-old rituals, such as rubbing against the stone or sitting on it. Some holy wells had the reputations of curing barrenness. Sexual carvings of men and women displaying their genitals can be found on some Christian churches, though no one knows for certain why they were fashioned.

The agricultural cycle has always incorporated many fertility customs. A most popular custom still practised today, though lacking its original earthiness, is dancing around the maypole. On the night before May Day, young people would go into the woods to fetch the maypole tree and to make their own personal contributions to the fertility rites. The maypole itself was a blatant phallic symbol around which the people would dance. Significantly, The Trendle earthwork at Cerne Abbas was, until quite recently, the location for such May Day festivities. A fir tree was taken up the hill and erected during the night inside the earthwork, and the villagers would dance around it on May Day.

The Cerne Abbas Giant himself was believed to have the power of fertility for obvious reasons. Barren women would sit on the giant, presumably on his 9m (30ft) phallus, in the hope of becoming pregnant. Some even believed it was necessary for sexual intercourse to take place there before conception could occur. And unmarried girls, hoping for a wedding and many children, would sleep the night on the giant's white outline.

One further mystery is how the giant has survived for so long, especially since a religious house was founded in the village in the 6th century. Is it even possible that the monks themselves were responsible for cutting the figure? While it sounds unlikely, it has been suggested that in the days when Christian and pagan rituals were performed side by side, the figure could have been cut by monks to represent the pagan god of fertility. Moreover, in earlier centuries, a naked figure like the giant would not have been considered as obscene. Another suggestion is that it was cut at the time of the dissolution of the monasteries during Henry VIII's reign in the 16th century, as a comment on the personal habits of the monks and the abbot.

The missing letters between the giant's feet have been seen as an attempt by the monks to counteract the strong influence of the giant's pagan and virile attributes. Not having the authority to actually destroy the figure, they added the letters JHD, 'God has overthrown this', to try to cancel its power. While the true history of the giant, his ancestry and identity, will probably remain unknown, it is sufficient that he has survived at all to provide an intriguing glimpse into the beliefs and customs of ages past.

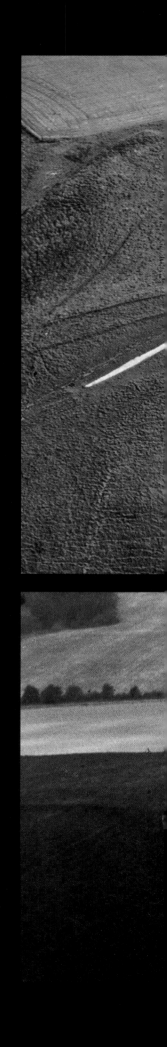

The huge stylized drawing of the White Horse near Uffington village in Oxfordshire is a complete mystery. Best seen from a distance or from the air, the figure is 111m (365ft) from head to tail. It was probably carved by the Iron Age Celts around 100 BC – the horse was highly venerated in Celtic times as the goddess Epona.

The White Horse may be a dragon, according to local tradition, and not a horse at all. Close by is Dragon Hill where St George is said to have killed the dragon; no grass grows on the top of the hill where the beast's blood was spilt. The figure may therefore be a graphic commemoration of St George's triumph.

HILL FIGURES OF OLD ENGLAND

THE LONG MAN OF WILMINGTON
Cut into the northern slope of Windover Hill, at the eastern end of the South Downs near Wilmington in Sussex, is a giant man, 70m (230ft) tall and carrying a long staff in each hand. His age is uncertain although his present form dates back to 1874 when he was restored. The Long Man of Wilmington has been identified variously as a local giant, St Paul, a Roman soldier, a Saxon haymaker or as a prehistoric surveyor, or dodman, who used his two staffs as sighting poles. Whoever he was, he most likely dates back 2,000 to 2,500 years.

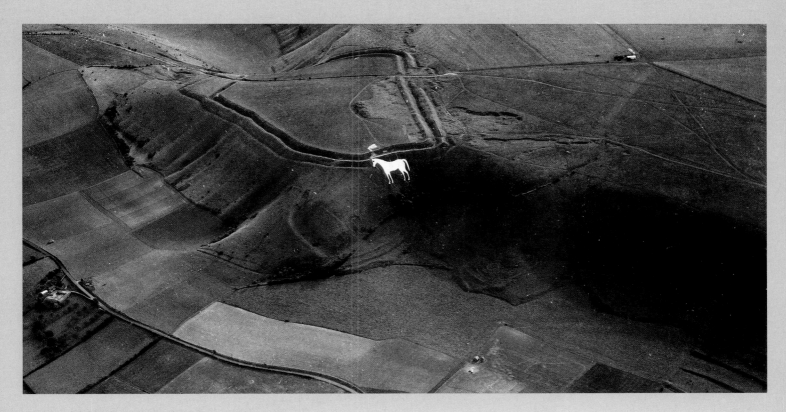

THE WESTBURY WHITE HORSE

The chalk figure carved on the hillside at the edge of Salisbury Plain in Wiltshire dates from only 1778, when the local lord decided to remodel the original horse. The latter was far more mysterious than today's figure; a drawing from 1772 shows the original horse with a long thin body, a big eye on its head and a slim tail that ended in a crescent shape. The age of the original Westbury carving is unknown – some say it was made by the Celts; others that it commemorates King Alfred's victory over the Danes in AD 878; still others reckon it to be an 18th-century folly.

DANCING AROUND THE MAYPOLE

A major fertility ritual held on May Day each year was 'dancing around the maypole'. The Trendle, above the Cerne Abbas Giant in Dorset, was one site used for this ancient festivity. Maypoles, usually painted in red and white stripes, were about 25m (82ft) high; some maypoles were taller – one at Barwick-in-Elmet in West Yorkshire, for example, is some 27m (90ft) high, while the last one to be erected in London in 1661 was 41m (134ft) tall.

ANCIENT CITIES

'. . . Between the walls of mighty mountains crowned
With Cyclopean piles, whose turrets proud,
The homes of the departed, dimly frowned
O'er the bright waves which girt their dark foundations
round.'

Percy Bysshe Shelley

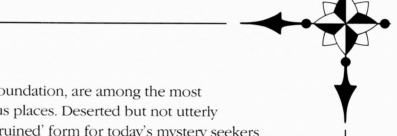

Ancient cities, often of shadowy foundation, are among the most enduring of the world's mysterious places. Deserted but not utterly destroyed, these cities remain in 'ruined' form for today's mystery seekers to marvel at. How, for example, did the Incas erect so accurately the massive walls of Machu Picchu? What secrets were used to build the Pyramid of the Sun at Teotihuacan? How were the gigantic temples at Angkor built in such close conjunction to its complex of waterways?

The purpose of these ancient cities may be as puzzling as their construction. Some, such as Great Zimbabwe, were probably trading capitals, but others had more spiritual uses. Thus the *kivas* of Chaco Canyon feature 'spirit-tunnels', while Petra is, in effect, a vast necropolis built to house the dead.

As cities with wonderful cultures were born and thrived, so others were doomed to destruction and decay. How and why they were deserted or ruined remains, in many cases, unknown. But the edifices survive, poignant reminders of their mysterious past.

MACHU PICCHU: FABULOUS INCA CITADEL

The last refuge of the Incas is thought to be a beautiful city high up in the Andes Mountains. How was it built and when? What was the purpose of the sacred stone, the Intihuatana? Why was the city deserted so suddenly leaving little trace of its former inhabitants?

When Gonzalo Pizzarro and a tiny force of Spaniards came to Peru in the early 1530s they must have been surprised at the ease with which they conquered the country. The ruling Inca Empire was severely embroiled in civil war and their foot soldiers had no answer to the Spaniards' cavalry. In 1536 the defeated Inca ruler, Manco Capac, fled from his capital Cuzco and founded another city called Vilcabamba where his Inca dynasty survived for a further 36 years.

Hiram Bingham of Yale University came to Peru in 1911 to find Vilcabamba and to establish the location of the Inca's last refuge. Basing himself at Cuzco, he explored the surrounding country-side. After several days walking along the banks of the Urubamba River, he met a peasant who offered to show him some ruins at the top of a nearby mountain which he called Machu Picchu, or 'old peak'. Strenuous climbing through dense jungle and across fragile rope suspension bridges brought Bingham's party to what is known today as the Royal Tomb. Despite the thick vegetation covering it Bingham realized this was no ordinary ruin. The pure white granite stone walls astonished him. He wrote: 'Dimly, I began to realize that this wall with its adjoining semicircular temple over the cave were as fine as the finest stonework in the world . . . It fairly took my breath away. What could this place be?'

Believing it to be Vilcabamba he organized an expedition the following year to clear the area of trees and to clean the monuments. Thus was the fabulous citadel of Machu Picchu revealed to the modern world. But it was not Vilcabamba, for Spanish documents have since come to light suggesting that the city lay in the opposite direction from Cuzco. Even today scholars are not agreed on its exact whereabouts.

The city and its people

Only from the nearby hilltop observatory of Intipunku can the visitor realize the full extent of Machu Picchu's colossal conception. The citadel is a stupendous achievement – in urban planning, civil engineering, architecture and stonemasonry. Who built this symphony in stone, this vast complex of buildings so well constructed that even five centuries in the inexorable grip of the Peruvian jungle have deprived them only of their thatch and reed roofs? The architectural forms are unmistakably characteristic of the Incas but beyond that its origins are veiled in a mystery as thick as the early morning mists swirling around its craggy fastnesses. At any moment, it seems, a gold-encrusted and befeathered Inca warrior will materialize between the curiously sloping door jambs.

The enigmatic Incas knew neither the wheel nor any written language, but forged an empire stretching 3,680km (2,300mi) along the mighty Andean heights. What is this city of theirs,

Precariously perched on a mountain shoulder, high up in the Andes, the citadel of Machu Picchu remained hidden for four centuries until Hiram Bingham drew back the green veil of the jungle in 1911. Steep stairways lead to granite shrines, fountains and flowers adorn dwelling places of marvellously carved stone. Thought by some to be the last refuge of the Incas, Machu Picchu was more likely to be a ceremonial city where Inca lords and the Virgins of the Sun worshipped their gods and consulted the heavens.

The ruins of Machu Picchu stand about 450m (1,500ft) above the waters of the Amazon-bound Urubamba River in Peru. The citadel lies about 112km (70mi) northwest of the Inca capital of Cuzco, 'the navel of the world' that was laid out in the shape of a giant puma.

perched on a rocky outcrop at 2,300m (7,000ft) on the eastern Andean slopes 112km (70mi) northwest of Cuzco? The word 'city' is not strictly accurate for these stone terraces and stairways never echoed to the clamour of everyday folk going about their common business.

Machu Picchu was a complex of temples, palaces and observatories and was the home of the Inca ruling classes. On the west side of the city is the sacred stone, the Intihuatana, whose name means 'the hitching post of the sun': a small flattened pyramid topped by a huge stone 'sundial' carved out of the natural rock into a sinuous shape of great beauty. From here, high priests made observations and calculations enabling them to chart the round of the heavens – knowledge which gave them both religious authority and temporal power. Prediction of the climate and consequent harvest was carried out by the examination of the entrails of sacrificed llamas.

The citadel sits upon a craggy mountain shelf with huge drops on each side, providing magnificent natural defences and commanding an excellent view of the narrow valley of the Urubamba, along which enemies would have to pass to reach the capital, Cuzco. Whatever the spiritual values of the site, strategic considerations were not neglected – only what might be expected from a people who had carved out an empire the size of Julius Caesar's.

While human sacrifices may have taken place in times of catastrophe, the Incas certainly indulged in other practices which seem equally bizarre by modern standards. Skull deformation, for example, was performed on high-status females, presumably in the name of fashion. At birth, a child's head would be tightly bound with straps and boards, which remained in place until the head was fully formed in late adolescence. By this time the skull had been elongated upward and backward to a truly alarming degree. This strange practice perhaps made necessary the even stranger one of trepanning, in which quite large areas of the skullbone were cut out with ritual knives called *tumis*.

The fall of Machu Picchu

Hiram Bingham found many objects of stone, bronze, ceramic and obsidian, but no gold or silver. There should have been fabulous riches of these metals comparable to those found at the Temple of the Sun in Cuzco where even the garden contained lifesize gold replicas of maize and other plants. It is unlikely the Spaniards stole the gold and silver, for it seems they never found Machu Picchu. They always took great pains to visit every inhabited settlement in Peru and record it in detail before relieving it of everything worth taking. But there is not a single reference to Machu Picchu in the Spaniards' chronicles. The Peruvian scholar Dr Victor Angles Vargas thinks the city became depopulated toward the end of the 15th century before the Spaniards arrived. What brought this about is one of the deepest enigmas surrounding this sacred site.

Wars between rival Inca tribes were common and bloody, often resulting in the annihilation of whole communities. When the Inca ruler, Wayna Capac, defeated the tribe of the Caranques, for example, he ordered the execution of all the remaining members. The citizens of Machu Picchu may well have suffered such a fate. Another possibility is that a novice priest defiled one of the sacred *ajllas*, the Virgins of the Sun. Garcilaso de Vega, the son of a Spaniard and an Inca princess, wrote exhaustive commentaries on Inca customs. According to him, anyone found guilty of sexually violating an *ajlla* was not only put to death himself, 'but servants, relatives and neighbours, inhabitants of the

The Tower of the Sun, in the centre of the photograph, displays Inca stonemasonry at its best. Roughly shaped like a horseshoe, the wall of the tower was assembled from perfectly made stones without the use of mortar. Each course of stones is slightly smaller than the one below. A trapezoidal window appears to have been placed to permit observation of the midwinter solstice.

The extraordinary skill of the Incas in working granite and other stones is illustrated by the close-up of a wall at Ollantaytambo, a fortress near Machu Picchu. The blocks of stone are so neatly cut and fitted that lichens can grow across the tiny gaps between them.

The Intihuatana, a sacred Inca stone dedicated to the mighty sun god Inti, was carved from a single outcrop of rock. Each winter solstice, at the festival of Inti Raymi, the god was symbolically tethered to the stone to ensure his return the following summer. Also used as a sundial, this 'hitching post of the sun' was a scientific instrument able to indicate solstices, equinoxes and lunar movements.

same town and their cattle were all killed. No one was left … The place was damned and excommunicated so that no one could find it, not even the animals.' Was this, then, the fate of the inhabitants of Machu Picchu?

Epidemics are common enough even in modern times – in the 1940s malaria decimated the population of an area near Machu Picchu. And the skeleton of a rich woman found by Hiram Bingham showed she had suffered from syphilis and was unlikely to have been alone in this. Perhaps the city was ravaged by a plague so terrible it was permanently quarantined by the authorities. Modern scientific analysis of the city's skeletons, using methods such as X-rays which were unavailable to Bingham, might prove illuminating, but otherwise the cause of the sudden depopulation of Machu Picchu may remain hidden forever.

Constructing the sacred city

What most fascinates the visitor today is the grandeur of the stonemasonry. The Incas had no draught animals yet they erected massive walls made of stones weighing many tons which, even now, fit together so closely a penknife blade cannot be inserted between them anywhere along the joints.

One characteristic of Inca masonry is the way the stones are carved with many edges which lock together perfectly without any mortar to form a kind of three-dimensional jigsaw puzzle. Such a design greatly increases the stability of the wall, which is necessary to endure the frequent earthquakes that shake the Andes. In Cuzco, there is a famous stone in a surviving Inca wall with 12 angles between the sides. At Torontoy, one of the smaller sites clustered around Machu Picchu, there is a stone with 40 such angles.

How did the Incas reach these unsurpassed standards of the stonemason's craft? Manpower problems were resolved by putting to work all the able-bodied men from captured tribes. The nearby temple complex at Ollantaytambo, for instance, was built by the Colla Indians from the shores of Lake Titicaca. But how did the Incas carve the hard granite into prodigiously long and straight lines? Although the Incas were exceptionally skilled at smelting and alloying soft metals – they did inlay work and cloisonné with gold, silver, copper and bronze – they never discovered how to make iron tools.

No artefacts hard enough to work such unyielding stones have ever been found. The Incas simply did not have the technology for such carving and yet they managed it. This is another great enigma presented by this mysterious race. Many explanations have been offered. The guide at Sacsayhuaman, near Cuzco, says it was done with fragments of meteoric hematite. If this is true, the Andes must have suffered a huge meteor bombardment, for hematite would not last long when made into tools, yet there are millions of man-hours of carving on display.

The use of laser technology by extraterrestrial visitors is a better-known theory sometimes invoked to explain the quality of the stonemasonry. This theory, by denying the Incas the ability to do the job for themselves, is based on the deep-seated modern assumption that the 20th century represents the pinnacle of human achievement. This view of the world, with its simple series of causes and effects, has, of course, helped conquer diseases and span the globe. But such a view could mean that humankind has lost certain powers available to ancient races. The Druid initiate is said to have had the powers of flight, time travel and weather control. Did the Inca shaman-priest use occult forces to raise and shape Machu Picchu from untamed rock? The answer may never be known.

Carved from solid granite, the Royal Tomb lies immediately below the Tower of the Sun. A throne of solid rock, walls faced with carefully worked stone slabs, and an exalted position under the sacred tower, indicate that this was the mausoleum of a high-ranking Inca official.

The Temple of the Three Windows is so called because of its three trapezoidal windows. No evidence regarding its purpose has been discovered except for a rectangular stone standing a short distance away from the windows in the middle of the temple. This stone could be a backsight for solar observations.

EXPLORING OLD PERU

MOCHICA EFFIGY POTS

Vigorous portrayals of everyday life were a hallmark of the Mochica culture which thrived on the north coast of Peru from 200 BC to AD 900. Effigy pots, such as this Mochica warrior, were mass-produced and depicted scenes showing animals, plants, mountains, fish, people – even a puma attacking a man.

THE PARACAS SHROUDS

Richly embroidered mantles were found wrapped around many of the mummified bodies in cemeteries near Paracas, on the south coast of Peru. Regarded as some of the world's finest weavings, the shrouds – together with other multicoloured textiles, such as shirts, turbans and pouches – indicate the importance of the afterlife to the people who lived in southern Peru some 2,000 years ago.

CELEBRATIONS OF THE SUN

The Inca sun festival of Inti Raymi, as re-enacted at Sacsayhuaman near Cuzco, was held in June and December at the midwinter and midsummer solstices. The festival would last for eight days and included prayers, thanksgivings, animal sacrifices, offerings of coca leaves and a ritual tethering of the sun to the ceremonial Intihuatana stone.

THE ADVENTUROUS SCHOLAR

To his dying day, Hiram Bingham remained convinced that the mountain citadel he had discovered in 1911 was Vilcabamba, the legendary last refuge of the Incas. But soon after his death in 1956, this American professor from Yale, who had combined the learning of a historian with the courage of an explorer, was to be proved wrong. Vilcabamba lies elsewhere and is still undiscovered. As for the citadel Bingham had unveiled, called Machu Picchu after a neighbouring mountain, no one knows its real name to this day.

CHACO CANYON: THE PUEBLO COMMUNITIES

A canyon in New Mexico is the site of one of North America's earliest civilizations. Who lived there? What was the function of the huge circular kivas? What was Pueblo Bonito? Why did the inhabitants of the canyon disappear so suddenly?

Cowboy movies nearly always encourage their viewers to see North American Indians as bloodthirsty whooping savages who eke out a meagre existence living in their wigwams. But a visit to the Four Corners Country of the southwestern United States would dispel forever this erroneous public image. For, at a time when the ordinary folk of Europe lived in rude hovels of wood and thatch, the inhabitants of Chaco Canyon dwelt in sophisticated urban complexes of skilfully constructed stones.

Chaco Canyon winds through arid sagebush country where vicious dust storms whip up at a moment's notice. Yet, over 1,000 years ago, the people there were making baskets with a weave so tight that even today they will hold water. The extraordinary geometric patterns they used to decorate their pottery illustrate a highly developed artistic sense. These people are today known as the Anasazi, from the later Navajo name for them.

The Great House of Pueblo Bonito

The earliest dwellings in the canyon are sunken pit-houses. Surface houses were built about AD 750, followed by many mud-and-sandstone villages of a dozen or more adjoining rooms. It is not to see these that tourists come to this parched canyon, but to view the remarkable towns called Great Houses on its north side.

The time when these Great Houses were constructed has been determined with precision by dendrochronology, the tree-ring dating technique pioneered in this region in the 1920s. At one Great House, where the arid climate has preserved a wooden roof intact, the season of felling each log was discovered. The roof had been assembled in the spring of AD 1040.

The most awe-inspiring of the 19 Great Houses today is Pueblo Bonito, literally 'pretty village'. This was begun around AD 1000 as a cluster of 20 rooms, but by 1150 had grown to a huge complex of 800 contiguous rooms in four storeys of superbly tooled masonry. The alternation of thick and thin stones gives a graceful banding effect which relieves the massiveness of the semi-circular wall that acted as a defensive backdrop to the horseshoe-shaped complex of rooms. The symmetry and geometrical precision of the various building phases suggests a high degree of central planning. And the fact that all the rooms are of much the same size – there are no palace suites or vast halls for an élite – points to a lack of social hierarchy.

The absence of furniture suggests everything from craftwork to cooking was done on the floor. Food was all-important. Corn was a staple because it is easily stored and ground into flour. By about AD 1000, the Anasazi had bred an eight-rowed variety of corn as big as those in today's supermarkets. They also cultivated beans and squash, and supplemented their diet by gathering wild seeds. Hunting deer, sheep, birds, rabbits and other animals would have been vital to the community in leaner years.

A multi-storeyed Great House with large curving walls and 37 ceremonial *kivas* once dominated the communal life of Chaco Canyon. This is Pueblo Bonito where an estimated 1,200 Anasazi Indians lived in the 11th and 12th centuries. Associated with Pueblo Bonito was a temple mound and discovered in its ruins were turquoise mosaics, conch-shell trumpets and copper bells.

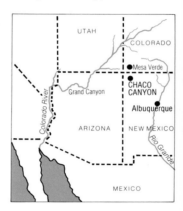

Chaco Canyon is located in the Four Corners Country where New Mexico, Colorado, Arizona and Utah meet. It lies 160km (100mi) northwest of Albuquerque and about the same distance southeast of Mesa Verde. The canyon is about 19km (12mi) long, 1.6km (1mi) wide and although it is dry today it was once well watered.

The Great Kiva at Pueblo Bonito is the largest of the 37 underground ceremonial chambers in the community. About 16m (53ft) in diameter, the *kiva* is perfectly circular and symbolizes a womb in the body of mother earth from which the people of the community were born.

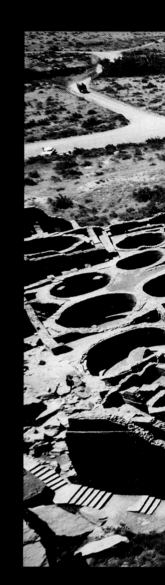

CHACO CANYON: THE PUEBLO COMMUNITIES

The importance of the spirit-tunnels

Every Chacoan community had a *kiva* – Pueblo Bonito had 37. This is a sunken circular chamber with a central hearth and a log roof. A hole in the centre of the roof functioned as both a smoke outlet and an entry hole. Remains of potters' tools and weavers' looms indicate that such crafts were carried on in the *kivas*. These chambers may have also served as a kind of men's club where they could find occasional refuge from a society which seems to have been significantly more matriarchal than today's.

Much more than local gossip occupied those who frequented the *kiva*. For it was here that the spirit life of the Anasazi community was controlled, although the form of the rituals involved will forever be a closed book. Most *kivas* feature a *sipapu*, a small round hole in the floor behind the central hearth. The spirits of tribal ancestors were thought to have emerged from this hole which represented the point of communication with the spirit world. Opposite the *sipapu* was a ventilator shaft to the outside which was needed for the proceedings in the *kiva* to continue. But its Indian name, which translates as 'spirit-tunnel', indicates a purpose beyond that of keeping the fire going and providing fresh air.

The subterranean nature of the *kiva* suggests that the Anasazi religion involved tapping the energy available from the earth. This might have been seen as arising from the *sipapu* in the form of spirits, beneficial ones if the ritual had worked properly. These would then pass through the 'spirit-tunnel' to the outside world – it may be significant that, on the way from the *sipapu*, they first had to pass through the fire. Once outside, they would bring good fortune to the people and their crops.

The sudden disappearance of the Anasazi people

Effective propitiation of the spirits of nature would have been especially important in the Four Corners Country. The climate is never the same from one year to the next – the only dependable meteorological fact is the near-absence of rain, often no more than 15cm (6in) falling in a year. A cold dry winter and the consequent crop failure would have had a devastating effect on the Anasazi people, as the excavated mass graves of starvation and malnutrition-related disease victims tragically demonstrate.

The climatic variability may provide a clue to the greatest enigma surrounding the Anasazi – their rapid and mysterious demise. In the early years of the 12th century, the people of Chaco Canyon represented the peak of Anasazi cultural progress. But, by 1150, they had almost completely disappeared.

Recent research suggests that rainfall patterns in the area follow a 550-year cycle, with an optimum just after AD 1100. With good harvests and plenty of game, the population would have expanded to as many as 5,000, an unprecedented figure for a pre-metalworking society. But when the climatic cycle reversed, the rain spirit withdrew its favours, causing yields to fall and the Anasazi people to go hungry.

In a desperate attempt to appease the rain spirit, huge *kivas* were built outside the towns, such as Casa Rinconada, which stands opposite Pueblo Bonito, and Kin Nahasbas. But even the frantic building of *kivas* beside the drying-up watercourses could not avert disaster. Faced with increasingly severe drought and erosion of their croplands, the Chacoans seem to have decided to cut their losses and abandon the canyon wholesale. They migrated southeast to the more reliable Rio Grande, where they merged with the ancestors of the Hopi and Zuni tribes. Thus, dried up in its prime, ended one of the great civilizations of pre-Hispanic America.

A huge recess in a canyon wall shelters the ruins of Cliff Palace, one of several Anasazi community dwellings in Mesa Verde, Colorado. Discovered in 1888 by trader Richard Wetherill and his cousin Charlie Mason, Cliff Palace once contained more than 200 rooms, 23 *kivas* and, in places, stood four storeys high.

Cliff Palace was probably a regional centre of the Anasazi Indians who came here for ceremonial, political and trade purposes. To reach it, they had to negotiate an easily defended but tricky series of footholds in the rock face. No one knows what happened at Mesa Verde, but it is clear that the complex of cliff dwellings was abandoned by the end of the 13th century.

THE FOUR CORNERS COUNTRY

RELICS FROM CLIFF DWELLINGS
Archaeological finds from the ancient
Pueblo communities in New Mexico
reveal a number of domestic items.
Among them are cooking implements,
beads, pottery with designs distinctive of
the Four Corners Country, samples of
basketry and several needles.

THE HOPI INDIANS
The oldest, continuously inhabited
settlement in the USA is the Hopi village
of Oraibi situated on a mesa in northern
Arizona. A deeply religious and esoteric
people, the Hopi are the inheritors of
the pueblo-style communities found in
Chaco Canyon. In their inhospitable
environment – the Hopi Reservation
covers an area of about 10,350sq.km
(4,000sq.mi) of arid land – the Hopi
grow corn and beans, and hunt rabbits
with curved sticks resembling the
boomerangs of Australia's Aborigines.

THE KATCHINA DOLLS

Dances and rituals play a vital role in the Hopi communities and ceremonies to appease the invisible spirits, or *Katchinas*, are common. To instruct children in ritual procedure, the Hopi make teaching aids of masked wooden dolls depicting the various *Katchinas*.

THE NAVAJO INDIANS

The most populous of all American Indian groups, the Navajo derive much of their culture from the Pueblo Indians who lived in the Four Corners Country around AD 1000. Agriculture, sandpainting, rituals, matrilineal clanship and weaving came from the ancient Pueblo peoples. Turquoise is also a feature of the Navajo culture, as it was in Chaco Canyon nearly 1,000 years ago – about half a million pieces of turquoise were found at Pueblo Bonito alone.

TEOTIHUACAN: MYSTERIOUS CITY OF THE GODS

An ancient religious capital of Mexico thrived a thousand years before the height of the Aztec Empire. Who built it? What were the Pyramids of the Sun and Moon? What caused its downfall?

The awe-inspiring ruins of the vast city of Teotihuacan lie at almost exactly the same altitude as that other great New World city, Machu Picchu, in Peru. But there the resemblance ends, for whereas the latter is squeezed into precipitous ravines, Teotihuacan is laid out on a spacious plain in the Valley of Mexico.

This topographical *carte blanche* gave free rein to the city's designers to try out their ideas about the relationship of mass to area, of light to shade. For Teotihuacan indeed feels to the visitor like a great experiment in the organization and control of a large population by means of fear and authority.

The Pyramids of the Sun and Moon
Teotihuacan covers an area of 23.5sq.km (9sq.mi) and is dominated by the gigantic Pyramid of the Sun which was built on the ruins of an earlier structure in the 1st century AD. Each side is 225m (738ft) long – a similar dimension to its Old World counterpart, the Great Pyramid of Cheops, though its height of 70m (230ft) is less than half the latter. This in no way belittles the organization required to assemble nearly two and half million tons of sun-dried brick and rubble into one structure.

Archaeologists accidentally discovered in 1971 that, some 6m (20ft) below the pyramid and running for some 100m (328ft) to the east, is a natural cavern which was used as a sacred centre both before and after the construction of the pyramid. Prior to the Spanish conquest, Mexicans considered such caverns as wombs from which the sun and moon, as well as the forerunners of the human race, had emerged in remote antiquity.

The recently restored Pyramid of the Moon is a similar edifice, constructed in the second half of the 2nd century AD on a smaller scale with sides 145m (476ft) long at the base. The disparity in size between the solar, or masculine, and the lunar, or feminine, monuments is not confined to the New World. For example, the spire of Chartres Cathedral which is crowned with the sun is appreciably taller than the one surmounted by the moon.

Running south from the Pyramid of the Moon and stretching for about 3.2km (2mi) is the Avenue of the Dead. This is, in fact, a series of open courtyards, each up to 145m (476ft) wide and lined with small platforms which the Aztecs believed to be tombs. This was not so, for the inhabitants of Teotihuacan cremated their dead and wrapped the remains in a shroud before burying them in the floor beneath their houses.

The avenue passes the Ciudadela, 'the citadel', a huge enclosure about 640m (2,100ft) square. On its eastern side is the Temple of Quetzalcoatl, a six-tiered step pyramid constructed in the characteristic 'talud-tablero' fashion with rows of rectangular panels superimposed on the sloping walls. Here, carved with extraordinary boldness, alternate the Fire Serpent, bearer of the Sun on its daily passage, and the Feathered Serpent, Quetzalcoatl, who represents the union of air and land, heaven and earth.

The mighty four-tiered
Pyramid of the Sun took an estimated 3,000 men 30 years to build. Its axis is aligned in an east–west direction, an orientation that follows the path of the sun across the sky. The pyramid was probably built to represent the centre of the universe, its four corners symbolizing the four directions and its apex the heart of life.

The city of Teotihuacan
stands on a plateau more than 2,286m (7,500ft) above sea level. It was strategically placed at a point where several important routes converge and where the Valley of Mexico is linked with the Gulf of Mexico near modern Veracruz.

TEOTIHUACAN: MYSTERIOUS CITY OF THE GODS

Recent excavations have shown that the Avenue of the Dead continues for a further 3.2km (2mi) beyond the Ciudadela, where it was bisected by an east–west avenue of equal length. Thus the city has been divided into quarters, like the much-later Aztec capital of Tenochtitlan in the heart of modern Mexico City.

The builders of Teotihuacan

The people responsible for constructing the largest city of pre-Colombian times have not been identified. They were once believed to be Aztecs, but when this race discovered the city it had already been in ruins for seven centuries. Indeed, the ruins so impressed the Aztecs that they named the place Teotihuacan which, in their own Nahuatl language, means 'the place of those who have the road of the Gods'.

Whoever did build this magnificent city were masters of both the architectural and governmental arts. Their sculpture is at its most impressive in the austere stone masks fashioned from greenstone, basalt and jade, with eyes of mussel-shell or obsidian. Their characteristic ceramics are vase-shaped pots and cylindrical vessels with three slab-shaped feet and decoration reminiscent of Chinese bronzes.

Obsidian, obtained from the volcanoes that ring the plain, was highly prized in the ancient world owing to the keenness to which it could be sharpened. At least 350 places in Teotihuacan were used for working obsidian and these probably represented the foundation of the city's mercantile wealth.

Teotihuacan traded with, and may even have ruled over, the central highlands of Mexico and possibly much of Central America. Elegant vases manufactured in this mysterious city are found in the graves of important people all over Mexico during the period 150–600 AD, when Teotihuacan was at the height of its power. The population at this time would have approached 200,000, making it the sixth largest city in the world.

The excavation of bone needles and bodkins shows that the people manufactured clothing and basketry. Though none have survived, there must have been books, for they certainly knew how to write. Although this writing has not yet been decoded, it is known that they used bars and dots for numerals as did their predecessors, the Olmecs. And their diet makes mouth-watering reading even by today's standards: deer, rabbits, turkeys, ducks, geese, fish, maize, climbing beans, squash, pumpkins, tomatoes and avocado pears.

What befell this magnificent metropolis?

The end of Teotihuacan is as shrouded in mystery as its beginnings. The seeds of ruin probably set in as the climate became increasingly arid, so causing agricultural yields to diminish. But the *coup de grâce* was delivered in about AD 700 when the heart of the city was put to the torch by barbarian invaders from the north, who lived on in the city for a further 200 years.

Thus ended one of the most brilliant civilizations of the New World. Its ruins are spectacular enough today, but how much more impressive it must have been when the black basalt was stuccoed and painted in all the colours of the rainbow. The fragments of boldly designed frescoes in blue, red, yellow and brown that still adorn some palace walls provide a tantalizing hint.

At a time when the grandeur of Rome had crumbled into dust, and Europe was reeling under the assault of barbarian hordes, Mexico produced a civilization embodying the highest order of social cohesion and artistic sensitivity. But years of painstaking research lie ahead before the mysteries of Teotihuacan can be unearthed from the shifting sands of the Valley of Mexico.

The Avenue of the Dead stretches south from the Pyramid of the Moon, past the Pyramid of the Sun, to the Ciudadela and the Temple of Quetzalcoatl. This misnamed artery at the heart of the city – it has nothing to do with the dead – has been seen as the union of heaven and earth. This is because it joins the celestial area where the pyramids stand, with the earthly section of the city where the Ciudadela is located.

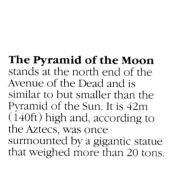

The Pyramid of the Moon stands at the north end of the Avenue of the Dead and is similar to but smaller than the Pyramid of the Sun. It is 42m (140ft) high and, according to the Aztecs, was once surmounted by a gigantic statue that weighed more than 20 tons.

AZTECS, TOLTECS AND OLMECS

OLMEC HEAD
Colossal stone heads, each carved from a single block of basalt rock, are the legacy of the Olmec people who thrived in Mexico between 800 and 500 BC. The heads are about 3m (10ft) high, weigh about 18 tons and are believed to be busts of Olmec leaders. They were found at San Lorenzo, Tres Zapotes and La Venta on the Mexican coast of the Gulf of Campeche.

THE DEFENCE OF CACTUS ROCK
Aztec warriors had to defend their shining capital city of Tenochtitlan, 'Cactus Rock', from the conquistadors of Hernando Cortez at the beginning of the 16th century. But much bloodshed was to follow and, by 1521, the Aztecs would be conquered, betrayed by their great king Montezuma and by Cortez whom they mistook for their god Quetzalcoatl.

TOLTEC STATUES
Standing in awesome silence upon a large pyramid at Tula, 80km (50mi) north of Mexico City, are four massive stone warriors. Once the supports of a temple, these statues are over 4.5m (15ft) high and were built by the Toltecs in about AD 900. Tula was the capital of the Toltec Empire which must have included Teotihuacan, less than 100km (62mi) away.

SYMBOL OF THE WATER GOD
The Aztec high priest of Tlaloc, the water god, wore as a breastplate a turquoise-encrusted, double-headed serpent with teeth made from shell. This symbol of the rain and storm god, whose special effects were to plague Hernando Cortez throughout his exploits in Mexico, was given to the Spanish commander by the Aztec leader Montezuma.

GREAT ZIMBABWE: AFRICAN TRADE CENTRE

The only major Iron Age civilization of the southern hemisphere flourished in southern Africa. Was the citadel of Zimbabwe the capital of an empire? Was it the centre for a slave trade? Was it the site of King Solomon's Mines?

In the lands between the Zambezi and Orange rivers lie the ruin fields of southern Africa. To date, around 8,000 ruins have been discovered; of these the most remarkable is Great Zimbabwe. The greatest stone monument on the African continent outside Egypt, this impressive complex was built by a culture that flourished before the coming of the Arabs or European settlers.

The Hill Fortress and Great Enclosure

After the rainy season, the ruins are surrounded by green rolling hills and outcrops of rock that overlook valleys of acacia trees. Two main groups of buildings dominate the site. One, located among huge surreal rocks on a hilltop, is known as the Acropolis or Hill Fortress. This seemingly impregnable structure looks down on a large elliptical building, the Great Enclosure, a short distance away in the valley below.

Bounded by a stone wall 253m (830ft) in circumference and ranging in height from 4.9m (16ft) to 10.7m (35ft), the Great Enclosure took an estimated 18,000 man-hours to construct. The walls were built from pieces of granite deliberately cut like bricks and laid without mortar in courses. The outer wall is at least 1.2m (4ft) thick and considerably wider than this in places. Inside, the Enclosure is subdivided by other walls forming narrow passageways, three platforms and many unidentifiable 'rooms'.

The most enigmatic feature of the Enclosure is the conical tower. Close to the outer wall and constructed by the same technique, the tower captures the imagination, not least because it appears to have no function. Without doors, windows, stairs or any other discernible feature, the tower has given rise to some ingenious theories about its use. Was it a phallic symbol involved in local religious rites or a symbolic grain bin to promote fertility? Perhaps it was a fire-tower for signalling to distant points on the surrounding landscape or a vantage point for observing the moon, stars and planets.

The history behind the ruins

For many centuries, Arab and European explorers sought the fabulous mines of Ophir from which King Solomon obtained his treasures. The legend of the great Christian king Prester John, whose domains included the land of the mines, was known to Portuguese explorers in the 16th century, and they thought Ophir must lie in southern Africa. In 1502, an Arab told a Portuguese trader that Sofala – now a port in modern Mozambique – was Ophir.

In 1552, Portuguese historian João de Barros wrote a book, *Da Asia*, in which he described a stone fortress in Sofala 'in the centre of the mining country'. This fortress had an indecipherable inscription over the door. Built in stone without mortar, the buildings were called Symbaoe by the local inhabitants, a name

A superb blend of drystone walls and huge surreal rocks forms the Hill Fortress, once a military stronghold and a sanctuary at Great Zimbabwe. Narrow stairways with room enough for only one person to pass lead into its labyrinthine interior consisting of a series of small enclosures. The Hill Fortress is a natural vantage point for observing the Great Enclosure in the valley below and for watching the only approach road to the southeast. On its south side and located under a large rock is a cave with remarkable acoustic properties. Anyone speaking in the cave can be clearly heard in the valley, especially in the Great Enclosure.

Great Zimbabwe is the most astonishing of the roughly 8,000 ruins known to exist in the region between the Zambezi and Orange rivers. Situated in the country which has taken its name from this ancient site, Great Zimbabwe lies in bush country 400km (250mi) inland from the Indian Ocean and 480km (300mi) south of the Zambezi. As the centre of a large trading nation, Great Zimbabwe's main link with the rest of the world was along the eastern trade route to Sofala.

close to the modern Zimbabwe. Barros believed the buildings were very old and, since neither Arabs nor Africans could read the inscription, of non-African origin.

Great Zimbabwe was almost certainly the centre of a great Bantu-speaking mining nation which thrived until the 15th century. The folklore of the BaLemba, an offshoot of the BaVenda tribe in southern Africa who were descended from the builders of Zimbabwe, tells of an ancient northern homeland ruled by King Mwali.

Mwali lived in a hilltop town whose walls were built with large stones. He was a god-king whom no one was permitted to see, for to lay eyes on him meant death. People could only hear what he spoke to the high priest in a tremendous voice that reverberated in a terrifying manner. On his death, civil strife led to the abandonment of the town and a migration to the south where, at the Nzhelele River, they built a new stone-walled capital, Dzata, which still exists today.

Rediscovering Great Zimbabwe

In 1867, Adam Renders, an old hunter living in southern Africa, and Karl Mauch, a German explorer, discovered the ruins and publicized them as the Palace of the Queen of Sheba. In 1891, the first investigator of the ruins, J. Theodore Bent, concluded that the conical tower was the object of phallus worship, and that the Great Enclosure had been an astronomical observatory.

At the beginning of the 20th century, Richard Hall, an English lawyer and journalist, surveyed the ruins. He favoured the Queen of Sheba theory on the grounds of the similarity he saw between the Great Enclosure, which he called the Elliptical Temple, and the Temple of Haram of Bilkis in south Arabia.

The English archaeologist David Randall-MacIver excavated parts of the Enclosure and dated them to the period AD 1000-1500. Moreover, he dismissed the Queen of Sheba theory as fanciful, since the ruins showed nothing but African origins. In 1929, English archaeologist Gertrude Thompson confirmed Hall's findings. She believed Great Zimbabwe was founded in the 9th century as a trading centre having important links with Arabia, India and China – fragments of pottery and beads from these places had been found throughout the ruins.

Great Zimbabwe is currently thought to be purely African in design and construction; the ruins show many affinities with the village designs of various southern African tribes. But this does not explain why the builders of Zimbabwe departed from the traditional African materials of wood and earth to build in stone. In the neighbourhood of the ruins were mines from which precious metals were obtained and probably used in trade with other nations. Studies of the ancient gold mines of Zimbabwe by English archaeologist Roger Summers show that there was Indian influence operating there, since the same mining methods had been employed at Mysore and in the Kolar district of India.

The most recent research into the mystery of Great Zimbabwe was conducted by Wilfrid Mallows, a South African city planner and journalist. He supports the view that it was a major trading centre but also asserts that Zimbabwe was used in the 9th century as a black slave centre for transporting many thousands of Africans to Arabia.

The uniqueness of Great Zimbabwe, its tenuous and fascinating links with Arabia, India and the Far East, the conflicting stories and theories, all conspire to make any conclusions open to question. Yet it cannot be denied that Zimbabwe is one of the great ancient monuments of the world, and will continue to inspire scholar and romantic alike.

The Great Enclosure is at the heart of the Zimbabwe enigma for within its unique walls lie many riddles. Roughly elliptical, the Enclosure has three narrow entrances which lead into an interior whose remains make little sense.

The massive granite wall around the Enclosure illustrates the architectural artistry of Zimbabwe's builders. Constructed of carefully shaped bricks that have no mortar to bind them, the wall curves gently upward to a double-chevron design. With no apparent means of reaching the top, the inhabitants of Zimbabwe could have had little military use for the wall.

The most mysterious feature of the Great Enclosure is the conical tower. Standing 9m (30ft) high with a circumference at its base of 17.4m (57ft), the tower is completely solid and offers no clues as to its purpose.

THE RICHES OF GREAT ZIMBABWE

THE QUEEN OF SHEBA

Great Zimbabwe was not the home of the Queen of Sheba. She is most likely to have come from Marib, now in Yemen, across the Red Sea from Ethiopia. An old Ethiopian painting on sheepskin tells of the Queen of Sheba's meeting with King Solomon, where gifts of gold, ivory and a lion were exchanged. Soon they fell in love and the queen bore the king a son.

GREAT ZIMBABWE'S GOLD

The legends of King Solomon's mines, the riches of the Queen of Sheba and the kingdom of Prester John have led many gold-hungry people to seek the treasures of Great Zimbabwe. They may not have found mountains of gold, but they did find many artefacts and evidence of extensive mining operations. Most of the gold from Great Zimbabwe was plundered at the end of the 19th century by a group of white settlers who called themselves the Ancient Ruins Company.

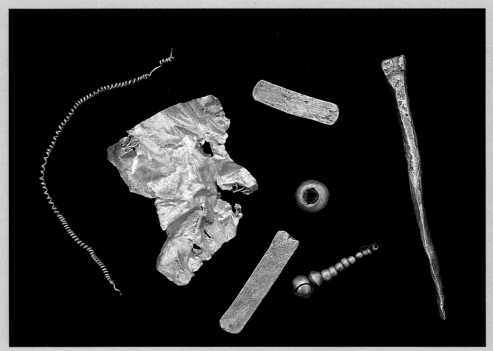

ZIMBABWE'S NATIONAL EMBLEM
Eight soapstone birds carved on poles were discovered at Great Zimbabwe, seven of them in one of the inner sanctuaries of the Hill Fortress. The birds are thought to be cult objects, symbols of power and identity. The finest and most elaborately carved bird, found in the ruins between the Great Enclosure and the Hill Fortress, has a crocodile crawling up toward it. The bird is now the Zimbabwe national emblem, shown here behind Robert Mugabe, who led the country to independence.

ANGKOR: THE HINDU TEMPLE CITY

The city containing the largest religious building in the world lies crumbling in the jungles of southeast Asia. Who lived there? Why was it built on waterways? Why did the Khmer Empire collapse and the city's inhabitants flee?

Until French naturalist Henri Mouhot ventured deep into the heart of the Cambodian jungle in 1860, the history of its people stretched back no further than the 15th century. What Mouhot was seeking was confirmation of rumours that a ruined city lay hidden in the green tyranny of the forest.

The rumours were probably started by Mouhot's fellow countryman, Father Charles-Emile Bouillevaux, who had visited the same jungle in 1850. The missionary had written: 'I discovered some immense ruins which I was told were the site of the royal palace. On the walls which were carved from top to bottom I saw combats between elephants, men fighting with clubs and spears, and others firing three arrows at a time from their bows.' However, it was Mouhot's own description and survey of the crumbling metropolis of Angkor that opened up the Cambodian past and posed many questions about its builders and inhabitants.

The city of Angkor covered almost 100sq.km (38sq.mi) and was full of temples, shrines, houses, causeways, reservoirs, irrigation canals and terraces. Said by some to be the world's largest city in AD 1000, Angkor's sprawling conurbation of squares and straight lines could possibly have accommodated half a million people. Everywhere there are statues, reliefs and carvings depicting scenes from Hindu mythology, bare-breasted dancing girls, a king mounted on an elephant and carrying a fly-whisk and parasol, an emperor leading his army into battle.

The people who inhabited Angkor were the Khmers, and their religion was obviously a form of Hinduism. It is thought that much Indian blood is mixed with Khmer, since Indian traders, travellers and missionaries came by sea in the first centuries after Christ to colonize southeast Asia – close to the southern tip of Vietnam, for instance, there was an Indian-based civilization in a kingdom the Chinese called Fu Nan.

The beginnings of Angkor's supremacy

Despite the fact that, by 1000 BC, southeast Asia was well-populated and technologically advanced, towns and cities did not develop until the 7th century AD. At this time, for some reason which archaeologists cannot fathom, civilization flowered in this part of the world. Monumental art and architecture appeared in many places, Angkor having the greatest influence.

Khmer documents were written on animal skins and palm leaves and so have not survived the test of time. Information about Angkor comes instead from more than 1,000 inscriptions, in both Sanskrit and Khmer, as well as Chinese, Moslem and Indian histories. These show that the founder of the Angkorian period of Cambodian history was Jayavarman II who freed his people from the Javanese at the beginning of the 9th century. He worshipped the Hindu god Shiva, and established the cult of the

The towers of the temple of Angkor Wat, fashioned like lotus buds, rise from the tangle of the Cambodian jungle, still extravagantly splendid after more than eight centuries. Covering an area larger than the Vatican, Angkor Wat was dedicated to the Hindu god Vishnu and designed as an astronomical observatory.

Angkor, the city of temples, is about 242km (150mi) northwest of Phnom Penh, the capital of present-day Kampuchea (formerly Cambodia). The great lake of Tonle Sap nearby is part of the Mekong River system and its flood waters may have been one of the factors contributing to the decline of Angkor in the 15th century.

Angkor was built over many centuries with slave labour and, in its heyday, the city covered an area of over 100sq.km (38sq.mi). Possibly the largest city in the ancient world, it housed some 500,000 people. This plan shows the well-ordered layout of causeways (**1**), irrigation canals and great reservoirs (both shown in blue). A wide crocodile-infested moat (**2**) surrounded the cosmic shrine of Angkor Wat (**3**). Behind is the great square of Angkor Thom (**4**), built by Jayavarman VII in the late 12th century, with the Bayon temple at its centre.

god-king, which meant that he was endowed with the creative energy of Shiva. Each king after him had a special temple built to house his linga, the phallic symbol of his authority. The temples were also symbolic representations of Mount Meru, the Hindu place of the gods and the centre of the universe.

The finest building in the whole of the Khmer metropolis is Angkor Wat. This is the funerary temple of Suryavarnam II who built it in the early 12th century. He dedicated it to Vishnu rather than Shiva and, unlike all the other temples in the area, its main entrance faced west, toward the land of the dead. Possibly the largest religious edifice ever built, Angkor Wat has a labyrinth of corridors lined with elaborate sculptures and carvings. Covering an area of nearly 2.6sq.km (1sq.mi), it features a number of towers – the tallest and most central is over 61m (200ft) high – built in the form of lotus buds.

This cosmic Hindu shrine is laid out on a plan of five rectangular and concentric enclosures. To reach the centre of the temple beneath the tallest tower, worshippers had to walk along a 305m (1,000ft) causeway whose carvings symbolized the sacred history of the Hindus. Angkor Wat was also designed and arranged to enable it to function as an astronomical observatory. For example, the temple of Prasat Kuk Bangro, 5.6km (3.5mi) away to the southeast, makes a midwinter solstice alignment with the temple of Angkor Wat.

The city built on waterways

The location of Angkor has several natural advantages which contributed to the city's success. First, the land was fertile and, if kept well irrigated, would yield three or even four crops of rice each year. Second, Tonle Sap, the huge, shallow lily-covered lake nearby, was reputed to contain one of the world's largest stocks of fish. Third, the rich forests supplied all the building needs, especially the thick teak for the floors of the temples and galleries. Fourth, the geology of the area offered a plentiful supply of sandstone, iron ore, gold, silver, copper and tin.

The people of Angkor built long stretches of irrigation canals and two huge reservoirs, the East and West Baray, each of which could store more than two billion gallons of water used in the six-month dry season to irrigate agricultural land. At such times, Tonle Sap would cover an area similar to the Great Salt Lake in the United States, but in the monsoon season would swell to the size of Lake Ontario.

One of the enduring mysteries of Angkor is why it was abandoned. Some authorities suggest that the doctrine of renunciation taught by the new Hinayana Buddhism at the end of the 13th century weakened the military ambitions of the Khmers. Instead, they became pacifists, non-materialists and altruists. So when, in 1431, the Thai armies descended on Angkor, they sacked it after a seven-month siege, meeting resistance only from the ruling classes. When the Thais left, the Khmers were unable to restore Angkor to its former glory.

Weak leadership, rebellious slaves and malaria all contributed to this loss of national vigour. In addition, a drought or an excessive monsoon may also have crippled the agricultural economy. A Buddhist legend tells of a king who had the son of a priest drowned in Tonle Sap because he offended the royal family. The angry snake god caused the lake to overflow, destroying Angkor. Even today, Tonle Sap floods dramatically when immense volumes of water flow along the Mekong River. In the 15th century the lake is thought to have been much closer to the doomed city of waterways, so it would not be surprising if the legend is based on truth.

A faint smile graces the stone face of the Buddha, his features modelled from the god-king Jayavarman VII. Unlike his predecessors whose gods were Hindu, Jayavarman was a Buddhist and, on being crowned king in 1181, declared he was the living Buddha. The towers of the Bayon temple in Angkor Thom are alive with these faces, about 200 of them, each 2.5m (8ft) high. Though encrusted with lichen, chipped and entwined with vines, they still look down in remote aloofness, making the blood of the unexpecting visitor curdle.

Thousands of young girls were trained as *apsaras* or holy dancers, to perform in the religious festivals of the Khmers. The stone carvings on the walls of Angkor's temples feature these ladies, who used to dance half-naked. When the Thai armies finally swamped the capital in 1431, they took the temple dancers back to Thailand and clothed them in heavy elaborate costumes, which the Cambodian Royal Ballet still wear to this day – a legacy of modesty imposed on them by an alien culture 500 years ago.

THE LEGACY OF THE KHMER PEOPLE

THE INHERITORS OF ANGKOR
Descended from the inhabitants of Angkor, these young soldiers belong to the Khmer Serei, the free Khmer, who are fighting to retrieve Kampuchea from Communist Vietnam. They are little different from their forefathers of the 13th century who were described by a Chinese envoy Chow Ta Kuen. On average, they are 1.6m (5.3ft) tall, and have pale brown skin, rounded heads and strongly defined features.

THE BUTTERFLY SPECIALIST
When French naturalist Henri Mouhot asked the local inhabitants about the ruins of Angkor, they replied, 'It is the work of giants', or 'It built itself'. A specialist in tropical butterflies, Mouhot had been sent by zoological societies to explore the jungles of Indo-China. He made many notes, drawings, sketches and surveys of Angkor but, in 1860, before excavation and restoration of Angkor could begin, Mouhot died of a tropical fever.

THAI DANCERS
The exquisite hand gestures of the ancient Khmer dancing girls are today expressed by Thai dancers. The bare-breasted temple dancers of Angkor, the *apsaras*, were captured when the city fell in 1431 and forced to cover up their bodies in glittering apparel before entertaining the dignitaries of the Thai royal court.

KNOSSOS: THE LABYRINTHINE CITY

The first major Aegean civilization flourished on the island of Crete in the Mediterranean. Was Knossos the capital of this Minoan Empire? What was the significance of the bull? How and when did Knossos fall?

On a simple earthenware jar in the Archaeological Museum of Heraklion, Crete, the Greek hero Theseus gazes into the eyes of his beautiful Ariadne. On another jar in the Vatican Museum he grasps the horns of the Minotaur and plunges his sword into its heart. Is the story of Theseus killing the Minotaur just a myth or could it really have happened? This is one of the many mysteries half-answered by the ruins of the Palace of Minos at Knossos.

Approaching the palace from the sea only 4km (2.5mi) away, the visitor sees it as Theseus would have done as he travelled along the walled road to its north entrance. For a nation of sea-farers and traders, as the Minoans were 2,000 years before Christ, this entrance to the palace flanked by its 'custom halls' would have been the most important. Upon entering here, the eye is caught by the huge relief fresco of a powerful bull struggling with its captors in terrified frenzy in an olive grove. Behind the bull stretches a veritable labyrinth of 1,500 rooms laid out in an intricate pattern of narrow corridors which would have bewildered all but the most familiar inhabitants of the palace..

There had been a settlement at Knossos since the fifth or sixth millennium BC. A series of magnificent palaces was built toward the end of the third and at the beginning of the second millennium BC. Each was destroyed by earthquakes and each was rebuilt on the ruins of the old. But between 1400 BC and 1250 BC a devastating offshore volcanic eruption on the island of Santorini obliterated city, palace and populace for the last time.

Not until 1878 did the work of Greek archaeologist Minos Kalokairinos and the subsequent comprehensive excavations by English archaeologist Sir Arthur Evans reveal once again the majesty of the Palace of Minos. The Knossos they discovered evokes an enviable way of life in which function and aesthetics had reached a remarkable harmony.

From the palace drains to the processional way

The quality of a civilization can perhaps best be judged by its drains. Those of the Minoans, particularly between 1700 BC and the final disaster, have seldom been surpassed. Few of the many wonders at Knossos make more impact than the three neatly dovetailed clay drainage pipes that lie as snug-fitting in their inspection pits today as when they were first laid 4,000 years ago. The pipes are carefully tapered to slow the water flow and, like the parabolic drainage gutters and their settling tanks for sediment beside the paved roads, they are just one of the many examples of the Minoan mastery of hydrodynamics.

The approach to the palace at Knossos from its western 'commercial' entrance leads to an apparently insignificant trio of walled pits. It was here that, after the Minoan religious ceremonies, the blood and bones of the sacrificed animals, together with the honey, wine, oil and milk of the libations, were returned

The Queen's Hall, as envisaged by Arthur Evans, must have been the epitome of Minoan comfort, complete with bathtub, running water, sophisticated drainage system of earthenware pots and a wooden-seated flushing privy. Vivid frescoes decorate the walls, with symbolic spirals and lively dolphins – the Minoan emblem for the joy of life. The Queen's Suite is even more labyrinthine than the rest of the palace; there are five ways in and out of the bathroom alone.

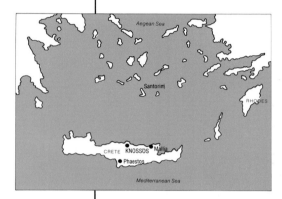

The ancient Minoan city of Knossos lay 4km (2.5mi) inland from the north shore of Crete, an island roughly equidistant from mainland Greece and Turkey. At its height, the great sea empire of the Minoans – based at Phaestos as well as Knossos – held dominion over the Aegean Sea.

Sir Arthur Evans stands by the great earthenware jars, discovered in the cellars of the palace. Each jar contained a special liquid tribute for use in ceremonies and was closed tight with an individual seal to denote ownership. Over 4,000 exquisite miniature seals have been found – no two of them are alike, suggesting a highly organized heraldry system in Crete.

A plan of the Palace of Minos shows the arrangement of the buildings around a central courtyard. Entrance was gained through the guardroom (**1**). A staircase (**2**) in the east wing led to the upper chambers, such as the Queen's Suite (**3**). A ground floor passage (**4**) in the west wing gave access to numerous storerooms. The throne room (**5**) faced the courtyard and the Grand Staircase (**6**) led to the Royal Apartments.

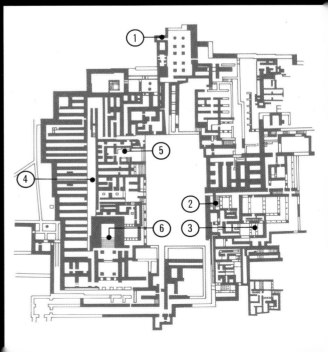

to the earth from which they sprang. This appositeness, this literal sense of propriety, pervades the site at Knossos.

Little is left of the nearby guardroom whose function would have been primarily administrative rather than military. Indeed, one remarkable feature of all Minoan palaces is that, of the thousands of artefacts recovered, there are few weapons and these are usually of a ceremonial nature. The palaces themselves are in no way fortified and it appears that, for most of their history, the Minoans lived at peace with their neighbours.

The guardroom marks the entrance to the processional way, which ends in a broad flight of stairs leading up to the level of the grand courtyard. One of the astonishing life-size frescoes which have captured so much of the Minoan past here greets the eye. A procession of priests and priestesses bearing flasks and pouring out liquid offerings to their deities stalks by with lifelike dignity.

The acrobatic bull-leapers

Beyond the stone cellars lies a room where vivid and dramatic Minoan frescoes have been recreated. The most famous grippingly shows, in a kind of ancient stop-frame photographic reconstruction, the grace and daring of the bull-leapers as they take part in an event which is part sport, part ritual and part test. As the bull charges, each leaper – they are of both sexes – seizes its horns in turn and flips on to the beast's back before somersaulting nimbly to the ground. A single slip could cost the leaper's life.

As leaper after leaper embraced and then eluded the charging bull in quick succession, it must have been hard to distinguish beast from human and, as a result, easy to see how the image of the Minotaur, half bull and half man was created. Whether the bull-games were performed in the great courtyard is not known, but this area was certainly the focal point of palace life, an eye of open space in the whirling pattern of daily routine. The stark symbolism of the homes of consecration, which dominate the courtyard with all the simplicity of a modern sculpture, suggest that it was more than just the nexus of palace life.

The heart of the palace

Above the level of the courtyard, the east wing of the palace was cut into the hillside. At one end were the Royal Apartments, while at the other end were the workshops of the carpenters, potters, stonemasons and jewellers who provided the comforts and artistic luxuries evident in the apartments themselves.

The Royal Apartments are reached by the so-called Grand Staircase which, while not particularly grand in scale, is undeniably grand in sophistication and artistry. The black and red pillars, tapering inward toward the base, enclose a light well that not only illuminates the apartments below, but provides a kind of bellows for the palace's natural air-conditioning. The 11 pier and door partitions of the King's Hall could be opened and closed to regulate the inflow of the cooler air, scented with wild thyme and lemon, from the colonnade outside as the warm air rose up the stairwell. In winter, the doors could be closed while portable hearths were brought in to provide heat.

The centre of power was the throne room where King Minos held court. Outside it stands a great porphyry basin, placed there by Arthur Evans because he believed it was used in purification rituals before entering the innermost chamber of the palace. Such a placement epitomizes the Knossos that can be seen today: an extraordinary reconstruction of the Palace of King Minos as it was in 1600 BC, as visualized by an English archaeologist whose sole purpose was to capture in time the Golden Age of the Minoan Empire.

The Minoan bull in fine relief greets all who enter the palace at Knossos from the north. The Charging Bull fresco was found in fragments in 1900 and erected on the West Portico of the northern entrance in 1930. The angry beast in the olive grove epitomizes the Minoan bull cult and, at the same time, advertises the dramatic games of the bull-leapers.

Symbols of royal and divine power, two fabulous griffins flank a replica of the oldest throne in Europe. This throne was used as a model for the chair of the President of the International Court at The Hague in Holland. King Minos' throne room, on the ground floor of the west wing of the palace, would have accommodated about 16 people for meetings with the sovereign.

SUSA: GLORIOUS CITY OF THE PERSIANS

The remains of a metropolis in Iran have revealed that, in 4,000 years, 13 cities were superimposed and 15 different languages used. When did Susa begin? Was it the capital of an empire? How did Susa fall?

Standing out against the horizon on the baked plain of Khuzistan, in southwest Iran, looms the great bulk of Susa. Here, beneath a series of mounds lie the remains of a once-great city which controlled important routes stretching from ancient Mesopotamia eastward through the Zagros Mountains.

Persian tradition claims that Susa was the first city in the world, built by the legendary King Hushang who discovered how to make fire with steel and flint. It is certainly one of the oldest. Urban life was thriving there at the beginning of the fourth millennium BC when its craftsmen were producing some of the world's most elegant pottery – slim beakers decorated with stylized birds and hunting dogs.

The Thousand-Year War

By about 2500 BC, Susa had become the capital of the kingdom of the Elamites, a vigorous but enigmatic people related culturally to the Sumerians in Mesopotamia. For 1,000 years, Elam was at loggerheads with the city-states of Mesopotamia. But in about 2350 BC, Susa became part of the world's first major empire when it fell to Sargon the Great of Akkad.

When Sargon's empire fell, the prosperity of the Elamites was renewed. Around 2100 BC, they beautified their capital with a holy precinct containing the temple and ziggurat of Inshushinak, 'Lord of Susa', the god of storm and the patron god of the city whose emblem was the zebu or humped-back bull.

But the tides of power in the Mesopotamian city-states continued to shift. The Babylonians seized Susa around 1000 BC and crippled its power. The Assyrians swept into Elam around 645 BC at the heels of the conquering Assurbanipal who burned Susa to the ground and took the kings of Elam home in chains to drag his chariots through the streets of Nineveh.

The mounds of Susa were rediscovered in 1850 and identified as the Susa of classical times by the British archaeologist William Loftus. The site consists of four mounds: the Acropolis, the Apadana, the Royal City, and the Artisan's Town. The earliest of 13 different settlements was on the Acropolis where the foundations of a temple from the fourth millennium were found. Here, too, was the site of the main royal Elamite buildings, among them the temple and ziggurat of Inshushinak, crowned with the bronze 'Horns' looted by Assurbanipal.

The Susa of the Elamites has all but disappeared. An idea of their city at its height lies 32km (20mi) to the southeast where King Untash-Gal, in about 1250 BC, built the royal city named after himself: Dur-Untashi, now known as Choga Zanbil. This was one of the most ambitious building schemes ever envisaged in the ancient world. Inside huge ramparts and stone walls stood temples of the many Elamite gods and, towering over all, a great ziggurat dedicated to Inshushinak.

The bare 'bones' of the ancient city of Susa reveal little of its former glory or splendour. Yet, buried beneath centuries of dust and earth, archaeologists have exposed the long history of the site: the comings and goings of the Akkadians, the Babylonians and the Greeks, as well as the intermittent resurgences of the Elamites and the 'world' domination of the Achaemenian kings.

The ruins of the city of Susa lie just to the east of the River Kharka in southwestern Iran. It was regarded as an important crossroads that controlled vital trade routes between the Zagros Mountains and the fertile Mesopotamian city-states to the west.

The waters of Choaspes

Although Assurbanipal had put Susa to the torch, the city flowered again. Cyrus the Great (*d.* 530 BC), who ruled from the Aegean Sea to the River Oxus, made it the capital of his Persian Empire. He chose Susa because it stood conveniently between the two halves of his empire, but perhaps also because it lay beside the River Kharka, famous for its purity.

The Greek historian Herodotus relates that whenever Cyrus went on an expedition, he took with him 'water from the Choaspes [Kharka] . . . whereof and of none other he drinks. This water of the Choaspes is boiled, and very many four-wheeled wagons drawn by mules carry it in silver vessels, following the king whithersoever he goes.' 'Whithersoever' might be a great distance. The energy of Cyrus and the Achaemenian dynasty he founded was prodigious. They would spend the winter at Susa, the spring 800km (500mi) away in the ceremonial capital of Persepolis, and summer 1,280km (800mi) from Persepolis in the cool mountains at Ecbatana. From Ecbatana back to Susa was another 480km (300mi). They would travel in the heat of summer and the cold of winter, through some of the harshest landscapes in the world, with all the elaborate paraphernalia of the court – not least the pure waters of Choaspes.

The Achaemenians were not unnaturally great road builders. Their Royal Road from Susa to Sardis in Asia Minor, covered more than 2,563km (1,600mi) with 111 post stations for changing horses. It was patrolled by military detachments while a relay of couriers maintained a swift postal service for the monarch – a journey which could at a pinch be made in a week.

The great palace of King Darius

In 517 BC, Cyrus the Great's next-but-one successor, Darius I, began to build a glorious palace on the Apadana mound, recording the construction on a clay tablet: 'I constructed this palace . . . And the ground that was dug out . . . and the bricks that were moulded – they were the people of Babylon who did the work. The wood called cedar was brought from a mountain called Lebanon. The people of Assyria brought it up to Babylon and the people of Karkha [in Anatolia] and Ionia [Greece] brought it from Babylon, to the land of the Susians.' From every corner of the empire and beyond came men and materials. Caravans arrived bearing gold – with Medes and Egyptians to work it – ivory, silver, ebony, lapis lazuli and turquoise.

No wonder that the Bible simply calls Susa 'Shushan the Palace'. Here was set the romantic story of Esther, and in the Book of Esther its luxury is described in vivid detail. As the Persian Empire expanded to encompass parts of Greece, the glories of Susa became as well known to the Greeks as to the Hebrews. After Alexander the Great had defeated the Persian king Darius III in 331 BC, he marched on Susa where he discovered fabulous riches. After seven years of conquest which took him across the River Indus to India, he returned and at Susa announced plans for uniting Greece and Persia into one great empire. He made a beginning by himself marrying Darius' daughter, Stateira, and holding a mass wedding of 10,000 Greeks to Persian wives.

After Alexander's death in 323 BC, Susa dwindled to a provincial capital. Later it was a Christian bishopric, and the Sasanian king Shahpur II, a fervent Zoroastrian, had it trampled underfoot by several hundred elephants. The Mongols delivered the final blow in the 13th century, and Susa thereafter remained a dead city, left to the wind which transformed it in time into just another Middle Eastern mound.

The glorious palace which Darius I built at Susa was decorated on the outside with glazed bricks of various delicate hues, designed and assembled by imported Babylonian artisans. Among the many images fashioned on the palace wall was this pair of winged genii or sphinxes, 70cm (28in) high, which acted as guardians.

The conical white shrine known as the Tomb of Daniel stands on the east bank of the River Shaur, not far from the site of Susa. For a long time, Moslems have attributed to the Hebrew Prophet's remains powers of preventing drought. In the 12th century, when Daniel's Tomb is thought to have been originally built, the local Sultan ordered Daniel's coffin to be wrapped in crystal and suspended from a bridge across the River Shaur.

THE LEGENDARY CITY OF TROY

The great city with powerful walls described by Homer was thought to have been discovered a century ago. Was it Troy? If not, where else could Troy be? What was the Trojan War?

Certain great and ancient legends burn with a light so bright and powerful as to remain inextinguishable for thousands of years. The sack of Troy on the northwest coast of Turkey is one of these. Despite a lack of factual proof, or even until recently the lack of a known site, the belief in the tale of the Trojan War has never dimmed.

When German adventurer Heinrich Schliemann discovered Troy he forged for the world a link with the past. For he gave concrete reality to a story from the Bronze Age as subtle and moving in its themes and passions as a play by William Shakespeare, but concerning a people hitherto thought of as little more than savages. In the case of the Trojan War, the legend owes its stature, if not its endurance, to one of the most famous epic poems ever written: *The Iliad.*

The story of ancient Troy

This tale of the long war between the Greeks and the Trojans is now thought to have been an assembly of oral traditional verse inspired by the story. The poet Homer, if he lived at all, was probably born on one of the Ionian islands, such as Chios, or at Smyrna, in the 8th century BC. He undoubtedly had a reputation beyond the limits of his lifetime for, even while the telling of the tale remained an oral tradition, the bard performing it would always finish his piece with the words 'as Homer sang it'.

The story of the fall of Troy begins when Paris, the son of Priam, the King of Troy, was given the dubious and dangerous honour of adjudicating a contest of beauty between the goddesses Hera, Athene and Aphrodite. These goddesses were unscrupulous about offering bribes. Consequently, Paris was obliged to make his choice not simply from natural inclination or fear of revenge from the losers, but also between, respectively: wealth and the lordship of all Asia; wisdom and invincibility; or the love of Helen of Sparta, wife of King Menelaos and reputed to be the most beautiful woman in the world. His choice of Helen set in motion a tragedy which was to span ten long years, lay waste his people's city, and cost the lives of countless men, women and children.

The problems of locating Troy

Even since classical times, the precise whereabouts of King Priam's Troy has been uncertain and a subject of controversy. When the Greek inhabitants of Ilion in northwest Turkey claimed their town was the true successor to Troy, students of Homer called them vain. For was not the Roman geographer Strabo (*c.* 60 BC–21 AD) correct when he stated the true site to be 5.6km (3.5mi) nearer the mountains, at the 'Village of the Trojans'?

The Iliad locates Troy at two springs that feed the River Skamander, one hot and steaming, the other always icy and cold. In 1791, the French traveller Lechevalier decided from this that

The epic story of the Trojan War has fascinated scholars for many centuries, not least the English Restoration poet Alexander Pope. In 1714 he drew up a detailed sketch to illustrate his translation of Homer's tale of *The Iliad.* Central to the sketch are the two main rivers on the coastal plain, the Skamander and the Simoeis, and the city of Troy on a hill in between.

The ruins of Troy stand on the mound of Hissarlik near the northwestern shores of Turkey. To the south lies Izmir, the modern name for the old town of Smyrna where Homer may have been born nearly 3,000 years ago.

A hundred Turkish labourers in the service of Schliemann dug a trench through the mound of Hissarlik and laid bare the archaeology of Troy. The engraving from Schliemann's *Troy and its Ruins* shows the workmen digging in the Temple of Athena.

SCAMANDER Fl.

SIMOIS. Fl.

Rhœteum

Sigeum

MARE ÆGEUM

Ostia Scamandri

Troy was sited at the village of Bunarbashi, which means 'spring head'. Above the village was a rocky hill, like a citadel, where a group of springs issue from the ground.

More than two generations of scholars ignored the fact that the springs were of the same temperature and so it was here that Heinrich Schliemann eventually came to look for Troy. After finding no trace of the expected city, he transferred his hopeful spade to the mound of Hissarlik. This low-lying hill is nearly 4.8km (3mi) from the seashore between the two main streams of the Trojan plain, identified from *The Iliad* as the Simoeis and Skamander. The citizens of Ilion had not been vain, for close to the ruins of their town Schliemann discovered Troy.

The nine cities of Troy

That buccaneer of archaeology, Dr Heinrich Schliemann, was a man of exceptional determination. His boyhood dream had been to discover Homer's lost city of Troy. He began his excavations at Hissarlik in 1870 and they lasted for 20 years.

In a rather bulldozing fashion, Schliemann dug a huge trench into the mound at Hissarlik, unfortunately eating into part of the layer he most longed to find – Homeric Troy. Schliemann was understandably confused by the multi-layered nature of the hill he was excavating. However, he came to recognize four separate successive cities beneath the classical Roman town of Ilium and decided that the second from bottom was the Troy he sought. This conclusion received little general acceptance among archaeologists which infuriated Schliemann and made him all the more proud when, in 1873, he discovered the 'Treasure of Priam' as he described it.

Schliemann's story is that as he dug out the golden treasure he handed it to his young and beautiful Greek wife, Sophia. She bundled it into her shawl, hiding it from Turkish officials and workmen alike. A photograph exists of her looking resplendent in the 'Jewels of Helen'. Together with this treasure trove was a fund of cups, lanceheads and earrings which probably all came from Troy II or Troy III (*c.* 2200 BC) – quite the wrong period for Homer's Troy, Troy VI, whose destruction probably occurred in 1260 BC. Sadly, all but one pair of earrings and a few other small objects disappeared from Berlin in 1945 – they would have been invaluable in learning more about those early cities.

What remains of the cities of Troy?

Many travellers have dismissed the site of Troy as too small and dull. Certainly, it is astonishingly small when compared with the classical dream of the mighty towered citadel of Priam. Only 137m (450ft) by 183m (600ft), there is room for a few dozen households, with perhaps a thousand people living round it. But the size of Troy is one of its most moving features, for it looks so vulnerable.

The shore where the Greeks beached their ships is now 15km (9.4mi) farther away than when Achilles dragged Hector's broken body round the walls of Troy in his rage. Two qualities remain of the Troy that Homer described: the wind blowing ceaselessly through the long grasses (it blows nowhere else in this area) and the tiny stunted oak trees which seem only to exist in this one place. The English author Rose Macaulay, in *The Towers of Trebizond*, has perhaps the last word on Troy's magic: 'I thought there were enough cities standing about the world already, and that those which had disappeared had better be let alone, lying under the grass and the asphodel and brambles, with the wind sighing over them, and in the distance the sea, where the Greek ships had lain waiting ten years . . .'

The best preserved building of all the nine cities of Troy is an amphitheatre on the south side of the site. The legacy of the rebuilding programme that Julius Caesar initiated in the 1st century BC, it forms part of the last and largest city of Troy – Troy IX – which was finally abandoned in about AD 350.

The turning point in the Trojan War came when the Greeks built a huge wooden horse; they hid a small band of warriors inside and then pretended to leave the battlefield. The horse had been constructed on the orders of Athena, the goddess of wisdom, seen on this Greek vase stroking the animal's head. After the Trojans took the horse into their city and had celebrated their victory, they fell asleep. The Greeks climbed down from the horse, opened the city gates to their returning army who proceeded to massacre the Trojans.

ΗΒΟΥΛΗΚΑΙΟΔΗ
ΛΟΥΚΙΩΟΥΙΝΟΥΛΕΙΩΤ
ΤΑΙΚΙΩΕΠΑΡΧΩΣΠΕΙ
ΡΗΣΧΕΙΛΙΑΡΧΩΛΕΓΙΩΝS
ΕΚΤΙΣΕΠΑΡΧΩΕΙΛΗSΕΠ
ΤΡΟΠΩΑΥΤΟΚΡΑΤΟΡΟS
ΚΑΙSΑΡΟSΟΥΕSΠΑSΙΑΝ
SΕΒΑSΤΟΥΕΠΑΡΧΕΙΟΝ
ΛΙΒΥΗSΑSΙΑSΘΡΑΚΗS

THE PROTAGONISTS OF TROY

THE BUCCANEER OF ARCHAEOLOGY

The son of an impoverished German parson, Heinrich Schliemann (1822-1890) started work in a grocery at the age of 14. Signing on later as a cabin boy, he was shipwrecked and ended up in Holland where, with his boundless energy, he set up a successful business that included smuggling tea into Russia. When he was 36, Schliemann retired a millionaire. Having studied the embryonic science of archaeology in Paris for two years, Schliemann settled in Greece and began the detective work that was to culminate in his discovery of the lost city of Homer's Troy.

THE JEWELS OF HELEN

The daughter of an Athenian draper, Sophia Engastromenos married Heinrich Schliemann in 1869, when she was 17, becoming his second wife. Sophia conspired with her husband to smuggle the 'Treasure of Priam' out of Turkey and was later photographed wearing the most beautiful part of the trove: the Jewels of Helen. These consisted of necklaces, bracelets, a headband, earrings and two diadems, all of gold.

PARIS AND HELEN

The unfortunate adjudicator of a beauty contest between goddesses shares a quiet moment with his reward, the woman whose face launched a thousand ships. One of the most famous couples in history, they have often become a subject for artists. 'Paris and Helen' was painted by Jacques-Louis David for the Comte d'Artois in 1788.

ACHILLES AND HECTOR

The tale of the Trojan War inspired many Classical artists, especially in Greece. On the side of a Black Attic vase of the 5th century BC, the Greek hero Achilles moves in to kill Hector, the commander-in-chief of the Trojan army. The image does not show the fury of Achilles who has just learnt that Hector had killed his friend Patroclus. Achilles dragged the dead body of Hector behind his chariot and then returned it to Troy for the funeral rites.

PETRA: THE CITY OF TOMBS

A curious and secluded necropolis is carved out of the rock in the Jordanian desert. Who built it? What happened to its inhabitants? Why did the city remain hidden for so many centuries?

Tales of returning travellers inspired the Victorian scholar John Burgon, later Dean of Chichester in England, to immortalize the ancient city of Petra: 'Match me a marvel save in eastern clime/ A rose-red city half as old as time.' Equally inappropriate, for Petra is not rose-red, but perhaps more evocative of the colours of the place, was the comment made by Edward Lear's Italian cook, Giorgio: 'O master, we have come into a world where everything is made of chocolate, ham, curry-powder and salmon.'

Petra is hewn out of the rock within a ring of almost impenetrable mountains in the Jordanian desert, and even today can be reached only on foot or on horseback. From the *wadi Musa*, or valley of Moses, close to the village of Elji, the path to Petra narrows to become the *siq*, a dark defile little more than one metre (3ft) wide in places. The *siq* winds its way through the mountains for nearly 1.5km (1mi) while cliffs tower above the humans and horses below. On both sides are decorated carved blocks of golden brown stone with channels cut into the rock to bring in water. Without warning the *siq* emerges from the gloom into the sunshine and the visitor sees the first and most dramatic sight of Petra: the Khazneh, a glowing, dusky red Nabataean temple carved from the rock.

Petra's ancient ruins

The well-preserved Khazneh or Treasury shows distinct Greek influence in its statues, niches and columns. Was it temple, tomb or treasury? It was possibly all three, although its name is derived from a legend that a Pharaoh's treasure was hidden in the urn at the top of the monument. For many years until the practice was officially forbidden, the local Bedouin would fire their guns at the urn in the hope of being showered with its glittering contents. The building was probably used as a tomb since tombs abound in Petra: from the royal Urn Tomb carved into a cliff side, to the public tombs with burial chambers set in the walls and the horrific shaft tombs into which criminals were pushed alive.

Roman ruins become apparent as the visitor progresses into the heart of the city, particularly the immense theatre on a hillside with 33 rows for over 3,000 spectators. The Romans also created the Colonnade Road through the once-bustling central area of 2nd-century Petra: markets lined the road and the public drinking fountain, the Nymphaeum, dedicated to water nymphs, provided shade and cooling water in the heat of summer.

The Colonnade Road leads to the sacred Temenos area, originally protected by doors. At its heart is the freestanding Nabataean temple Kasr El Bint, which is now in ruins and probably dates from the 1st century BC. Although a shrine to the deity Dusares, its name means the Castle of the Daughter of the Pharaoh – why it should be so remains a mystery. Just to the west is the modern museum housed in a tomb or temple. Much less accessible is the Deir or Monastery, one of the most striking

Man's work is fused magically with that of nature in the extraordinary collection of tombs and temples carved into the raw red sandstone of Jordan's Petra mountain. A vast and prosperous city developed here in the 1st century under the Nabataeans, formerly a nomadic tribe of Arabic origin. At its peak, the city would have housed over 20,000 people, but most of their freestanding stone dwellings have long since disappeared. Only the gods and the dead now inhabit Petra.

The earliest tombs and temples, sculptured from the rock in about 300 BC, were in the traditional, somewhat austere, Egyptian and Assyrian styles. But as Greek, and later Roman, influences permeated the Middle East, the Nabataeans absorbed them and developed their own flamboyant style.

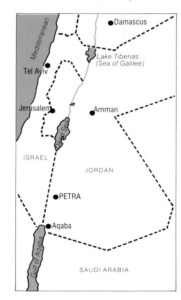

Petra lies in present-day Jordan, to the east of the great valley that connects the Dead Sea to the Gulf of Aqaba. A tributary of that valley leads toward the mountain of Petra in the Esh Shara range, some 190km (120mi) southwest of Amman and 96km (60mi) northeast of Aqaba.

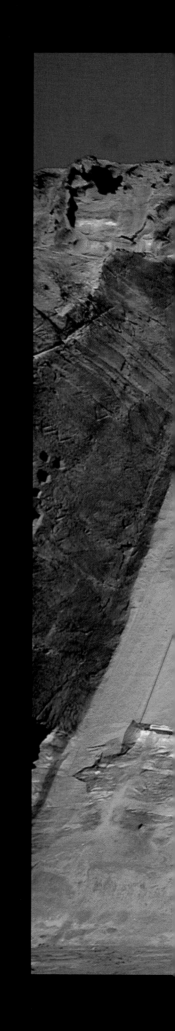

sights of Petra, built into a shoulder of the mountain and also surmounted by an urn. On the long climb up the *wadi al Deir* are a series of caves full of carved crosses which recall the short Christian era of Petra but whose function remains unresolved.

Who were the inhabitants of Petra?

An extraordinarily skilled nomadic tribe of shepherds called the Nabataeans made Petra the centre of their empire over 2,000 years ago. They originated in northwest Arabia and over a period of 600 years from the 5th century BC spread their dominion as far north as Damascus. An even earlier settlement of Edomites – Edom, meaning red, is the Biblical name for this region of the Middle East – predated the Nabataeans, but it was the latter who carved the city out of rock. They also developed their own style of architecture, a unique and delicate pottery and, vital to the history and success of Petra, a sophisticated system of water engineering.

Strategically situated at the crossroads of ancient trade routes, Petra thronged with merchants bringing goods from the Mediterranean, Egypt, Damascus and Arabia. With Petra as an almost impregnable base, the Nabataeans controlled the caravan routes, grew wealthy and prospered. Rock was all important, so it was not surprising to discover their chief god, Dushara, was symbolized by blocks of stone and by obelisks found in the *siq* and throughout the city. And sometime later the city was called Petra, meaning rock.

In the centuries before and after the birth of Christ, the Nabataeans were at the height of their power, and a population of around 20,000 lived within Petra. From time to time they had to defend themselves from attacks by their neighbours, particularly the Romans from the north who, in 63 BC, had planned to take Petra by storm. They finally succeeded in AD 106 when, seemingly without a struggle, the city of Petra became part of the Roman province of Arabia.

Although the Nabataean dynasty had come to an end, the people coexisted with the Romans for more than a century. During this time, Petra continued to prosper, and the Romans added the theatre and the colonnaded street. When Petra became part of the Christian Byzantine Empire in the 4th century AD, one of the largest Nabataean tombs, the Urn Tomb, was converted into a church and the city became the seat of a bishop. But after the rise of the Moslems in the 7th century AD, history is silent on the fate of Petra, save for a brief sojourn by the Crusaders who built a small castle on top of a hill to the west.

The rediscovery of the city

A young Anglo-Swiss explorer, Johann Ludwig Burckhardt, on his way from Damascus to Cairo in 1812, heard rumours of an ancient city set in a mountain fastness and he determined to find it. He had already learned to speak Arabic so he disguised himself as a Moslem trader, one Ibrahim ibn Abdallah, who had vowed to God that he would sacrifice a goat to the Prophet Aaron at his tomb on top of Gebel Haroun, a high hill overlooking the rumoured city.

This elaborate cover story was made necessary by the mistrust of strangers felt by the local Bedouin tribesmen. At Elji, Burkhardt persuaded two Bedouin to guide him along the *wadi Musa* through the *siq* to the Khazneh, where under the cover of his robes he managed to make a drawing of the building. He made a brief excursion around the city and, with darkness falling, he sacrificed the goat at the foot of Aaron's shrine before returning to Elji, his mission accomplished.

Access to the ancient rock city of Petra is gained through the *siq*, a narrow pass that winds its way between towering walls of rock. The first thing to confront the traveller on emerging from the dark passage is the classical, essentially Greek, facade of the Khazneh. So incongruous is this building in the middle of the desert mountains that it looks like part of a film set left over from a Hollywood epic.

After its discovery in 1812, other explorers revealed Petra's splendours to the world. Two Frenchmen – the scholar Count Leon de Laborde and the engineer Maurice Linaut – came in 1826 and made romantic, but wonderfully accurate, drawings of the city, including this sketch of the Khazneh.

For many centuries, Petra remained unknown to the Western world, visited only by the Bedouins. But in 1812, a young Anglo-Swiss explorer, Johann Ludwig Burckhardt, entered the hidden city and made hasty covert sketches of the wonders he saw.

MOHENJO-DARO: THE FIRST PLANNED CITY

A port on the River Indus had no palaces or temples but a highly organized urban development. When did the city thrive and what caused its downfall? Who lived there? How was it built?

Myths and legends from India give tantalizing hints of the existence of a forgotten civilization, long vanished. According to the Sanskrit *Rigveda*, from the second millennium BC, the Aryan invaders who poured into India around 1500 BC were led by the Hindu god Indra, called 'the fort destroyer' because he had 'destroyed ninety forts and a hundred ancient castles'. Until the 20th century these 'forts' were assumed to be purely mythical. Archaeology has since proved otherwise.

A civilization contemporary with those of Egypt and Mesopotamia came to light through excavations made in the 1920s and 1930s. Like those more renowned civilizations, it was based in a river valley – that of the Indus in modern Pakistan – but flourished over a wider area. Indeed, the Indus valley civilization is now thought to have formed the largest preclassical empire in the world. Almost a hundred villages, towns and cities have been discovered in a rough triangle, its apex 800km (500mi) up the Indus and its base stretching 960km (600mi) along the coast at the river's mouth.

The world's first urban planners

When Sir Mortimer Wheeler became Director-General of Archaeology in India in 1944, he re-excavated the huge mounds concealing the two greatest cities of the Indus valley civilization: Harappa in the north and, 560km (350mi) to the southwest, Mohenjo-Daro, the 'mound of the dead'.

The two cities Wheeler laid bare were built almost entirely of kiln-fired brick between 2500-2100 BC and were probably the twin capitals of what is now known as the Harappan Empire. Astonishingly well organized, and bearing a remarkable similarity to one another, the two cities were, at the time, the world's largest urban settlements. Each metropolis had a perimeter of over 5km (3mi) and only Uruk in Mesopotamia came close to rivalling them.

Originally square in outline, Mohenjo-Daro was laid out along the lines of a grid. Twelve main streets of beaten earth, between 9m (30ft) and 14m (45ft) wide, divided the city into a dozen blocks. Eleven of these were residential, composed of many standardized and close-packed houses of brick, and including artisan dwellings, shops and workshops. The twelfth block, set aside from the main city, dominated the urban dwellings. Here, an artificial rectangular mound about 6m (20ft) high forms the citadel, whose chief buildings have been called the Great Bath, the Granary and the Assembly Hall. Today the citadel is crowned by the imposing *stupa* of a Buddhist monastery erected in the 2nd century AD.

Many houses conformed to a basic but spacious pattern of a central courtyard surrounded by several rooms with a well and stairs leading to an upper storey. Few houses either opened on to, or had windows overlooking, the main streets. Perhaps

The Great Bath of Mohenjo-Daro is a brick-built tank, 12m (40ft) by 7m (23ft) and 2.5m (8ft) deep. It was sunk into the brick platform supporting the citadel and made watertight with gypsum. Flights of steps originally fitted with wooden treads led down to it at each end and surrounding it were wooden changing rooms. Some archaeologists regard it as a kind of municipal swimming pool, while others see it as a centre for ritual bathing.

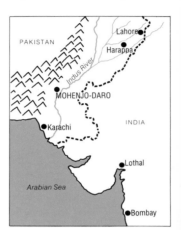

The numerous towns of the Indus civilization were located in and around the valleys of the Indus River, from Harappa in the north to Mohenjo-Daro, some 560km (350mi) to the southwest. Other towns thrived to the southeast, where Lothal was the main trading port.

Finely carved stone seals have been found in abundance at Mohenjo-Daro and are evidence not only of a high level of craftsmanship, but of an advanced economy. They were used in the trade of such goods as pottery, ivory, timber and cotton textiles with Mesopotamia and the Arabian Gulf via the ancient mercantile emporium of Dilmun, now present-day Bahrain.

An important clue to the enigma of Mohenjo-Daro's rulers is this small broken steatite figure. It is one of 11 stone sculptures found in the city. All but two show men with shaven upper lips and neatly trimmed beards, hair done up at the back and kept in place by headbands. The trefoils on this figure's robes probably had a religious meaning. Haughty and self-possessed, he may be a god or else a priest-king of the Indus civilization in ceremonial attire.

because of the need for privacy and security, or simply to keep out the noise and dust of bustling urban traffic, all the houses in Mohenjo-Daro had access only to the numerous narrow lanes that honeycombed the city.

Who governed Mohenjo-Daro?

One of the many unsolved mysteries of the Indus civilization is the absence of recognizable temples. Other ancient civilizations were ruled by priest-kings or living gods from elaborate temples or palaces. But no clear evidence of Mohenjo-Daro's rulers has been unearthed. There are hints that the religion of the Indus civilization was a precursor of Hinduism. The Indus people had several deities including, probably, a mother-goddess represented by many small figurines, and a three-headed god with horns thought to be ancestral to the Hindu god Shiva.

That the Indus people did possess an organized religion with a professional body of priests is suggested by the Great Bath on Mohenjo-Daro's citadel. Ritual bathing is still a vital part of Hinduism today, and many archaeologists think the Great Bath was once the scene of communal ceremonies for spiritual cleansing conducted by a college of priests.

Mohenjo-Daro conjures up a lifestyle both disciplined and efficient, perhaps with distinctions of class between workers and the merchants who controlled the wealth, not unlike the caste system in India today. Another notable building on the citadel was once the Civic Granary. A number of working platforms for pounding grain, storage space for wheat and rice, and a system of underground air ducts for drying the grain, all amount to what Wheeler called 'the economic focus of the city'.

An early totalitarian state is how archaeologists have interpreted assorted signs that Mohenjo-Daro was tightly controlled. The lack of evidence for any Mesopotamian-style ruling class to act as patrons might explain why the Harappan people produced scarcely any art of quality. A few statuettes, such as an erotic dancing girl, some fine stone seals engraved with animals and gods, several lively clay models of bulls and various decorated pots, are a poor reflection of what was once an organized and probably affluent society. For the most part, the artefacts at Mohenjo-Daro are as standardized and utilitarian as its city planning. More answers to the questions the Indus cities pose may be revealed when the inscriptions on the stone seals, the only Indus writing, are finally decoded.

The end of a civilization

The alluvial plains of the Indus valley have flooded many times. Much of Mohenjo-Daro lies below the water-table and many of its secrets may lie in the grip of sand. By 1900 BC the cities were in decline, either because of constant flooding or because their inhabitants had exhausted the supply of timber from the forests, which was essential to fire the huge quantities of brick needed to repair and rebuild them.

When the Aryans reached the Indus, they probably found a degenerating people of mixed blood doing little more than scraping a living in their ancestors' great towns. 'He rends forts as age consumes a garment', says the *Rigveda* of Indra; and if it really was he who led the invading Aryans, he showed little mercy. For on the last level of occupation at Mohenjo-Daro, many skeletons with skulls bearing sword-cuts have been found. Men, women and children were butchered, some in their homes. Beside a public well, four men and women lay where they had fallen, a grim epitaph to the last descendants of a once successful and unique trading nation.

A noteworthy aspect of urban planning in Indus civilization cities was an elaborate drainage system. The sewers, clearly laid out and maintained by a central authority, had manholes at intervals to allow workers to remove rubbish. Connected to the sewers by open brick gutters were the house drains, each consisting of an enclosed system of clay pipes. Some houses even had built-in Western-style lavatories equipped with seats.

LOST
LANDS

'Groves where rich trees wept odorous gums and balm,
Others whose fruit burnished with golden rind
Hung amiable, Hesperian fables true
If true, here only . . .'

John Milton

Tales and legends of lost lands abound in history, myth and folklore. The memories and remnants of these 'dream worlds' may, at the least, provide some insights into the lifestyles of other worlds and other ages. At most they could hold the keys to the very genesis of civilization.

The ocean depths may one day yield the secrets of once fertile and prosperous lands such as Lyonesse and Atlantis. Victims, perhaps, of great deluges or tidal waves, they are symbols of Golden Ages past, of romance, idyll and 'paradise lost'. Utopian, also, is the land of Shangri-La, the legendary ideal community set somewhere in Asia and isolated from the corruption of the modern world.

A thirst for riches and for knowledge has inspired the quest for lost lands. Eldorado, the 'place of gold', has been sought – but never found. Lemuria, by contrast, is a continent whose past existence has been proposed to explain unusual evolutionary phenomena. But whether fact or fable, these lost lands remain alluring to successive generations. As long as they stay enigmas, the search for them will never cease.

ATLANTIS: A PARADISE LOST?

The lost continent of Atlantis still remains one of the world's greatest mysteries. Is it fact or fiction? Where should Atlantis be sought today?

Everyone has heard of lost Atlantis but did it really exist? Was it an island in the Atlantic Ocean or in the Mediterranean? Was it to be found on land in Africa, America or Europe? There are many theories and it has been looked for in many places. The search for Atlantis, however, would never have begun if it had not been for the Greek philosopher Plato (*c.* 427–347 BC), who in two of his dialogues, the *Timaeus* and the *Kritias*, tells the following story:

Atlantis was a vast island, bigger than Asia Minor and Libya combined, lying beyond the Pillars of Hercules (Straits of Gibraltar). Beyond Atlantis again, there lay an archipelago of lesser islands. Some 9,000 years before Solon (*c.* 640–559 BC), Atlantis had been a powerful kingdom, with a high civilization and an ideal political constitution, which dominated the Mediterranean. When it became aggressive and imperialistic, it had been, through the anger of the gods, overwhelmed by the sea.

Plato's tale purports to come originally from Kritias who heard it when he was ten from his grandfather (then nearly 90), who had heard it from *his* father. And Kritias' great grandfather had been told it by Solon, who learned it in Egypt from the priests of Sais. Plato, being a philosopher and not a storyteller, wrote the account he received with a moralistic end in mind, not just for the sake of telling. How far is Atlantis Plato's invention and how far is it based on facts of which no other record remains?

After removing Plato's additions – his 'Atlantean' institutions, for example, were often modelled on those of the Persians – there remains, as the core of the tale, a vast island with its flourishing civilization which sank without trace, except for unnavigable shoals, somewhere under the Atlantic. Did this really happen? No writer before Plato mentions it – not even the Greek historian Herodotus (*c.* 484–420 BC) who had questioned the priests at Sais and would surely have been told if they had thought of it as history.

The Shipwrecked Traveller

If the account of Atlantis is not fact, then it is not fable either – at least not Plato's, for a similar tale was known in Egypt at the time of the Middle Kingdom (2000–1750 BC). A papyrus now in Leningrad tells the tale of the Shipwrecked Traveller, an Egyptian on his way to the Pharaoh's mines when his ship was hit by a big wave and broken to matchwood. All aboard were drowned except the traveller, who clung to a timber and was cast upon an unknown island. Here lived a golden dragon who carried him to its lair but did not harm him. The dragon told him that the island, a land of heart's desire where wealth abounded, was formerly home to 75 happy dragons of whom he himself was the lone survivor. The rest had been burned to a crisp by a star that had fallen there in his absence. The dragon prophesied that an Egyptian ship would soon rescue the traveller, but said that

Proof of the existence of Atlantis appeared to be at hand when Paul Schliemann, grandson of the archaeologist who discovered Troy, announced in 1912 that he had Atlantean artefacts in his possession. Even the map that he drew seemed to echo most people's impression of where Atlantis was and what it looked like. The dark oval lines represented the capital city as described by Plato. But Schliemann's revelations, published as a sensational article in the *New York American*, turned out to be based on faked evidence and ideas taken from other writers.

Among the most famous philosophers of all time, Plato was one of several ancient Greeks who laid the foundations of present-day Western thought. He was the first man to write down the story of the disappearance of Atlantis.

'never more shall you see this island because it will be swallowed by the waves'.

The tale of a happy and prosperous island later submerged was evidently well known to the Egyptians, as indeed it was elsewhere – it appears, for instance, in the Indian *Mahabharata*. It may even be a basic myth shared by different peoples. This does not mean that an Atlantis never existed – legends often consist of myth, supposition and invention laid on a hard core of fact. Many seekers after Atlantis have recently come to believe they have found this core on the Greek island of Thera.

A source for the lost continent

In 1967, the Greek archaeologist Professor S. Marinatos began excavating on the small volcanic island of Santorini in the Aegean Sea. He found the centre of a large city, where some houses still had two or three floors and rooms decorated with frescoes depicting scenes of everyday life. The remains of furniture were discovered as well as fine pottery utensils and the bones of food- and work-animals – but no human remains and no jewellery.

Archaeologists have determined that Thera, as Santorini was once known, had been a commercial centre of the Minoan civilization. It was not, as was originally thought, a colony of Crete, which in the first half of the second millennium BC had dominated the Aegean. Instead, it had its own independently developed culture dating back to 2500 BC. A flourishing commerce brought Thera prosperity – hence the frescoes displaying an art of considerable richness. The Spring Fresco in particular expressed the spirit of Theran culture: painted round three walls of a smallish room, it recreates a spring day with swallows 'kissing' in the air above wind-tossed red lilies on highly stylized rocks.

Then calamity overtook the island. Earth tremors must have sounded an alarm, for over a period of months, the Therans left, taking their valuables with them. They evidently expected to return, for they had placed *pittoi* – huge storage jars containing olive oil, seeds and grain – under the door jambs, often the strongest part of the house. Earthquakes destroyed part of the town before a lull encouraged a few people to return. They managed to escape, presumably in ships, when Thera's volcano erupted, leaving a fine pumice stone layer all over the town.

The volcano finally exploded with a crack that could have been heard more than 3,000km (1,875mi) away – the eruption is calculated to have been four times as powerful as that of Krakatoa, between Sumatra and Java, in 1883, which was heard in Australia. Thera's volcano spewed out enough ash to cover parts of the island in a layer 30m (98ft) thick and to bury the main city completely. Even though this eruption occurred about 1520 BC, the ash is still 4m (13ft) thick in places. Some 40 years later, the volcano's cone collapsed, causing the sea to rush in and leaving Thera the knife-edged arc it is today. Huge tidal waves wreaked such havoc that they are thought to have destroyed Cretan civilization almost overnight.

Was this the end of Atlantis? Many people think so. It is also possible that Crete itself was the site of the lost civilization, an idea first mooted in 1909. Crete's contacts with Egypt were suddenly broken at the same time as the drowning of Thera. Egyptian tradition may well have combined what was known of Thera's destruction with the abrupt and final break with Cretan civilization to explain the disappearance of this 'world power'.

Plato's '9,000 years before Solon' would be correct for equating Thera with Atlantis if the figure is divided by ten, as suggested by Greek seismologist A.G. Galanopoulos, since 900 years before Solon coincides neatly with the eruptions on Thera. Galano-

A great volcanic eruption decimated Thera in the Aegean Sea around 1520 BC. The area of fall-out (*below*) was enormous. Much of the centre of Thera disappeared underwater, leaving the small group of islands visible today.

One of these, often called Santorini after the patron saint of the island, St Irene, bears the colours of the volcanic fall-out (*right*). Rocks and beaches are black, red or white, or mixtures of these colours and, according to Plato, these hues were incorporated in the buildings of Atlantis.

Archaeological excavations begun in 1967 have revealed the remains of a Bronze Age city at Akrotiri at the southern end of Santorini. A room in one of the buried houses contained a remarkable fresco which depicted a coastal city, surrounded by seas full of dolphins and fish, and a fleet of elegant ships. If Santorini was the site of Atlantis, could this be a picture of the lost land?

poulos argues that the discrepancy might have arisen when the Egyptian scribe confused the symbol for 100 with that for 1,000. Another plausible explanation is given by Marinatos who suggests the priests of Sais multiplied the true figure by ten to project events into a dim and distant past. This reflects an age-old predilection of storytellers for round numbers and 'long ago'.

Beyond the Pillars of Hercules

The location of Atlantis in the Atlantic, while attractive because of the name, is much more difficult to justify. It may be that, following the Phoenician's circumnavigation of Africa (*c.* 600 BC), which made people realize how vast the Atlantic was, some story-teller in the development of the Atlantis legend decided to match 'long ago' with 'far away'. Whatever the reason, the search for Atlantis still continues beyond the Pillars of Hercules.

Medieval writers, who received the Atlantis story by way of Arab geographers, believed Atlantis was a real place, a belief encouraged by a widespread myth of an island paradise in the west. The Fortunate Isles, the Island of the Seven Cities, St Brendan's Isle – all were marked on 14th- and 15th-century maps and were the objects of voyages of discovery.

Many old maps reflect the imagination of the cartographer as much as the true reckoning of distant places. And so scholars received cautiously the conclusions of American historian Charles Hapgood, who in the 1960s became interested in medieval navigation charts. In the Library of Congress he found a map dated 1531 showing the Antarctic coast free of ice. So far as was known, oceanic seafaring did not begin until about 2000 BC and yet the scientific evidence shows that Antarctica has been frozen for roughly 6,000 years. Could its coast have been charted by seafarers before then?

Hapgood compared medieval maps known as portolans and gathered enough evidence to suggest that a great maritime civilization existed thousands of years before the Egyptians. This civilization, argues Hapgood in his *Maps of the Ancient Sea Kings*, was so completely destroyed that scarcely a trace remains except odd pieces of its seafaring knowledge handed down via generations of maps. Although Hapgood does not suggest this civilization could be that of Atlantis, similarities do exist.

The return of Atlantis

The American psychic and healer Edgar Cayce (1877–1945) prophesied that Atlantis would soon begin to rise again. In June 1940 he predicted: 'Poseidia will be among the first portions of Atlantis to rise again. Expect it in '68 and '69; not so far away!' He even specified the location – in the Bahamas. By an extraordinary coincidence, airline pilots photographed in 1968 what appeared to be buildings off the coast of North Bimini in the Bahamas. Undersea exploration has revealed stone formations resembling huge cobbled roads on the seabed, and mention has also been made of cyclopean walls, pyramids and stone circles. So far such descriptions lack tangible evidence – underwater archaeologists have yet to be convinced that the 'Bimini Roads' are manmade.

This is, of course, a good area in which to seek Atlantis. The Sargasso Sea, on the other side of the Bahamas, was long believed to be the 'unnavigable shoals' left by the sinking of Plato's Atlantis. But submerged 'roads' and 'walls' have for centuries been cited as proof of the truth of 'sunken city' legends along Europe's Atlantic coasts. In fact, anything resembling a manmade structure will sooner or later be linked with the idea of a 'sunken city'. The powerful impact of Plato's Atlantis has had much to do with this. As for Atlantis itself – the search goes on.

Six volcanic eruptions in the last 2,000 years have rocked Thera in the Aegean. In 1866, an eruption brought French vulcanologist Ferdinand Fouqué to Thera and led him to uncover a Bronze Age settlement at Akrotiri which had been buried by volcanic ash more than 3,000 years before.

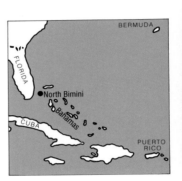

North Bimini in the Bahamas is not the only place in the Caribbean where underwater sightings have been made. A flight of stone steps off the northern coast of Puerto Rico also indicates that there were manmade structures in this region before the polar ice-caps melted and the waters rose sometime after 10,000 BC.

The discovery of huge 'stone walls' underwater off the coast of North Bimini boosted the theories of those who believed Atlantis was located in the Atlantic Ocean. Divers also found an encrusted pillar of worked marble and a stone artefact which resembled a fragment of tongue-and-groove masonry.

THEY FOUND ATLANTIS?

THE FATHER OF ATLANTOLOGY
American writer, scholar and politician Ignatius Donnelly (1831-1901) was the man who, more than anyone else, resurrected the study of Atlantis. His 1882 book, *Atlantis: The Antediluvian World*, became the 'bible' for all who believed in the former existence of the lost land. Donnelly's thesis appeared to explain mysteries such as the similarities between pre-Colombian culture and ancient Egyptian civilization, the mysterious migration of eels and the origin of the Basque people. Donnelly managed to generate a controversy so great and lasting that it has taken modern science and technology to disprove many of his assertions.

THE QUEEN OF THE OCCULTISTS

Russian spiritualist and co-founder of the Theosophical Society, Madame Helena Blavatsky (1831-1891) is regarded by many as a charlatan. But for her, and her occultist court, Atlantis and Lemuria might never have become so established in the legends of lost lands. Blavatsky maintained that Atlantis lay in the North Atlantic and was peopled by highly civilized Atlanteans who, as the Fourth Root Race of humankind, were descended from Lemurians. Humans today are the Fifth Root Race which will soon evolve, via the Americans, into the Sixth Root Race. Eventually, South America will generate the last Root Race of all.

THE MAN WHO DREAMED ATLANTIS

American commercial photographer Edgar Cayce (1877–1945) became a renowned healer, prophet and clairvoyant. In his many trances, he had extraordinary dreams and visions of Atlantis, a civilization of high spiritual and technological standards. Cayce believed that the Atlanteans had successfully harnessed atomic energy and had mastered the principles of flight. Their brilliant civilization, however, was destroyed in three nuclear disasters, the first in 50,000 BC and the last in 10,000 BC. Having foreseen the coming catastrophes, most Atlanteans had escaped to Central America and Egypt.

THE VANISHED DOMAIN OF LYONESSE

Medieval tradition describes a former land beyond southwest England. Is there any factual truth in this? What connection does Lyonesse have with King Arthur or the Celts?

Anyone standing at Land's End, at the southwest tip of England, looking out on a clear day toward the Isles of Scilly, can easily imagine that in between once lay a prosperous country. This was, in the words of the English poet Alfred Lord Tennyson, 'the lost land of Lyonesse, where, save the Isles of Scilly, all is now wild sea'. But was the existence of Lyonesse ever more than a poet's romantic dream?

A great deluge appears in the traditions of many peoples in different parts of the world – Asia, Australia and the Pacific, as well as the Americas. The best known in the West is 'Noah's Flood' from the Book of Genesis, a tale derived from ancient Mesopotamia. Curiously, Africa has no universal deluge legend. Neither, folklorists believe, had western Europe until the Mesopotamian myth reached it as the Greek legend of Deucalion and Pyrrha, and as the Biblical story of Noah.

What Europe may have had instead was a legend of a more local flood caused not by rain but by the encroachment of the sea, perhaps following land subsidence – a 'lost land' story like that of Atlantis. Several such tales survive from medieval and later times, particularly along the coasts of Britain and Brittany in France. The most celebrated of these 'lost lands' is undoubtedly Lyonesse, because it has become part of the legend of Arthur.

How Lyonesse was lost

The earliest written report of a lost land off the coast of Cornwall is to be found in the 15th-century *Itinerary* of William of Worcester. He refers to 'woods and fields and 140 parochial churches, all now submerged, between the Mount and the Isles of Scilly'. But he does not give the drowned land a name.

The Cornish antiquary Richard Carew may have been the first to identify this lost land with the Lyonesse of Arthurian legend. His report of it appeared in William Camden's *Britannia* and later in his own *Survey of Cornwall* (1602). He wrote: 'And the whole encroaching sea hath ravined the whole land of Lioness, together with divers other parcels of no little circuit; and that such a Lioness there was, these proofs are yet remaining. The space between Land's End and the Isles of Scilly, being about 30 miles, to this day retaineth that name in Cornish – Lethosow – and carrieth continually a depth of 40–60 fathoms, a thing not usual in the sea's proper dominion.'

Moreover, midway between Land's End and the Scilly Isles lay a group of rocks called the Seven Stones, bounding an area known in Cornish as *Tregva*, 'a dwelling'. Here fishermen reported drawing up pieces of doors and windows. The tale told of Lethosow in Carew's day was that, when the sea rushed in and drowned it, a man called Trevilian made his escape galloping on a white horse just ahead of the waves. This was commonly thought to explain the arms of the Trevelyan family: a horse rising from the sea.

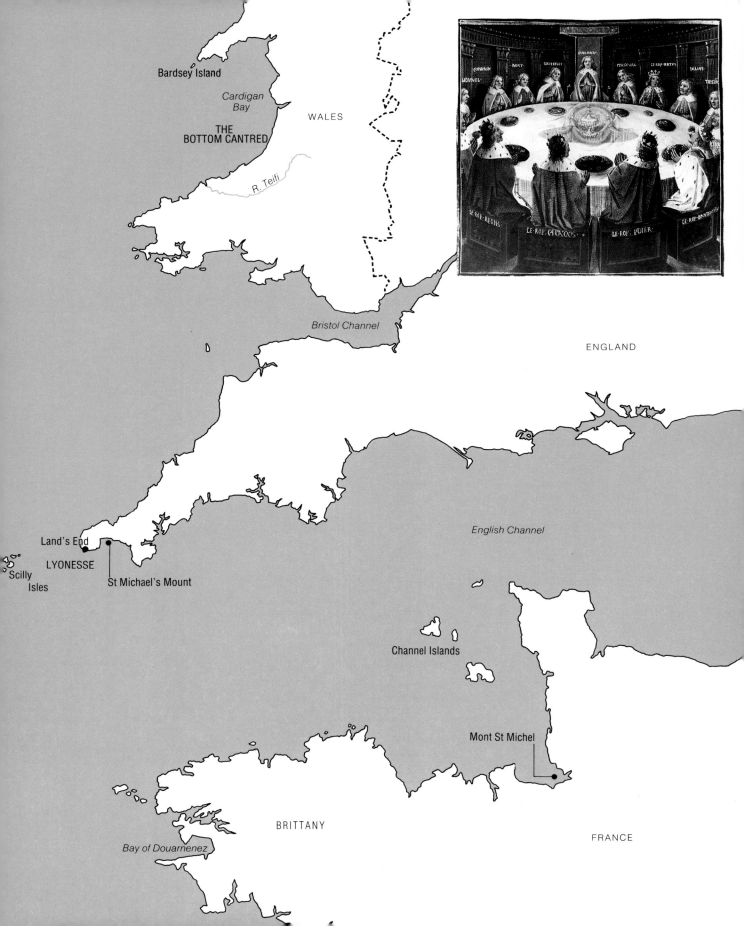

Bardsey Island

Cardigan Bay

WALES

THE
BOTTOM CANTRED

R. Teifi

Bristol Channel

ENGLAND

English Channel

Land's End

LYONESSE

Scilly
Isles

St Michael's Mount

Channel Islands

Mont St Michel

BRITTANY

Bay of Douarnenez

FRANCE

THE VANISHED DOMAIN OF LYONESSE

In Arthurian romance, Lyonesse is the name of the homeland of the hero Tristan, nephew of King Mark and lover of Mark's wife, Iseult. Because Mark was King of Cornwall, Carew or another author assumed that the Cornish 'lost land' and Lyonesse were one and the same. But medievalists believe this is an error and that 'Lyonesse' is a corrupt form of an earlier name given to Tristan's country. This was *Loenois*, actually Lothian, in Scotland. Such a location agrees with the fact that Tristan's own name belonged to a Pictish prince of the 8th century.

Once Cornwall's lost land had been identified with Lyonesse, it became bathed in the glow of Arthurian legend. New connections were made. Alfred Lord Tennyson placed Arthur's court of Camelot there, and mystics expected to see Lyonesse rise again from the waves or to behold it off Land's End in vision.

The truth behind the legend

Like Atlantis, Lyonesse has become a potent symbol, expressing regret for a Golden Age that has perished and for a Cornish past more glorious than its present. But is there any evidence that reality underpins tradition? The Cornish historian William Borlase, writing in 1753, pointed out, as suggestive of a lost land, lines of stones running out from the shore on Samson Flats in the Scilly Isles. Looking like field walls, they were thought to be manmade and, in the 1920s, it was suggested that they were indeed ancient field boundaries built in the Bronze Age.

Oceanographers today, however, say that to submerge what were once tilled fields, a rise in sea level of more than 3.7m (12ft) would be needed over the past 3,000 years. This does not agree with what is known of recent sea-level changes around Britain.

The theory that the 'walls' were fish traps, and always covered at high tide, is more plausible. If so, they are not alone in suggesting that the Scilly Isles have lost ground to the sea. On the foreshore of the islands of St Martin's, Little Arthur and Tean, there are partially submerged hut circles and cists thought to have been encroached on by the sea in Roman times. Certainly, classical writers speak of the Scilly Isles as one (or substantially one) island as late as the 4th century AD. But widespread subsidence such as this was taking place around the coast of Britain in the Iron Age only very slowly. Submergence must have been gradual and intermittent, not a single traumatic event such as one man might witness, remember and hand down as tradition.

The Celtic connection

The story of Lethosow/Lyonesse has its counterpart in Brittany, where under the Bay of Douarnenez lies drowned the great city of Ker-Is. Only King Gradlon escaped, riding like Trevilian on a white horse ahead of the flood. Both tales are attached to heroes of the 6th century and both belong to the Celtic world. Although there is no evidence of a widespread flood in the Celtic area around that time, there may well have been a *local* disaster caused by exceptionally high tides, such as those the east coast of England witnessed in 1953.

It is possible that when monks from the abbey of Mont St Michel in Brittany founded the Cornish daughter-house of St Michael's Mount in Cornwall, they brought the flood story with them. Wherever the tale started, it is not hard to believe there was once a flood which, like all disasters, was improved in the telling: a lost village became a town and the town eventually became a whole kingdom. People forgot exactly where it happened and set it where there was 'proof' of the tale – in the shape of submerged 'buildings'. As to when it happened – why, of course, in 'storytime', in the Celtic heroic age, the age of Arthur, Gradlon and Tristan.

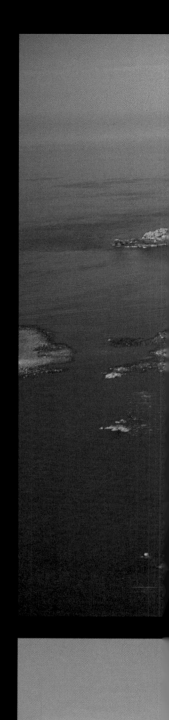

A cluster of islands located 32km (20mi) southwest of Land's End may be all that remains above water of the vanished domain of Lyonesse. These Scilly Isles contain on their foreshores and beneath the waves at low tide remarkable ruins of a bygone era.

'The hoary rock in the wood' is the old Cornish description of the conical hill which today is the island of St Michael's Mount. Lying a short distance out to sea, the mount is surrounded by the fossilized remains of a forest which may be seen at low tide.

Atlantic breakers crash on to the rocks of Land's End where, it was once thought, the domain of Lyonesse was joined to England. Looking out to the Scilly Isles from the top of the cliffs, it is occasionally possible, according to tradition, to see the remains of Britain's most famous lost land.

LEMURIA: THE ELUSIVE CONTINENT

Scientists of the 19th century proposed a lost continent to explain the unusual distribution of flora and fauna around the Indian Ocean. What is the evidence for this? Was there once a race of humans called Lemurians?

From the observation car of the train carrying him through the night to Portland, Oregon, a newspaper reporter looked out and saw some curious red and green lights on California's Mount Shasta. The conductor of the train, when asked about them, said they were the lights of 'Lemurians holding ceremonials'.

So wrote Edward Lanser in an article published in the *Los Angeles Times Star* on 22 May 1932. In the hope of a further story, Lanser travelled to Mount Shasta where, in the town of Weed, he met others who had seen the lights. He also heard talk of a 'mystic village' on the slopes of the mountain to which no one had ever been and returned. An 'eminent scientist', Professor Edgar Lucin Larkin, had observed the village with the aid of a powerful telescope.

The Lemurians were 'tall, barefoot, noble-looking men with close-cropped hair, dressed in spotless white robes'. The ceremonials with lights were performed in memory of their lost home of Lemuria. They had lived undetected in North America for several thousand years by using the 'secret power of the Tibetan masters' which enabled them to blend with their surroundings and to vanish at will. Their village was defended against intrusion from the outside world by an invisible barrier.

Had someone played a joke on Lanser? Or was this his own fiction? Later investigators have never found any traces of Lemurians on Mount Shasta; and Professor Larkin was, in truth, an occultist who ran the Mount Lowe Observatory as a tourist attraction. He had died in 1924 and could not deny Lanser's statements. Lanser's Mount Shasta colony was undoubtedly inspired by *A Dweller on Two Planets*, an occult novel published in 1894 by 'Phylos the Tibetan', alias Frederick Spencer Oliver. In this, Mount Shasta is the retreat of a community of sages founded to preserve the ancient wisdom.

The origins of Lemuria

The publication of naturalist Charles Darwin's *On the Origin of Species* in 1859 had placed scientists in a quandary. If similar species had evolved in one place from a common ancestor, how were scientists to account for such creatures as the lemur, which lives mainly on the island of Madagascar – with some in nearby Africa – but is otherwise only found in India and the Malay archipelago? Other fauna, and likewise flora, raised the same question. How did they cross the Indian Ocean?

The obvious answer was a land bridge. Geologists added to the debate by pointing out a similarity between certain rocks and fossils of central India and southern Africa – and a new 'continent' was born, connecting Africa to India, and deemed to exist when lemurs were evolving. An English zoologist, Philip Sclater, suggested a name for this continent: Lemuria.

Darwin's theory of evolution implied that humans were

Psychic memories, a badly preserved document and a broken terracotta model inspired British occultist William Scott-Elliott to draw a map of Lemuria at its greatest extent. According to Scott-Elliott, the elusive continent probably took this form from about 280 to 180 million years ago.

Natural catastrophes began to break up the landmasses of Lemuria between 136 and 60 million years ago, according to Scott-Elliott's second map of Lemuria. But the complete submergence of the continent did not take place until much later, at a time the occultist was unwilling to specify.

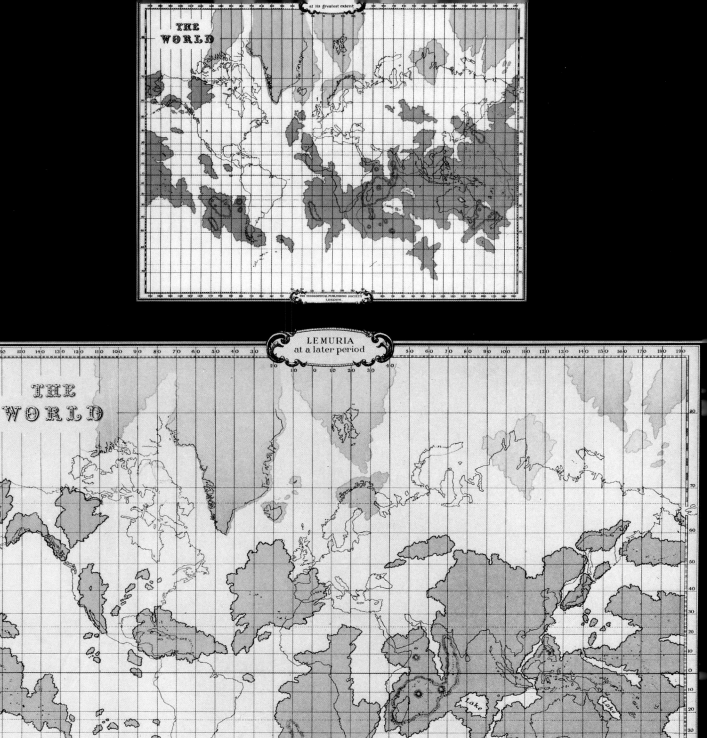

descended from apes, but no fossils had been found to prove the connection. The German naturalist Ernst Haeckel seized on Lemuria as the possible cradle of humankind – the fossils needed to demonstrate this had sunk with the continent under the sea.

Today's scientific world-picture has no need of a Lemuria since other theories, such as continental drift, are used to explain the distribution of lemurs and the cross-matching of geological strata between Africa and India. Even if Lemuria had existed, it would have been submerged millions of years before primitive humans evolved. Nevertheless, the idea of a lost land that was the cradle of humankind proved irresistible to many occultists and Lemuria has taken its place beside Atlantis in their cosmos.

What was Lemuria to the occultists?

The founder of theosophy, Madame Blavatsky (1831–1891), is regarded either as a great mystic or as an outrageous charlatan. But no one can deny her remarkable powers of imagination. In a racy career, ranging from circus bareback-rider to spiritualist medium, she acquired a working knowledge of western magic and eastern philosophy. She also picked up the Lemuria theory.

Blavatsky claimed to have travelled the world in search of occult wisdom which she found in Tibet at the feet of the 'Mahat-mas', whom she said ruled the world by sending out streams of occult force. The many difficult, some would say confused, volumes of her masterwork *The Secret Doctrine* were supposed to be derived from *The Book of Dzyan*, an ancient Atlantean text which the 'Mahatmas' had shown her in a trance.

The Secret Doctrine proclaimed the evolution of humankind through seven Root Races, the third of which was that of the Lemurians. These ancient beings lived in a continent occupying most of the southern hemisphere. They were giant apelike creatures. Some had four arms while others had a third eye in the back of the head. They had no spoken language but used tele-pathy, and although they had no proper brain they could, by the exercise of their will, quite literally move mountains. Eventually, Lemuria broke up and was followed by Atlantis, then the world as it is today. Descendants of the Lemurians, according to occultists, still survive – as Aborigines, Hottentots and Papuans.

After Blavatsky's death, other theosophists built a more detailed picture. In his *Story of Atlantis and the Lost Lemuria*, William Scott-Elliott reports that Lemurians were almost 4.5m (15ft) tall with brown skins. Their faces were flat, without fore-heads but with protruding jaws. Their eyes were so far apart they could see sideways, like birds, as well as forward. Most bizarre of all, their heels stuck out so far behind them they were able to walk backward as easily as they could forward.

Lemurians were once egg-laying hermaphrodites but eventually reproduced as humans do. When they interbred with animals, producing apes, the supernatural beings helping the Lemurians to evolve refused to assist them any longer. Their place was taken by the 'Lords of the Flame' who came from Venus and enabled the Lemurians to achieve immortality and reincarnation. But just when they had mastered civilization and begun to look human, Lemuria sank beneath the sea.

These heady ideas not surprisingly found their way into the *Martian Chronicles* of Edgar Rice Burroughs. In the meantime, other occultists had shifted Lemuria to the Pacific Ocean where it contributed to the lost continent of Mu proposed by the American James Churchward and held to explain the statues on Easter Island and the ruined city of Nan Matol in the Caroline Islands. But these are remote, not easily reached, and Mount Shasta remains the most alluring site to seekers after Lemuria.

The sensational news that Mount Shasta in California was host to a colony of Lemurians was announced by reporter Edward Lanser in 1932. The snowcapped mountain, 4,317m (14,160ft) high and located near the state border with Oregon, had been watched by a so-called eminent professor using a telescope. He had seen a splendid temple of onyx and marble, not unlike the Mayan temples of the Yucatan in Mexico. The Lemurians were reported to come into the local town of Weed to buy stores, paying with huge gold nuggets apparently mined from the mountain.

The ring-tailed lemur is the most familiar member of the Lemur family whose distribution caused such consternation among 19th-century scientists. Related to humans and monkeys, lemurs live mainly in Madagascar but may also be found in Africa, India and the Malay archipelago.

ADVOCATES OF LOST LEMURIA

SEEKING THE ORIGINS OF HUMANKIND

German naturalist Ernst Haeckel (1834-1919) fervently supported the idea of a lost land called Lemuria. A tireless proponent of Darwin's theories of evolution and natural selection, Haeckel believed that a continent which once stretched from Madagascar to Malaysia would explain the distribution of lemurs and other species. More significantly, he suggested that Lemuria may have been the site of the origin of human beings. He wrote in the 1870s that '. . . there are a number of circumstances (especially chronological facts) which suggest that the primeval home of man was a continent now sunk below the surface of the Indian Ocean . . .'

THE LOST CONTINENT OF MU

French physician Augustus Le Plongeon (1826-1908) was the first man to excavate the Mayan ruins in the Yucatan state of Mexico. He translated one of the few surviving Mayan books, the *Troana Codex*, and produced an extraordinary account of the alleged continent of Mu which had thrived in the Pacific Ocean before it was destroyed by an earthquake. Le Plongeon claimed he had evidence indicating that Muvians were the ancestors of not only the Maya but also of the Egyptians.

THE EMINENT EVOLUTIONIST

Charles Darwin was not the only British naturalist to arrive at a theory of evolution in the mid-19th century. Alfred Russel Wallace (1823–1913) developed his own independent ideas about natural selection and coined the phrase 'survival of the fittest'. Wallace lent his support to Haeckel's proposal about Lemuria. He wrote that Lemuria 'represents what was probably a primary zoological region in some past geological epoch . . . If we are to suppose that it comprised the whole area now inhabited by Lemuroid animals, we must make it extend from West Africa to Burma, South China and Celebes, an area which it possibly did once occupy.'

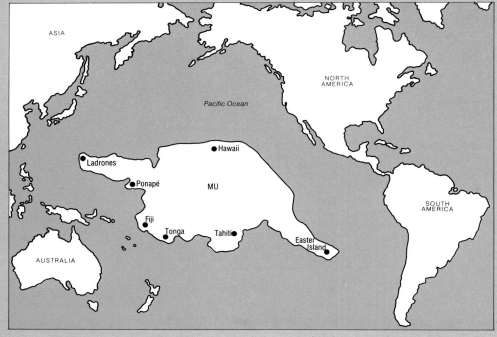

PUTTING MU ON THE MAP

In the 1920s and 1930s, an Anglo-American, James Churchward, produced a number of books relating to the history of the lost land of Mu. His map shows Mu covering much of Polynesia, including Hawaii and Easter Island. Churchward decided that Mu had disappeared beneath the waves about 13,000 years ago, leaving only the myriad islands of Polynesia behind.

SHANGRI-LA: THE SECRET UTOPIA

An ideal community somewhere in Asia, isolated from the corruptions of civilization, has captured the imagination of the 20th century. Does this paradise exist? How much of its reputation is true? Where is it most likely to be located?

'To Conway, seeing it first, it might have been a vision . . . It was, indeed, a strange and almost incredible sight. A group of coloured pavilions clung to the mountainside with . . . the chance delicacy of flower-petals impaled upon a crag. It was superb and exquisite. An austere emotion carried the eye upward from milk-blue roofs to the grey rock bastion above . . . Beyond that, in a dazzling pyramid, soared the snow slopes of Karakal. It might well be, Conway thought, the most terrifying mountain-scape in the world . . .' Such was Conway's first glimpse of Shangri-La, the hidden lamasery in Tibet described in James Hilton's romantic adventure novel, *Lost Horizon.*

Clinging to the slopes of Karakal, 'the loveliest mountain on earth', somewhere 'far beyond the western range of the Himalaya', the lamasery with its lay people in the fertile valley below forms a paradisal community. The inhabitants live in peace and harmony, governed by the principle of moderation. Says a lama-to-be: 'We rule with moderate strictness, and in return are satisfied with moderate obedience.' Later, the high lama explains further the operation of this benevolent autocracy: 'We have no rigidities, no inexorable rules. We do as we think fit, guided a little by the example of the past, but still more by our present wisdom, and by our clairvoyance of the future.'

The evidence for Shambhala

This secret community of lamas living beyond the normal span and able to foresee the future is dedicated to the preservation of civilization – including Chinese porcelain and Mozart – against the barbarism they predict will overtake the outside world. *Lost Horizon,* with its hidden monastery and poignant love story, captured the Western imagination and Shangri-La has, with Atlantis, Lyonesse and Eldorado, become part of popular mythology as an aspiration, a dream world, often sought but seldom found.

Lost Horizon is perhaps not pure invention. It may be based on traditions long current in the Far East of a hidden paradise. Early Buddhist writings call it Chang Shambhala and describe it as a source of ancient wisdom. Belief in it was once widespread – in China, the Kun Lun Mountains were rumoured to contain a valley where immortals lived in perfect harmony, while in Indian tradition there was a place called Kalapa, north of the Himalayas, where lived 'perfect men'.

In Russia, it was said that if the path of the Tartar hordes was followed all the way back to Mongolia, Belovodye would be found, where holy men lived apart from the world in the Land of the White Waters. Shambhala, now another name for Shangri-La, was reputed to lie in or north of Tibet, where seemingly impassable mountains enclosed secret valleys that were both fertile and verdurous. But did this hidden paradise ever exist or was its reality wholly spiritual?

Clouds of mystery hang over Shangri-La and mountain peaks look down on its treasured sanctuary, as they do here in Kathmandu, Nepal. The hopes of civilization may be stored within its archives for this secret utopia, protected by almost impenetrable landscapes somewhere in deepest Asia, could hold the key to a safe, secure future for mankind.

The precise location of Shambhala/Shangri-La is not shown on any map, yet tales and legends concerning it point to Asia north of India. Perhaps it can be found on the Tibetan side of the Himalayas, or among the Kun Lun Mountains of western China, or in the Altai Mountains of Mongolia. Wherever it lies, pilgrims will need more than a map to guide them – they must be spiritually prepared.

The mystics of Tibet

Until overrun by the Chinese in 1950, the high plateau of Tibet could claim to be the remotest place on earth. This circumstance helped foster a highly spiritual society ruled from his monastery-citadel at Lhasa by the Dalai Lama. Especially after the closure of Lhasa, which became 'the forbidden city' to Europeans in the 19th century, Tibet also nurtured among Westerners a climate of belief in which they would readily accept marvels.

Buddhist lamas, or monks, and mystics were credited with extraordinary powers. One of the most dramatic was *lung-gom*, a training that allowed adepts to overcome gravity and reduce their body weight, so enabling them to move with astonishing speed. In the early part of this century, the British traveller Alexandra David-Neel spent 14 years in Tibet and observed one of these runners bounding along like a ball. She later wrote: 'I could see his perfectly calm impassive face and wide open eyes with their gaze fixed on some invisible distant object situated somewhere high in space. The man did not run. He seemed to lift himself from the ground, proceeding by leaps . . . His steps had the regularity of a pendulum.'

David-Neel was a theosophist and it may be that her account of the Tibetan lamas was coloured by her desire to believe. But assuming she was an unbiased observer, should Shambhala be sought in and around Tibet? Her 'mystic masters' fit the description of the inhabitants of that utopia.

Heavenly domain or earthly paradise?

The Russian-born traveller, Nicholas Roerich, another member of the Theosophical Society, records in his *Shambhala* (1930) several visits to Tibet. In 1928, he asked a lama whether Shambhala was a real place and received the reply: 'It is the mighty heavenly domain. It has nothing to do with our earth . . .' Roerich, who believed he himself was under the protection of Shambhala, seems to have convinced himself that this was an evasion and the lama's consequent remarks indicated a real location.

The Buddhist tradition of a subterranean paradise known as Agartha has also been linked with Shambhala, perhaps by the celebrated medium Madame Blavatsky. Roerich, who called it Agharti, had heard of it on his 1924 expedition through the Altai Mountains, Mongolia and Tibet. A lama told him Shambhala was a great city at the heart of Agharti where ruled the 'king of the world'. Roerich became convinced Agharti was linked to all the nations of the world by subterranean tunnels.

Edward Bulwer Lytton, author of *The Last Days of Pompeii*, had expressed some of these ideas in his novel *The Coming Race* (1871). He describes a world under the earth's crust where live a superior race, the *Vril-ya*. By the exercise of *vril* – a psycho-kinetic energy more developed in the female, dominant, sex – they plan to conquer the 'upper world'.

The notion of this superior race and their mystical *vril* power proved a powerful attraction to both occultists and Nazis. Hitler is said to have believed in *vril* power and in a race of supermen living underground. He is supposed to have sent expeditions to search in German, Swiss and Italian mines for the entrance to their kingdom.

From the serenely tranquil Shangri-La to the rather more sinister associations of Agharti, it is ironic that the very barbarians foretold by the high lama in *Lost Horizon* should themselves seek to harness the legend of the secret utopia where holy men live in peace and harmony. The tale is perhaps one more example of how the forces of good and evil compete side by side even in the most treasured places of the world.

The Dalai Lama's palace at Lhasa in Tibet is reputed to be linked by subterranean tunnels with Chang Shambhala, 'a northern place of quietude'. Called the Potala, this fortress palace was once the national religious centre where the spiritual leader of the Tibetans governed his people. But since 1959, when the Tibetans rebelled against the occupying forces of the Chinese, the Dalai Lama has ruled from exile in India.

ELDORADO: THE FABULOUS GOLDEN REALM

A legendary 'place of gold' situated in northern South America has long eluded the most imaginative of explorers. What likely trails have so far been travelled? What sites have been explored? Who was El Dorado, the Golden Man?

'Gold', wrote the Greek poet Pindar, 'is the child of Zeus. Neither moth nor rust devour it but the mind of man is devoured by it.' Mankind's obsession with gold is immemorial. Despite appearances in Eastern bazaars, not to mention *Dallas* and *Dynasty*, gold has always been rare – the total ever mined is reckoned at less than a million tons. For this reason, gold has become the ultimate measure of value. Diamonds may be 'a girl's best friend', but people speak of a Golden Age, a heart of gold, a golden opportunity. As a medium for craftsmen, it is unequalled – responsive as clay, tough as stone. Gold's rarity and beauty made it the metal of kings.

The powerful mystique of gold originally had much to do with its colour. The Egyptians linked it to the sun and to the life-essence. On what was once the Gold Coast, now Ghana in West Africa, the famous Golden Stool of the King of the Ashantis embodied the nation's soul, and a pinch of gold dust tucked into a dead man's loincloth was his passport through the spirit world.

Gold was the ultimate treasure, guarded by dragons in the ancient North and picked by the handful in the kingdom of Prester John. It was the stuff that beckoned Alexander the Great to Persia, seduced the Portuguese into 'sailing off the map', brought the Spaniards to the New World, and launched a search lasting centuries and costing hundreds of lives – the pursuit of Eldorado.

The story of the Golden Man

'Gold is the most exquisite of all things . . .' wrote Christopher Columbus. 'Whoever possesses gold can acquire all that he desires in the world. Truly, for gold he can gain entrance for his soul into paradise.' Such was the view that, after 1492 when Columbus first crossed the Atlantic, launched the Spanish conquest of the New World. Within 50 years the Aztecs of Mexico and the Incas of Peru had succumbed to the conquistadors' voracious appetite for gold. In the high Andes of Colombia, there had been expeditions inland to loot the rich tombs of the Sinu Indians, and in 1539 Europeans first entered the territory of the Muisca people and founded the city of Bogota.

Among the Muiscas the Spaniards first heard of a ceremony that took place a little to the north of Bogota at Lake Guatavita. Indians were still alive who had seen the last of these ceremonies acknowledging a new king. The following is an eye-witness account recorded in 1636 by a Spanish chronicler:

'The first journey he had to make was to go to the great lagoon of Guatavita, to make offerings and sacrifices to the demon which they worshipped as their god and lord. During the ceremony which took place at the lagoon, they made a raft of rushes, embellishing and decorating it with the most attractive things they had. They put on it four lighted braziers in which they

Round and mysterious, Lake Guatavita is surrounded by desolate hills and is distinguished by the notch Antonio de Sepulveda made in the 1580s when he attempted to drain it. The lake was once sacred to the local Muisca people who made offerings to the spirit of a former chieftain's wife, said by legend to live in the depths of the lake in the company of a terrible monster.

No one knows where Eldorado can be found but Lake Guatavita, lying in the hills about 50km (31mi) northeast of Bogota, has been for many years among the leading candidates. Others sought the mythical land of Manoa, said to lie in the hills of Guiana beyond the Orinoco River.

burned much *moque*, which is the incense of these natives, and also resin and many other perfumes. The lagoon was large and deep, so that a ship with high sides could sail on it, all loaded with an infinity of men and women dressed in fine plumes, golden plaques and crowns . . .

'At this time they stripped the heir to his skin, and anointed him with a sticky earth on which they placed gold dust so that he was completely covered with this metal. They placed him on the raft on which he remained motionless, and at his feet they placed a great heap of gold and emeralds for him to offer to his god. On the raft with him went four principal subject chiefs, decked in plumes, crowns, bracelets, pendants and earrings all of gold. They, too, were naked and each one carried his offering. As the raft left the shore the music began, with trumpets, flutes and other instruments, and with singing which shook the mountains and valleys, until, when the raft reached the centre of the lagoon, they raised a banner as a signal for silence.

'The gilded Indian then made his offering, throwing out all the pile of gold into the middle of the lake and the chiefs who had accompanied him did the same on their own accounts. With this ceremony the new ruler was received, and was recognized as lord and king.'

The treasure of Lake Guatavita

The ceremony of El Dorado, the Golden Man, was the beginning of the legend. The conquistadors, although they had managed to loot many hundreds of pounds of gold from the Muisca and their neighbours, were convinced that the best was yet to come. This was the vast treasure which they thought lay at the bottom of Lake Guatavita.

The first attempt to dredge the lake was in 1545, but the most serious of the early ventures was that of a merchant from Bogota, Antonio de Sepulveda, who began drainage operations in the 1580s. Using a labour force of 8,000 Indians he cut a great notch in the rim of the lake – still a notable landmark – through which the water flowed, reducing the level by 20m (61ft) before the cut collapsed killing many workmen. The scheme was abandoned, even though gold had been found: the share sent back to Spain to King Philip II included a gold breastplate, a staff covered with gold plaques and an emerald the size of a hen's egg.

The quest for riches beyond the dreams of avarice was not long confined to the shores of Lake Guatavita. Even in the days of the conquistadors, rumour had run like wildfire of the Golden Man and his mythical city of Manoa, where even the cooking pots were made of gold. Believing it to be in the unexplored forests of the Amazon basin, explorers and adventurers vanished into the jungle year after year, many never to return.

Sir Walter Raleigh was one adventurer who did come back, though he lived to regret it. In 1595, he sought Manoa and its gold in the forests of Guyana for England's Elizabeth I. When he found the city he planned to ally himself with the Manoans to defeat the Spanish. But the expedition was not a success. The failure of a second expedition in 1617-18 was made the excuse for his execution.

As the Golden Man faded from memory, people assumed that his name applied to the place where unimaginable riches awaited them – Eldorado, hidden in the Andes or the Amazon jungle. For the next two centuries it was sought and, in a manner of speaking, found, though not in the way the conquistadors envisaged. For it was in pursuit of their dream of a fabulous golden realm that early explorers and prospectors opened up the secret heartland of South America.

222

A solid gold model depicting the Muisca ceremony of the Golden Man was found by two farm workers in 1969 in a cave near Bogota. This model was a votive figure or *tunjo* made by the Muisca as an offering to their gods.

German natural scientist Alexander von Humboldt published in 1810 the first illustration of Lake Guatavita (*below*). He also tried to calculate how much gold was contained in the lake, arriving at a figure which in 1807 would have been worth a current 300 million dollars.

The new Muisca ruler is prepared for the sacred ceremony on Lake Guatavita: one man smears resin on to his body, another blows gold dust through a pipe. The costumes the Muisca are wearing are the fancy of the engraver, Theodore de Bry, who published the illustration in 1599.

Golden artefacts have been discovered all over northern South America. Many were designed as votive offerings such as this gold face which was dedicated to the sun god.

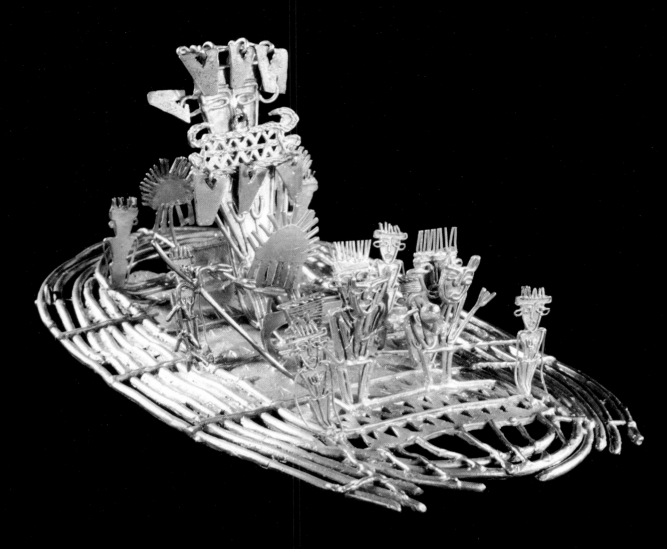

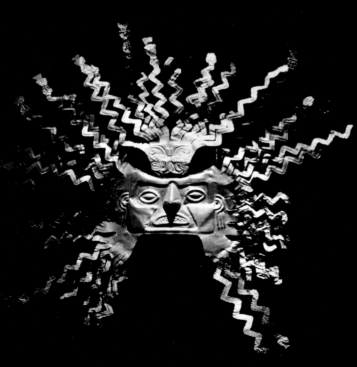

DIGGING FOR SOUTH AMERICAN GOLD

THE INDIGENOUS GOLD MINERS
Indians panning for gold were a common sight to the conquering conquistadors in South America. Spanish chronicler Juan Castellanos wrote in 1589 of the gold miners of Buritica, a town to the northwest of Bogota, 'Gold is what gave them breath; for gold they lived, and for gold they died.'

THE SEARCH FOR THE LOST GOLD-DIGGER
British adventurer Colonel Percy Fawcett, convinced he knew the location of Eldorado, set off with his son in 1922 to explore the Matto Grosso in Brazil. They were last heard of in 1925. A quarter of a century later, a Brazilian expedition claimed the Kalapos Indians had confessed to killing Fawcett and to burying him beside a lake between the Kuluene and Tanurio rivers. The leader of the expedition, Orlando Vilas Boas, held up the skull of the explorer for all to see and, in so doing, laid to rest the rumours that Fawcett had found the legendary kingdom.

GOLD FOR THE ENGLISH EMPIRE
English explorer, politician and scholar,
Sir Walter Raleigh (c. 1552-1618) set sail
for South America in 1595 intending to
find gold and establish an English
Empire. His friendship with the Indians
was essential to the success of his
mission. An engraving showing him in
conference with an Indian chief in
Guiana – now Venezuela – was used to
illustrate his account of the expedition,
published in 1599. Raleigh returned to
England with the news that the Indians
were willing to join with the English, that
Eldorado existed and that gold was to be
found in abundance beside the waters of
the Orinoco River.

GAZETTEER

The world is rich in mysterious places and while some countries are better endowed than others, few nations are entirely without them. This gazetteer offers essential information about 54 additional places, indicating what they are and where to find them.

*The gazetteer is divided into five regions: **The Americas,** including North, Central and South America; **Africa; Europe,** including western and eastern Europe, as well as Scandinavia; **The Near East,** including Turkey, the Middle East and Pakistan; and **The Far East,** including India, the Orient and the islands of the Pacific Ocean.*

The AMERICAS

Mystery Hill,
New Hampshire, USA
On a wooded rise just outside North Salem, and north of Boston, is the site of Mystery Hill. It consists of drystone walls, standing stones up to 1.5m (5ft) tall, dolmen-like stone slab chambers and a 4.5 ton slab which has been called a 'sacrificial table'. Some claim it to be an authentic megalithic site that dates back to 2000 BC. Allegedly Celtic inscriptions in ogham appear on a dedication tablet. Did the Celts from Spain and Portugal build the site? Was it used as an observatory, a shrine or for some other purpose?

Blythe Figures,
California, USA
As the Colorado River winds its way through the California desert, giant figures appear on the stony bluffs near the river's edge. About 29km (18mi) from the site is Blythe, a small town inland from Los Angeles. Drawn in stones are figures of a man 29m (95ft) long, a dance ring 43m (140ft) in diameter and an animal 11m (36ft) in length. The animal resembles a horse but the native American horse died out 10,000 years ago and its successor was not introduced until 1540 by the Spaniards. Were the figures drawn by local Indians? If so, what did they depict?

Bighorn Medicine Wheel,
Wyoming, USA
Near the top of a 3,000m (10,000ft) peak, high in Wyoming's Bighorn Mountains, is an elaborate pattern traced out in stone. It resembles a 28-spoke wheel, 24m (80ft) across, with six rock piles or cairns around its rim. To this date it is not known when it was built or by whom. Its pattern is similar to a Cheyenne medicine lodge which was used for sun-dance ceremonies. It may have been a rudimentary observatory. Were the cairns used as markers to show where the sun rises and sets? Did the Indians or some other race know more about the sky than is thought?

Monte Alban, Mexico
Around 600 BC, in the Oaxaca Valley, local inhabitants built a huge complex of ceremonial buildings on top of a mountain known today as Monte Alban. The site, south of Teotihuacan, has one of the most oddly shaped structures of the ancient world. No two sides or angles of the building are equal. Slabs on the outside are inscribed with symbols and hieroglyphs that cannot be fully deciphered. Was this particular building used for astronomical purposes? Why was it constructed in such an odd way?

Tenochtitlan, Mexico
The foundations of modern Mexico City were laid on the ruins of the magnificent city of Tenochtitlan, constructed by the Aztecs in the 14th century AD. Built on an island in what was then Lake Texcoco, it consisted of splendid houses, palaces and temples which were linked to the mainland by beautiful bridges. The Aztec ceremonies of human sacrifice were carried out in the city when as many as 20,000 victims would die at the same time. In the early 16th century the soldiers of Cortez destroyed the city and most of its inhabitants. Why did they do this and why did the Aztecs commit such acts of sacrifice?

Chichen Itza, Mexico
Little is known about the Mayan Indians who built this city which is sited 123km (77mi) southeast of Merida. It is estimated that the Temple of the Warriors was built around AD 1100. Although they knew the principle of the wheel, the Maya did not use it for construction purposes. One of the buildings functioned as an observatory and another as a ball-game court. The Maya built roads throughout the land and engaged in complex sacrificial rituals. Why was astronomy so important to the Maya? What were their religious beliefs?

Tiahuanaco, Bolivia
High on the arid windswept *Alti Plano* about 97km (60mi) west of La Paz lie the remains of an ancient culture, dating from about AD 600 to 1000. The Spaniards made every effort to destroy 'this pagan shrine' in the 16th century. Consisting mainly of a semi-subterranean temple, it also has many monoliths and strange-looking statues. Who built the site? Claims have been made that it was the earth-base of ancient astronauts. Is this a possibility?

El Panecillo, Ecuador
Quito, the second highest capital in the world, nestles in a high mountain valley. About 183m (600ft) above this old Inca city is a watchtower or observatory. It is shaped like a beehive and has a masonry tunnel entering the structure underground. The top of the beehive has an opening through which the sun's light enters. The structure was built around AD 1500 by the Incas. Was it an observatory or was it used for some other purpose?

San Agustín, Colombia
In the lush green valley of the Magdalena River that flows from the northern Andes lie the remains of a little-known South American culture. About 594km (369mi) southwest of Bogota, and near the town of San Agustín, the sites contain large stone sculptures, burial mounds and megalithic structures. They were built, or were already in use, 2,000 years ago. They were not abandoned until AD 1500. Who lived and worshipped here? Were the sculptures part of a more widespread cult?

AFRICA

Ife, Nigeria
To the west of the tropical rain forests and the Niger River lie the remains of the first Yoruba capital. East of Ibadan and 160km (100mi) northwest of Benin City, it was the seat of a sacred figure, the Oni. Afin, the Oni's palace, had floors of terracotta where many potsherds were found. Nearby, many intricate heads of bronze, copper, brass and terracotta were discovered. The city was inhabited by AD 600 and flourished until the rise of Benin in AD 1450. Is it possible that these works of art were made by another race? Were they part of an unknown cult?

Karnak, Egypt
Beside the fertile banks of the Nile lie the remains of one of the most magnificent building complexes ever constructed. Between the ancient cities of Thebes and Luxor, it is the work of several pharaohs. Dedicated to Amon-Ra, the site consists of huge temples, a forest of massive columns and avenues of sphinxes. An ancient obelisk still stands and is said to weigh 323 tons with a height of 29m (97ft). The complex was built around 1500 BC, although nearby ruins date to almost 2000 BC. How did the sphinxes originate? Who created such awe-inspiring architecture?

Merowe, Sudan
Away from the harsh desert and next to the Nile lie the remains of a city once inhabited by a people called the Kushites. They fled there from Egypt in 600 BC, bringing with them the custom of erecting pyramids. The burial chambers beneath the pyramids served as tombs for the ruling families. Nearby are the remains of temples and houses. The Meroites became famous for their ironwork, but about AD 350 they were conquered by people from Ethiopia and their empire disappeared. Where did they go? What do the Meroitic inscriptions mean?

Carthage, Tunisia
Overlooking the fine views of the Gulf of Tunis lie the remains of a city that was once on the richest part of the North African coast. It was here that the Carthaginians were defeated by the Greeks in 310 BC. To appease the Punic gods and gain their pardon, 500 children were sacrificed. A sacred enclosure containing small burnt bones has been discovered, confirming the story of the atrocity. Carthage was founded about 814 BC and was eventually destroyed by the Romans in AD 146. Why did the Carthaginians commit such acts? What were their religious beliefs?

Abalessa, Algeria
In the depths of the harsh Sahara desert and nestling in a valley surrounded by mountains lies the tomb of a queen called Tin-Hinan. About 55km (34mi) west of Tamanrasset, on top of a small hill, a stone structure consisting of several chambers was found, one of which contained the skeleton of a woman. She wore a leather dress and had gold and silver bracelets on her arms. Beside her were some Roman coins which were made between AD 308 and 324. Who was Tin-Hinan? Was her tomb a Roman construction?

EUROPE

Bryn-celli-Ddu, Wales
Along a farm track near
Llandaniel Fab on the Isle of
Anglesey lies the site of a
chambered cairn. About 6km
(4mi) from the Menai Bridge,
the burial site is located directly
on top of a former henge. Inside
the chamber is a tall smooth
pillar. Fragments of bones were
found inside the tomb, which
was constructed around
2000 BC. Who was buried here?
Was it haunted by the spirits of
the last Druids, who were killed
by the Romans?

Maes Howe, Orkneys, Scotland
In the windswept Orkney
Islands lies one of Europe's
most awe-inspiring monuments.
About 15km (9mi) west of
Kirkwall, the site contains a
series of passages, chambers
and alcoves. The entire site is
covered by an earthen mound,
11m (36ft) high and 46m
(150ft) in diameter. It was built
around 3100 BC and in the 12th
century the main chamber was
broken into by the Vikings. In
the 19th century bones of a
horse and a fragment of a
human skull were found in the
tomb. Who built it and what was
its purpose?

Callanish, Lewis, Scotland
Gale-force winds often sweep
the Isle of Lewis which, together
with its harsh terrain, has a
special mystique of its own.
About 19km (12mi) west of
Stornoway stands one of the
most dramatic megalithic
monuments in Britain. Avenues
of stones lead to a circle in
which stands a huge monolith.
The site was built about 2000 BC
and in some respects is similar
to Stonehenge. Who lived and
worshipped here? Was it used
for astronomical observations?

La Grotte des Fées, France
In the low-lying marshlands of
the Rhône delta is sited one of
the greatest known rock-carved
chambers. The tomb, 4km
(2.5mi) northeast from Arles,
has a 12m (40ft) antechamber
and at the far end an immense
burial chamber, 24m (80ft) long
and 3m (10ft) wide. There are
also two smaller side chambers.
They were constructed between
4000 and 3500 BC. Who built
them? Were they used as burial
chambers or for some other
reason?

Rennes-le-Château, France
A small and isolated village,
32km (20mi) from Carcassonne,
in southern France had a
penniless priest who in a few
years acquired a vast fortune. In
the church he discovered some
rolled parchments written in
Latin, two of which contained
cyphers. The locality was once a
stronghold of the Visigoths who
sacked Rome in AD 410. The
booty was said to include the
treasures of Solomon. The
priest died in 1917 leaving the
source of his wealth unknown.
Did he find these treasures in or
near his church?

Filitosa, Corsica, France
Along the mountainous main
road from Propriano northward
to Ajaccio lies the most famous
megalithic site in Corsica.
Consisting of five statue menhirs
and three monuments, it was
occupied from 4000 until about
1400 BC. Afterwards the Tower
People rebuilt it during their
occupation which lasted until
after 800 BC. None of the statue
menhirs are in their original
positions, since they were found
buried when excavated in 1954
and re-erected. Who were the
people who originally
constructed them? What was the
purpose of the site?

Los Millares, Spain
On a spur high above the
Andarax River in the midst of an
arid landscape lie the remains of
a megalithic settlement. The site
is about 20km (12.5mi) inland
from the port of Almeria. Early
this century extensive remains
were found which include a
large cemetery, dwellings, metal
implements and a major
chambered mound surrounded
by a circle of stones. The
settlement flourished between
3100 and 2500 BC. Did the
people originate from Iberia or
spread there from central
Europe?

Trepuco, Menorca, Spain
In the fertile southern part of
Menorca lies an evocative
megalithic monument. On the
outskirts of Mahón, the site
stands on a slight rise. It
contains a tower (*talayot*) and,
within a circle of stones, a table
(*taula*) which rises 4m (13ft),
with a capstone higher still. Built
by the Tower People after
1500 BC the site included
dwellings and fortifications.
Ashes of uncertain age and
bronze bulls have been found.
Were rituals performed on the
site? What is the meaning of the
circle of stones?

Talati de Dalt, Menorca, Spain
On a tree-covered hill on the
main road to Alayor, 3km (2mi)
from Mahón, stand the remains
of the most powerful Menorcan
megalithic site. It consists of five
talayot towers, circular houses,
stone circles and underground
chambers. Away from the main
tower stands a *taula* and a
boat-shaped setting of stones.
The site was built around 1000
BC. Who were the people who
lived there? Were the *taulas*
used as sacrificial tables?

Evora, Portugal
On the Guadiana River, to the
east of Evora, lies one of the
oldest cemeteries in Europe – a
group of seven round
chambered mounds, called
antas locally. Pottery bowls and
flint blades found in the tombs
dated the site to around 4000
BC. The sides of the tombs were
formed by great stone slabs,
about 1.5m (5ft) high, and the
roofs were corbelled. Who built
the mounds? Did the megalithic
tradition spread outward from
this region?

Val Camonica, Italy
In a rock-strewn valley 100km
(62mi) northeast of Milan lies
Val Camonica, where an
estimated 15,000 carvings have
been made on the rocks. They
depict a variety of scenes,
including houses, religious
practices and farming methods.
It is thought that they span a
period of 6,000 years, from the
New Stone Age until 16 BC when
the area was conquered by
Rome. Who were the carvers?
Were they minority groups
anxious to leave a record of
their culture before persecution
wiped them out?

Cerveteri, Italy
Within sight of the sea and inland from Lake Bracciano lie the remains of an ancient Etruscan city. Just outside the old city, which is northwest of Rome, stands the extensive cemetery of Banditaccia. At the sides of the principal funerary road there are numerous tombs. Some are enclosed within walls, others lie in neat rows. They were built between 700 and 600 BC. Evidence exists that a settlement thrived in the area from Villanovan times to the Roman period. Who built the tombs? Where did the Etruscans come from?

Castellucio, Sicily, Italy
On a spur with steep cliffs falling around it into the valley below lies the prehistoric village of Castellucio, between Syracuse and Ragusa. Into the face of the cliffs more than 200 'tombs' have been cut. Although amounts of pottery and debris were found on the site, there were no traces of human remains. The site has been dated to between 1800 and 1400 BC. Whose cemetery was it and where are the bones? What is the meaning of the carvings on the stone slabs filling the doorways to the 'tombs'?

Li Muri, Sardinia, Italy
In the fertile farming area of north Sardinia lie the oldest megalithic monuments on the island. About 8km (5mi) from Arzachena on the road towards Luogosanto, the site consists of five intersecting circles on a platform of a downward slope of a spur. Each circle has a small chamber of stone slabs and a surround of upright slabs and standing stones. Human bones, knives, pottery and beads have been found. The site is dated to around 2500 BC. Were the stones used for celestial observation? Who built and used the site?

Monte d'Accordi,
Sardinia, Italy
Near the middle of a rolling plain, with mountains in the distance and the sea nearby, lie the remains of a sacred mound. Beside the road to Sassari and 7km (4mi) southeast of Porto Torres, the mound is about 12m (40ft) high, with two stages of drystone walling. It dates from about 1700 BC. No trace of a chamber or an entrance to the mound has been found. A dolmen lies close to one side and a menhir by the approach ramp. A mysterious egg-shaped boulder, with a curve cut right through it, stands nearby. Who built the mound and what was its purpose?

Wéris, Belgium
The Ardennes, an area of flowing hills with many steep slopes, has one of Europe's most evocative megalithic sites. Near Erezée, 5km (3mi) from Wéris, starts a cross-country alignment of monuments. Three menhirs – the tallest is 2.4m (8ft) – create a haunting group. Nearby is a half-buried dolmen and in its chamber were found bones of humans and animals and also pottery. It is thought that the site was built between 3000 and 2500 BC. Who built the monuments? Was the alignment related to the seven stars of a constellation?

Drenthe, Holland
Along a strip of land bordered on each side by marshes, and concentrated between the towns of Assen and Emmen, lie over 50 *hunebedden* or long dolmens. Consisting of an extended chamber, each dolmen has a row of trilithons – two uprights roofed by a capstone – over it. The dolmens are surrounded by a circle of smaller stones. They are dated to between 3400 and 2300 BC. The chambers show signs of collective burials. It is thought that the style of construction originated from Poland or central Germany. Who built them and why did their construction decline with the arrival of the Beaker culture?

Visbek, Germany
Among the forest trees where once there was cleared farmland stands an enclosure surrounded by many long dolmens. About 50km (31mi) west of Bremen lie the sites of Visbeker Braut and Brautigam (Bride and Bridegroom). The quadrilateral enclosures are 80m (260ft) and 108m (350ft) long respectively. They both have varying formations of stones and each has a large sunken stone chamber. It is thought they were built around 3000 BC. Was this a centre where special festivals were held? Did people gather here for the sunrise at the summer solstice?

Tustrup, Denmark
In the gentle and rolling wooded countryside of north Djursland lie many megalithic monuments. Near the coast and the village of Vivild are several enclosed structures including dolmens and capstoned chambers. Various bowls and ladles were found in one enclosure, as well as some unidentified ashes. The site was built shortly before 3000 BC. Were the monuments part of the Funnel-Beaker culture? Were the complex rites that took place here connected with funerals?

Kong Asgers Høj, Denmark
On the island of Møn, facing across the sea to Zealand, stands 'King Asger's House', one of the best preserved mounds of the passage-grave type. Both the mound and the chamber, measuring 10m (33ft) long, are remarkably complete. Dating from the centuries around 3000 BC, they may be the work of the Funnel-Beaker culture. Were they used just for religious purposes, or for some form of astronomical activity?

Popovo Polje, Yugoslavia
Strange scenes and figures depicted on unusual funerary monuments give an air of mystery to an area located 48km (30mi) northwest of Dubrovnik. The site is attributed to a sect known as the Bogomils who settled in the region in the Middle Ages. The stone coffins have carvings of people, horses, the sun and moon, and a swastika. Although crosses appear on all the burial places, the monuments do not seem to be Christian. If the Bogomils did not make them, who did? Does their origin lie in a magic cult?

Biskupin, Poland
Extending from the Lusatia Mountains to northern and western Europe, the Urnfield culture existed during the first millennium BC. Biskupin, once on an island, is 225km (140mi) northwest of Warsaw. The entire city consisted of wooden houses and when discovered had been preserved under mud for 2,000 to 3,000 years. The city was enclosed by a stone wall and covered an area of about 2 hectares (5 acres). The inhabitants worshipped the sun and moon deities – were they Lusatians or some other race? Did the Druids inherit their culture?

Mycenae, Greece
The site stands on a hilltop and is said to be Greece's oldest city. Located 10km (6mi) from Argos, it includes the so-called Treasury of Atreus (*c.* 1400 BC) and an opening in the citadel walls called the 'Lion Gate' (*c.* 1260 BC) which led to a circle of royal burials. The Treasury has several beehive burial chambers built under a hill and is approached by a walled passageway. Gold death masks were found there – were they actual portraits of the deceased? Could one have belonged to King Agamemnon?

The NEAR EAST

Çatal Hüyük, Turkey
In an area of broad plains where stone was not readily available lie the remains of a city without streets. Located in southern Turkey, the city was constructed from about 6250 to 5400 BC. The houses were made of mud-bricks and wood. Many of the buildings were used as sanctuaries and shrines, and were decorated with wall paintings, reliefs and cult statues. Was this a holy city? Who were the people who lived and worshipped here?

Hattusas, Turkey
Standing on a plateau with sloping ground to the north and south lie the remains of the Hittite capital. The city, whose ruins lie at Boğazkale about 153km (95mi) east of Ankara, was protected by a stone wall 6km (3.75mi) long. There are numerous temples, shrines, storehouses and a library which yielded 3,300 clay tablets. The city was completely sacked and burned down about 1190 BC. Who conquered the Hittites and where did they go? What caused such intense heat that the bricks fused when the city was burned?

Nemrut Daĝi, Turkey
In an area often affected by earthquakes and sited on the peak of a mountain stand the ruins of several statues. Situated 563km (350mi) southeast of Ankara, the site contains the heads belonging to 9m (30ft) statues. They were made on the orders of King Antiochus I who ruled the area in the 1st century BC. Is it possible that tombs exist on the site which could reveal the unknown history of the statues? Do they also contain hidden treasure?

Karmir-Blur, Soviet Armenia
In the mountainous region surrounding Lake Van, a powerful kingdom once prospered. On the outskirts of Yerevan, near the border with Turkey, citadels were built of brick or cut into rock. It is believed that they were constructed between 900 and 700 BC. Half the area of one citadel was occupied by a 120-room palace which included workshops and storerooms. In some of these were found jewellery, ivory and bronze objects. Who made these superb artefacts? Was their culture passed on to others?

Alexandropol, Ukraine
When the Scythian nomads roamed the plains of the Ukraine, they established a reign of terror and performed acts of ritual brutality. At the height of their power and prosperity – 700 to 400 BC – they built funeral barrows, which rose like hills from the steppes, where they buried their chiefs. The one at Alexandropol, southeast of Kiev, is nearly 18m (60ft) high with several burial chambers. The barrows contained vast amounts of golden jewellery. Why did the Scythians choose Alexandropol? How could they have been so barbarous and yet such master craftsmen in gold?

Hatra, Iraq
On the west bank of the Wadi Tharthar lie the remains of a city that was once part of the Parthian Empire. About 100km (62mi) southwest from Mosul, the city was surrounded by a massive stone wall and within was a rectangular area containing temples and vaulted chambers. Numerous sculptures of humans and animals, together with a wide range of jewellery, were found. It is thought that the city was built between the 1st and 2nd centuries AD. Who inspired the people to create such beautiful jewellery? What were their beliefs?

Persepolis, Iran
On a high plateau in harsh and mountainous countryside stand the remains of a city of royal grandeur. About 48km (30mi) northwest of Shiraz, Darius the Great created a vast complex of splendid buildings and these were continued by his son, Xerxes. They included palaces, great columned halls and much fine sculpture. Construction of the city started about 520 BC and continued until after 470 BC. Why were no temples built in the city? What was the purpose of its fire-altar?

Dilmun, Bahrain
In the barren desert island of Bahrain, situated in the Persian Gulf, lie the remains of some 100,000 burial mounds. Known as 'the island of the dead', Bahrain has been shown by recent excavations to have been the site of an ancient city. Walls and houses, pottery and tools dating to about 4000 BC have been found. Where did the people come from who were buried here? Was Bahrain the same place as Dilmun, the Sumerian paradise?

The FAR EAST

Todai-ji, Nara, Japan
At the foot of a group of mountains, one of the finest Buddhist precincts in the world was built. Situated southeast of Kōbe, the central building (Daibutsen-den) houses the largest bronze statue of Buddha in the world. Measuring 16m (53ft) in height and weighing 560 tons, it was dedicated by Emperor Shomu in AD 752. During periods of anarchy starting in 1180, the temple was burnt down and the head of the Buddha melted. What priceless treasures were stolen by the vandals? Did people really believe the statue would come to life?

Borobudur, Java, Indonesia
On top of a hill covered with volcanic ash lies a complex of shrines dedicated to Buddha. Located 48km (30mi) northwest of Jogyakarta, the site is the architectural masterpiece of Indonesia. Erected by the Shailenda dynasty in the 8th century AD, the building has nine levels. On the higher tiers there are 72 bell-shaped *stupas* containing images of Buddha. Lower galleries contain more than 1,300 panels of relief sculptures depicting symbolic references to the life of Buddha. Did the number 72 have some astronomical connection? Did the building have a symbolic meaning?

Pagan, Burma
Along the wide Irrawaddy River as it passes through dense jungle lie the remains of a remarkable city. Located southwest of Mandalay, it once had more than 800 temples, the most ornate and imposing one being the Ananda, which was begun in the middle of the 11th century AD. Hundreds of statues of Buddha were found, including four enormous golden ones about 9m (30ft) high. The city was destroyed by Kubla Khan in AD 1287. Why has the city such an otherworldly aura about it? What is the symbolic meaning of the Buddha statues?

Anuradhapura, Sri Lanka
In an area clear of the dense jungle lies the ancient capital of Sri Lanka. Southwest of Trincomalee and 11km (7mi) east of Mihintale, this magnificent city was conceived by King Dutthagamani in the 1st century BC. Nine colossal public buildings were erected, together with an enormous reservoir constructed in AD 450. Sculptures and paintings adorned the buildings. One building, said to contain 900 rooms, had silver furnishings and gold studded with gems. What was the true meaning of these great works of art? Why was such a splendid city deserted?

Sanchi, Madhya Pradesh, India
On a peaceful hilltop overlooking woods lie the remains of a monumental burial tomb (*stupa*), located 48km (30mi) northeast of Bhopal. King Asoka is said to have distributed the remains of Buddha to 84,000 *stupas* in India, and this site is one of eight he built in the area in the 3rd century BC. It has four gateways covered in exquisite carvings that tell a multitude of stories. The *stupa* was looted in the 19th century, although the remains of two of Buddha's disciples have been recovered. Do the carvings tell other stories? Why was the site deserted in the 17th century?

Bhuvanesvar, Orissa, India
On the swampy coast of Orissa, about 20km (12mi) south of the Mahanadi delta, stands one of the wonders of India, known as the 'city of temples'. It is said that several thousand temples were built in the area, although only 30 now remain, together with some 500 tombs. They were constructed from the 7th to the 15th centuries, the most famous (Lingaraja) being built about AD 1000. Although stark inside, the exteriors feature highly decorative sculptures. Who created such sculptures? Were they associated with the worship of the god Shiva?

Ajanta Caves, Maharashtra, India
The Waghora River winds its way through a gorge, past manmade caves cut in the cliff face. Situated 113km (70mi) northeast of Aurangabad, the caves contain four sanctuaries and 25 monasteries. They are known for their murals, which depict the life of Buddha. Buddhist communities first lived here from about the 2nd century BC. Most of the paintings show familiar subjects, but others include 'super-humans' or strange animals. Do they relate to a cult or religion? Who were the artists?

Malekula, New Hebrides, Melanesia
Midway between Australia and Samoa lies the archipelago of the New Hebrides. Malekula is about 2,020sq. km (780sq. mi) in area and has several small islands offshore, all of which are volcanic and subject to earthquakes. The earliest archaeological site is dated to AD 350 and located on Efate Island. The Malekulans represent a Stone Age culture with megalithic elements including altars, monoliths and dolmens. What was the origin of their culture? Did their ancestors practise cannibalism?

Nan Matol, Caroline Islands, Micronesia
The Caroline Islands, to the east of the Marshall Islands, became a US Trust Territory after World War II. On the island of Ponapé, to the southeast of the group, lie the ruins of an old city, Nan Matol. It consists of 90 walled artificial islands – a kind of Venice divided by shallow canals and inhabited several hundred years ago by about 1,000 people. Its buildings are made of crystalline basalt logs, geometrically shaped and measuring around 4m (15ft) thick. Who lived here? Was the city residential or ceremonial?

GLOSSARY

A

Acropolis: the citadel at the highest point of a Greek city, containing its chief temples and public buildings.

Antiquary: a student or collector of old things whose interest is based more on curiosity than archaeology.

B

Barrow: a long or round mound covering one or more burials. In Britain, long barrows may be earthen (unchambered) or cover megalithic passage-graves. Long barrows are characteristic of the Neolithic Age, while most round barrows in Britain belong to the Bronze Age.

Breccia: a conglomerate rock composed of angular fragments of any material cemented together by a mineral such as lime.

Bronze Age: the second age of the archaeological 'Three Age System', when weapons and other implements were made of bronze. The first was the Stone Age and the third, the Iron Age.

C

Cairn: a small pyramid of rough stones assembled to mark a memorial, burial or path.

Ch'i: the breath of life, the cosmic breath, the vibrating energy which, the Chinese believe, permeates all living things. Its beneficial qualities are enhanced when *yin* and *yang* are in harmony, hindered when they are imbalanced.

Chthonic: relating to the Underworld.

Cist: a box-shaped container made of stone slabs and used for burial. It might be sunk into the ground or built on the surface, in which case it was covered by an earthen barrow.

Conquistadors: the Spanish conquerors of Mexico and Peru.

Continental drift: the movement of continents which takes place over millions of years as a result of the relative motion of huge 'plates' on the earth's surface.

Corbelling: a neolithic roofing method in which walls, built up by layers of flat stones protruding beyond the layer below, converge until the gap is narrow enough to be bridged by a large capstone.

Cosmology: the study of the universe, or cosmos, as an ordered whole.

Cyclopean: composed of large, close-fitting irregular blocks.

D

Dendrochronology: tree-ring dating method which uses the fact that the annual growth of trees varies from year to year, according to the climate. The comparison of young and old trees, especially the bristlecone pines of California, have provided an accurate system for dating wooden artefacts from the last 7,000 years.

Diorite: a crystalline igneous rock.

Dolmen: a megalithic tomb composed of two or more standing stones bridged by a huge capstone, the whole structure originally covered with earth.

Dowsing: the art of using a divining rod to locate something which is hidden, especially water.

E

Eclipse: the event in which one celestial body obscures the light of another, usually involving the earth, moon and sun. A solar eclipse occurs when the moon obscures the sun, a lunar eclipse when the moon moves into the earth's shadow.

Equinox: the time of year, in the spring and autumn, when the night and the day are of equal length.

F

Fresco: a watercolour image painted on to a wall or ceiling before the plaster dries.

H

Henge: a circular earthwork, surrounded by a ditch and bank, which often enclosed one or more stone or wooden circles. Henges are ritual monuments found only in the British Isles.

Hieroglyphs: picture writing, especially from ancient Egypt, which is used to express either ideas or sounds.

I

I Ching: the Chinese *Book of Changes,* which has been used for 3,000 years or more as a means of divining the future and as a source book of wisdom.

Iron Age: the third age of the archaeological 'Three Age System', characterized by the use of iron for weapons, implements and artefacts in general. It was immediately preceded by the Bronze Age.

K

Kiva: underground chamber common in the Pueblo communities of the southwest USA. Usually circular, they were used by men for secret meetings and ceremonies.

L

Lamasery: a Tibetan monastery where Buddhist priests, or lamas, live and study.

Legend: a fiction at some time popularly believed to be true, and sometimes based on real events, though embellished and exaggerated.

Libation: the wine or other liquid poured out in honour of a god or goddess.

M

Mansard roof: a type of roof in which the lower part is steeper than the upper part.

Megalithic: relating to the large stones found in neolithic tombs, graves, circles or standing in isolation.

Menhir: a tall upright standing stone.

Mesa: an isolated flat-topped hill or plateau.

Messianic: relating to the Messiah.

Monotheism: the belief in only one divinity.

Myth: a narrative involving supernatural persons and events, and expressing popular ideas concerning the universe and man's past.

N

Necromancy: the magic art of foretelling the future by communicating with the dead.

Necropolis: a city of the dead.

Neolithic Age: an addition to the classical 'Three Age System' of archaeology, the Neolithic or New Stone Age was that part of prehistory when people practised the cultivation of crops and the domestication of animals, but still used stone for tools and weapons as in the preceding Palaeolithic and Mesolithic (Old and Middle Stone) Ages.

O

Obsidian: a hard black or dark-coloured glass produced when hot volcanic lava cools rapidly.

P

Passage-grave: a megalithic tomb reached by a long passage. Both the tomb and the passage are usually covered by a barrow.

Pictish: belonging to the Picts, or 'Painted People'. This was a name given by the Romans to all the peoples who lived north of the Antonine Wall in Scotland. They remained independent until absorbed into the kingdom of Scotland in the 9th century AD.

Porphyry: a hard rock composed of red or white crystals and once venerated for its beauty.

Portal: a small entrance gate.

R

Radiocarbon dating: the method used to determine the approximate date when an organism died by measuring its level of radioactive carbon. Bone, natural fibres, shell and charcoal are the easiest materials to date.

Reliquary: a small casket in which relics are kept.

S

Sarcophagus: a carved stone coffin commonly used in ancient Egypt and among the Maya of Central America.

Sipapu: a small hole in the floor of a *kiva* representing the umbilical cord from mother earth and the path of man's journey from the Underworld.

Soak: a place where water seeps out of the ground.

Solstice: the time of the year, at midwinter and midsummer, when the sun reaches the turning point of its apparent course.

Stele: a column or upright slab of stone, often with carvings or inscriptions.

Stucco: a plaster made of gypsum and crushed marble for moulding cornices, bas-reliefs and other decorations.

Stupa: a Buddhist monument composed of a stone-lined mound and containing holy relics.

Sutra: a memorable saying from Sanskrit literature which encapsulates a ritual, philosophical or Buddhist principle.

T

Tao: the unimaginable ultimate reality which pulses through the universe, maintains all things and acts as a guide to all those who would order their lives.

Telluric: relating to the natural energy of the earth which emerges from the land at particular power points and can be detected by dowsers.

Trigrams: the eight essential elements used in the Chinese oracle known as the *I Ching*. Each trigram is composed of three lines and is in a state of continual transition. Taken together, the eight trigrams describe everything that happens in heaven and on earth.

W

Wattle and daub: a building technique using interwoven twigs and thin branches (wattle) smeared with clay or mud (daub).

Y

Yin and Yang: the two opposing energies found in all things according to ancient Taoist philosophy. They are both antagonistic and, at the same time, complementary. *Yin* is passive, dark, negative, receptive; *Yang* is active, light and positive.

Z

Ziggurat: a lofty ancient tower of the Near East in which usually rectangular stages of decreasing size are built to accommodate an important temple on the summit.

Zodiac: a heavenly ring of 12 constellations, called signs of the zodiac by astrologers, around which the sun appears to move each year.

INDEX

All places featured in main essays are illustrated. Subsidiary illustrations are in *italic*.

BIBLIOGRAPHY

Ashe, G. (Ed.) (1971) *The Quest for Arthur's Britain*. Paladin, London; (1980) Academy Chicago Publishers, Chicago, IL.

Atkinson, R.J.C. (1979) *Stonehenge*. Penguin, Harmondsworth.

Bivar, A.D.H. (1952–53) 'Lyonesse, the Evolution of a Fable'. *Modern Philology*, Vol. 50, p. 163*f*.

Blavatsky, H.P. (1888) *The Secret Doctrine*. Theosophical Publishing House, London; (1980) Wheaton, IL.

Bord, J. (1976) *Mazes and Labyrinths of the World*. Latimer New Dimensions, London.

Bord, J. and Bord, C. (1978) *A Guide to Ancient Sites in Britain*. Latimer New Dimensions, London; (1981) Academy Chicago Publishers, Chicago, IL.

Bord, J. and Bord, C. (1986) *Ancient Mysteries of Britain*. Grafton, London.

Brennan, M. (1983) *The Stars and the Stones*. Thames & Hudson, London; (1984) New York.

Browning, I. (1973) *Petra*. Chatto & Windus, London; (1982) Merrimack Pub. Corps., distributed by Associated Booksellers, Bridgeport, CT.

Burl, A. (1979) *Prehistoric Avebury*. Yale University Press, New Haven, CT.

Campbell, J. (1984) *The Way of the Animal Powers*, Vol. 1. Times Books, London; (1983) Alfred van der Marck Editions, New York.

Castleden, R. (1983) *The Wilmington Giant*. Turnstone Press, Wellingborough.

Ceram, C.W. (1952) *Gods, Graves and Scholars*. Gollancz/Sidgwick & Jackson, London; (1976) Bantam Books, New York.

Charpentier, L. (1972) *The Mysteries of Chartres Cathedral*. Research into Lost Knowledge Organization, London.

Chippindale, C. (1983) *Stonehenge Complete*. Thames & Hudson, London; (1983) Cornell University Press, Ithaca, NY.

Coe, M.D. (1971) *The Maya*. Penguin, Harmondsworth; (1980) Thames & Hudson, New York.

Cotterell, A. (1979) *The Minoan World*. Michael Joseph, London.

Couling, S. (1917) *Encyclopaedia Sinica*. Humphrey Milford, London. (Re-issued 1983 in facsimile edition by Oxford University Press.)

Crow, H.C. (1925) *Handbook for China*. Carl Crow, Shanghai. (Re-issued 1984 in facsimile edition by Oxford University Press.)

David-Neel, A. (1931) *With Mystics and Magicians in Tibet*. Bodley Head, London; (1971) *Magic and Mystery in Tibet*, Dover Publications, Mineola, NY.

Edwards, I.E.S. (1986) *Pyramids of Egypt*. Viking, London; (1986) Penguin, New York.

Evans, H. (1979) *Mysteries of the Pyramids*. Marshall Cavendish, London.

Frankfort, H. (1977) *The Art and Architecture of the Ancient Orient*. Penguin, Harmondsworth and New York.

Ghirshman, R. (1978) *Iran*. Penguin, Harmondsworth and New York.

Grant, M. (1971) *Roman Myths*. Weidenfeld & Nicolson, London.

Hapgood, C. (1966) *Maps of the Ancient Sea Kings*. Chilton Book Co., Radnor, PA.

Hawkes, J. (1974) *Atlas of Ancient Archaeology*. Heinemann, London; (1974) McGraw-Hill, New York.

Hawkes, J. (1976) *Atlas of Early Man*. Macmillan, London; St Martin's Press, New York.

Hawkins, G.S. (1970) *Stonehenge Decoded*. Fontana/Collins, London.

Herrmann, G. (1977) *The Iranian Revival*. Elsevier-Phaidon, Oxford.

Heyerdahl, T. (1958) *Aku Aku: The Secret of Easter Island*. Allen & Unwin, London.

Hilton, J. (1933) *Lost Horizon*. Macmillan, London.

Jennings, J.D. (Ed.) (1979) *The Prehistory of Polynesia*. Harvard University Press, Cambridge, MA.

Kenyon, K.M. (1974) *Digging up Jerusalem*. Ernest Benn, London.

Knight, W.F.J. (1936) *Cumaean Gates*. Blackwell, Oxford.

Koldewey, R. (Trans. A.F. Johns) (1914) *The Excavations of Babylon*. Macmillan, London.

Lampl, P. (1968) *Cities and Planning in the Ancient Near East*. George Braziller, New York.

Luce, J.V. (1970) *The End of Atlantis*. Paladin, London.

Lytton, E.G.B. (1871) *The Coming Race*. George Routledge, London. (1st Edition.)

Mallows, W. (1975) *The Mystery of the Great Zimbabwe*. Hale, London; (1984) W.W. Norton & Co., New York.

Marples, M. (1981) *White Horses and Other Hill Figures*. Alan Sutton Publishing, Gloucester; (1982) Humanities Press, Atlantic Highlands, NJ.

Matheson, S.A. (1976) *Persia: An Archaeological Guide*. Faber & Faber, London and Winchester, MA.

Matthews, W.H. (1922) *Mazes and Labyrinths: A General Account of their History and Development*. Longmans, Green & Co., London; (1970) Dover Publications, Mineola, NY.

Meyer, K.E. (1980) *Teotihuacan*. Newsweek, New York.

Michell, J. (1977) *A Little History of Astro-Archaeology*. Thames & Hudson, London; (1977) *Secrets of the Stones: The Story of Astro-Archaeology*. Penguin, New York.

Morrison, A. (1980) *Pathways to the Gods*. Paladin, London; (1983) Academy Chicago Publishers, Chicago, IL.

Mountford, C.P. (1965) *Ayers Rock*. Angus & Robertson, London.

Mullins, E. (1974) *The Pilgrimage to Santiago*. Secker & Warburg, London; (1974) Taplinger Publishing Co., New York.

North, F.J. (1957) *Sunken Cities*. Cardiff University Press, Cardiff.

O'Kelly, M.J. (1982) *Newgrange: Archaeology, Art and Legend*. Thames & Hudson, London; (1983) New York.

Perowne, S. (1976) *Holy Places of Christendom*. Mowbrays, London and Oxford.

Plato (Trans. Desmond Lee) (1965) *Timaeus and Kritias*. Penguin, Harmondsworth; (1972) Penguin, New York.

Renfrew, C. (1973) *Before Civilization*. Jonathan Cape, London; (1979) Cambridge University Press, New York.

Roerich, N. (1930) *Shambhala*. Jarrolds, London; (1930) Frederick A. Stokes, New York.

Roux, G. (1976) *Ancient Iraq*. Penguin, Harmondsworth and New York.

Scott-Elliott, W. (1896–1930) *The Story of Atlantis and the Lost Lemuria*. Theosophical Publishing House, London.

Sox, D. (1985) *Relics and Shrines*. Allen & Unwin, London.

Spence, L. (1933) *The Problem of Lemuria*. David McKay Co., New York.

Steiner, R. (1923) *Atlantis and Lemuria*. Anthroposophical Publishing Company, London.

Stevens, R. (1971) *The Land of the Great Sophy*. Methuen, London; (1979) Taplinger Publishing Co., New York.

Stewart, D. (1980) *Mecca*. Newsweek, New York.

Tompkins, P. (1978) *Secrets of the Great Pyramid*. Penguin, Harmondsworth; (1978) Harper & Row, New York.

Virgil (Trans. Robert Fitzgerald) (1985) *The Aeneid*. Penguin, Harmondsworth; (1984) Random House, New York.

von Hagen, V.W. (1974) *The Golden Man: The Quest for El Dorado*. Saxon House, Farnborough.

Waters, F. (1977) *Book of the Hopi*. Penguin, Harmondsworth and New York.

Watkins, A. (1971) *The Old Straight Track*. Garnstone Press, West Sussex.

Wauchope, R. (1962) *Lost Tribes and Sunken Continents. Myths and Method in the Study of American Indians*. Chicago University Press.

Wellard, J. (1980) *The Search for Lost Cities*. Constable, London.

Westwood, J. (1985) *Albion: A Guide to Legendary Britain*. Granada/Grafton, London; (1986) Merrimack Publishers' Circle, Manchester, NH.

Wheeler, M. (1968) *The Indus Civilization*. (Supplementary volume, *Cambridge History of India*, 3rd Edn.) Cambridge University Press.

Wilhelm, R. (Trans.) (1977) *I Ching*. Routledge & Kegan Paul, London.

Youde, P. (1982) *China*. Batsford, London.

ACKNOWLEDGEMENTS

Picture Credits

l= left; *r*= right; *t*= top; *c*= centre;
b= bottom

10/11 Aerofilms; 12/13*t* Zefa Picture Library; 12/13*b* Walter Rawlings/Robert Harding Picture Library; 13 Janet & Colin Bord; 14/15 Mary Caine; 17 Hawkshead Communications Ltd; 18 BPCC/Aldus Archive; 19 Sally & Richard Greenhill; 20/21 Adam Woolfitt/Susan Griggs Agency; 23 Topham Picture Library; 24*t* Sonia Halliday & Laura Lushington; 24*b* The Mansell Collection; 25 Giraudon; 26/27 Aerofilms; 29 Adam Woolfitt/Susan Griggs Agency; 30 National Portrait Gallery, London; 30/31 Homer Sykes; 31 Harper & Row Publishers Inc.; 32/33 Adam Woolfitt/Susan Griggs Agency; 34 Bodleian Library, Oxford; 35*t* Aerofilms; 35*b* Birmingham Public Libraries; 36 J. Catling Allen Photographic Library; 37 J. Allan Cash; 38 Yan/Rapho; 39 Robin Hunter Neillands; 41 Adam Woolfitt/Susan Griggs Agency; 42/43*t* Anthony Weir/Janet & Colin Bord; 42/43*b* Aerofilms; 43 Clive Hicks; 44/45 Louis Salou/Explorer; 46/47*t* Phelps/Rapho; 46/47*b* J. Allan Cash; 48/49 The Tate Gallery, London; 49 Archivo Iconografico, SA; 50 H. Roger Viollet; 50/51 Werner Forman Archive; 52 Konrad Helbig/Zefa Picture Library; 53*t* Sonia Halliday Photographs; 53*b* The Bridgeman Art Library/National Museum, Athens; 54/55 Archiv für Kunst und Geschichte; 56/57 Martzik/Bavaria-Verlag; 58/59 Schörken/Interfoto; 61 Adam Woolfitt/Susan Griggs Agency; 63 The Billie Love Collection; 64 Robert Harding Picture Library/British Museum; 65 Archiv für Kunst und Geschichte; 66*l* Murray Donald/Royal Society of Edinburgh; 66*r* Peter Clayton; 67 Mary Evans Picture Library; 68/69 Tony Morrison; 69 Janet Chapman/Michael Holford; 70 J.P. Courau/Explorer; 71 Bruno Leclerc/Agence Top; 72*t* Horst Munzig/Susan Griggs Agency; 72*b* Vautier-de-Nanxe; 73 Vautier-de-Nanxe; 75 C. Mould/NAAS; 76 Michael Holford; 76/77 NAAS; 78*t* Werner Forman Archive/Victoria & Albert Museum; 78*b* The Fotomas Index; 78/79 Raymond Depardon/Magnum/The John Hillelson Agency; 80 Sonia Halliday Photographs; 80/81 K. Chernish/The Image Bank; 82/83 F. Le Diascorn/Rapho; 84/85 Robert Harding Picture Library; 86/87 Roger Wood; 88 BPCC/Aldus Archive; 89*l* The John Hillelson Collection; 89*r* Bury Peerless; 90/91 The Bridgeman Art Library/Kunsthistorisches Museum, Vienna; 92 J. Catling Allen Photographic Library; 93 Dr. Georg Gerster/The John Hillelson Agency; 94 E.C.M. Lines/Daily Telegraph Colour Library; 95 Robert Harding Picture Library; 98/99 Cornell Capa/Magnum/The John Hillelson Agency; 100/103 Dr. Georg Gerster/The John Hillelson Agency; 104 W.A. Allard/Contact/Colorific!; 105*t* Larry Dale Gordon; 105*b* Marion Morrison; 106 The Mansell Collection; 107 Janet & Colin Bord; 108/109 Kunsthistorisches Museum, Vienna;

110*t* Janet & Colin Bord; 110*b* Mary Evans Picture Library; 111 Peggy Shortt; 112/113 J. Bunbury-Richardson/Daily Telegraph Colour Library; 113 John R. Brownlie/Bruce Coleman; 114 Robert Harding Picture Library; 115 The Photographic Library of Australia; 116/117 The Saint Louis Art Museum; 118 Peter Newark's Western Americana; 119 Dr. Georg Gerster/Photo Researchers Inc.; 120/121 Dr. Georg Gerster/The John Hillelson Agency; 121 Peter Newark's Western Americana; 122/123 Michael Holford/Science Museum; 124/125 Zefa Picture Library; 126/127 Mary Evans Picture Library; 127 British Library; 128*l* Hereford Library; 128*r* Fortean Picture Library; 129 Fortean Picture Library; 130/131 Colin Caket/Zefa Picture Library; 133 N. Saunier/Rapho; 135 Aerofilms; 136/137*t* Dr. Georg Gerster/The John Hillelson Agency; 136/137*b* Edwin Smith; 138 Dr. Georg Gerster/The John Hillelson Agency; 139*t* Aerofilms; 139*b* BBC Hulton Picture Library; 142/143 Tony Morrison; 144/145*t* Boireau/Rapho; 144/145*b* Walter Rawlings/Robert Harding Picture Library; 145 Walter Rawlings/Robert Harding Picture Library; 146/147 Tony Morrison; 148*t* Robert Harding Picture Library; 148*bl* Tony Morrison; 149 Tony Morrison; 150/151 Walter Rawlings/Robert Harding Picture Library; 152/153 M.P.L. Fogden/Bruce Coleman; 154 Peter Newark's Western Americana; 154/155 Peter Newark's Western Americana; 155 Walter Rawlings/Robert Harding Picture Library; 156/157 Charles W. Friend/Susan Griggs Agency; 158/159 H. Roger Viollet; 160*t* Robert Harding Picture Library; 160*b* Janet Chapman/Michael Holford; 161*t* Bibliotheque Nationale, Paris/BPCC/Aldus Archive; 161*b* Werner Forman Archive/British Museum; 162/163 Philip Sayer/Departures Magazine; 164 Robert Aberman/Barbara Heller; 165 Tom Nebbia/Aspect Picture Library; 166*t* Archivo Iconografico, SA; 166*b* Tom Nebbia/Aspect Picture Library; 167*l* Alain Keler/Sygma/The John Hillelson Agency; 167*r* Dr. Georg Gerster/The John Hillelson Agency; 168/169 Dick Rowan/Susan Griggs Agency; 170/171 Marc Riboud/The John Hillelson Agency; 172 Mary Evans Picture Library; 172/173 Burk Uzzle/Magnum/The John Hillelson Agency; 173 D. & J. Heaton/Colorific!; 175*t* Robert Harding Picture Library; 175*b* Ashmolean Museum, Oxford; 176/177 Bob Davis/Aspect Picture Library; 178/179 H. Roger Viollet; 180 Naud/A.A.A.; 181 Archiv für Kunst und Geschichte; 182 BPCC/Aldus Archive; 184 Scala/Museo Archeologico, Firenze; 184/185 P. de Prins/Zefa Picture Library; 186*l* The Mansell Collection; 186*r* BBC Hulton Picture Library; 187*t* BBC Hulton Picture Library; 187*b* Michael Holford/British Museum; 188/189 Lisl Dennis/The Image Bank; 190*t* Mary Evans Picture Library; 190*b* Historisches Museum, Basel/BPCC/Aldus Archive; 191 J. Allan Cash; 192/193*t* Christine Osborne; 192/193*b* Robert Harding Picture Library; 193 Robert Harding Picture Library; 195 H. McManus/Daily Tele-

graph Colour Library; 198 The Mansell Collection; 200/201*t* S.H. & D.H. Cavanaugh/Robert Harding Picture Library; 200/201*b* Ronald Sheridan; 202/203*t* J. Allan Cash; 203 Roger Haydock/BPCC/Aldus Archive; 204 Minnesota Historical Society/BPCC/Aldus Archive; 205 Mary Evans Picture Library; 207 The Mansell Collection; 208/209*t* Robert Harding Picture Library; 208/209*b* Croxford/Zefa Picture Library; 209 Adam Woolfitt/Susan Griggs Agency; 211 BPCC/Aldus Archive; 212/213 Keith Gunnar/Bruce Coleman; 214*l* BPCC/Aldus Archive; 214*r* BBC Hulton Picture Library; 215 BBC Hulton Picture Library; 216/217 Dave Paterson; 218/219 Peter Carmichael/Aspect Picture Library; 220/221 Adam Woolfitt/Susan Griggs Agency; 222 British Library; 223*t* Victor Englebert/Susan Griggs Agency; 223*bl* British Library; 223*br* Tony Morrison; 224 Popperfoto; 225 The Fotomas Index.

The publishers and authors would like to thank the following people from whom they received invaluable assistance in the compilation of this book:

Alison Abel
Donald Binney
Lucy Bishop
Mary Caine
Mary Corcoran
Katie Fischel
Mary Ingoldby
Jazz Wilson

Stone-cut lettering on front jacket by Catherine Lonsdale.

p. 9: lines from 'Thanksgiving for a Habitat' by W.H. Auden. UK Edition: Reprinted by permission of Faber and Faber Ltd. from *Collected Poems* by W.H. Auden. US and Canadian Editions: Copyright © 1965 by W.H. Auden. Reprinted from *W.H. Auden: Collected Poems*, by W.H. Auden, edited by Edward Mendelson, by permission of Random House Inc.

Maps and illustrations

Location maps and illustrations p. 28, 40, 169 by John Hutchinson.
Illustrations p. 22, 65, 102, 132, 175 by Stan North.
Illustration p. 94 by David Parker.
Illustration p. 212 by Graham Allen.
Maps pp. 6–7 and illustration p. 14 by Thames Cartographic Services Ltd.